Improving Project Performance

Also by Jerry L. Wellman

Organizational Learning (2009)

Improving Project Performance

Eight Habits of Successful Project Teams

Jerry L. Wellman

IMPROVING PROJECT PERFORMANCE
Copyright © Jerry L. Wellman, 2011.

First published in 2011 by
PALGRAVE MACMILLAN®
in the United States—a division of St. Martin's Press LLC,
175 Fifth Avenue, New York, NY 10010.

Where this book is distributed in the UK, Europe and the rest of the world,
this is by Palgrave Macmillan, a division of Macmillan Publishers Limited,
registered in England, company number 785998, of Houndmills,
Basingstoke, Hampshire RG21 6XS.

Palgrave Macmillan is the global academic imprint of the above companies
and has companies and representatives throughout the world.

Palgrave® and Macmillan® are registered trademarks in the United States,
the United Kingdom, Europe and other countries.

ISBN: 978–0–230–11217–9

Library of Congress Cataloging-in-Publication Data

Wellman, Jerry L.
    Improving project performance : eight habits of successful project
    teams / by Jerry L. Wellman.
        p. cm.
    ISBN 978–0–230–11217–9 (hardcover)
        1. Project management. 2. Teams in the workplace. I. Title.
HD69.P75W463 2011
658.4'04—dc23   2011018693

A catalogue record of the book is available from the British Library.

Design by Newgen Imaging Systems (P) Ltd., Chennai, India.

First edition: November 2011

10 9 8 7 6 5 4 3 2 1

Printed in the United States of America.

CONTENTS

FIGURES AND TABLES

FIGURES

TABLES

This book is for those with some practical experience with projects and project environments. The principles, examples, and recommendations herein will resonate with those who have engaged in project management activities and have no doubt been frustrated by that engagement. The intent is to help the journeyman and the craftsman better make sense of and have more influence over their environment, one that is both complex and challenging.

The project environment is often not well understood, even by its practitioners. Many of the executives and managers overseeing, supporting, or leading project activities do not appreciate the fundamental differences between projects and other sorts of work activity. This book offers some insight into those differences, and into their consequences.

The primary audience for this book is threefold. First, it is intended primarily for current project managers who will recognize situations and experiences that may be frustrating them today. Project managers are often chosen from among the cadre of individuals who have successfully demonstrated technical skills (e.g., engineering, science, or computer programming) then thrust into project leadership roles with little or no training, coaching, or mentoring. This book may help you make sense of some of the dynamics and pressures that impede project success. It will also suggest techniques that may help you influence the likelihood of project success. Second, it is intended for organizational leaders who will recognize herein cultural, environmental, and procedural challenges that are inhibiting the success of their project initiatives. This book points out factors within the organization and within the project teams that can be managed to facilitate, rather than impede, project success. Although it is written more from the perspective of the project manager than that of the organizational leader, it does address systemwide impediments to project success and offer insights about dealing effectively with them. Third, it is intended for other key project stakeholders, including customers who will use the results of the project activity and functional managers whose departments interact with project teams. These stakeholders will better appreciate the challenges faced by project teams and understand how stakeholders can exaggerate or minimize those challenges. Those who lack direct project management experience may find it difficult to internalize some of the specifics in this book, but the broader principles and perspectives may nonetheless prove enlightening and useful.

  This book does not attempt to be all things to all people, which would dilute its value to anyone. The book will likely not be useful for individuals who have no direct experience with projects or project management because it presumes some hands-on experience with projects and the organizational environment in which they are executed. Those who have found themselves thrust into a position of project management without direct experience or training should wait a year or two before reading this book. If you are a new project manager, you may find *Successful Project Management* by Milton Rosenau and Gregory Githens (2005) useful.[1] It is a straightforward classical description of the fundamental principles of engineering project management and a direct and specific how-to description rooted in sound principles. Leaders who find themselves suddenly responsible for overseeing a multiproject environment may find it useful to read the Rosenau/Githens book referenced above. Afterwards, you may find enlightening *Project Management: Strategic Design and Implementation* by David Cleland (1990),[2] a book with more of an organization-wide perspective on the challenges of project management.

WHAT THIS BOOK IS ABOUT

This book primarily looks at what it is that project teams try to accomplish, what principles are essential to project success, and why those principles are so important. It is less about specific tasks and tools, although these are mentioned as exemplars of the principles being described. Some people have written profusely and well about the mechanics of project management. There is no shortage of descriptions of project phases, tasks to be accomplished during each phase, and tools for carrying out those tasks, but practitioners seeking to understand the fundamental reasons for those tools and methods will find significantly fewer resources. This book may be helpful.

This book describes eight habits that successful project teams often display. Many failed project teams have also *not* displayed at least some of the eight habits described. This correlation between the habits described and project success is not absolute. Projects are often challenging and complex. Thus, they can easily fail in several ways, despite the best efforts of the project team and their organization. However, more than thirty years of personal experience managing complex projects, leading project-based organizations, and consulting with other project-based organizations has made it clear to me that practicing these eight habits improves a team's likelihood of success.

THE AUTHOR'S EXPERIENCE

I have enjoyed over thirty years experience working in complex project-oriented organizations in the aerospace industry as an engineer, project manager, functional manager, and general manager. From that experience, I developed a visceral understanding of how such organizations behave, how they evolve, and how their members both adapt to and shape them. The assertions herein emerged from those decades of personal experience. As a new project manager, I was fortunate to be working in an organization that understood deeply the nature of projectized work activity and was dedicated to creating an organizational culture and infrastructure that enabled effective project performance. Several years later I joined the leadership team of a struggling project-based organization with many troubled and very few successful projects. I was fortunate to be joined by other leaders who shared a commitment to transform the organization into a place where project success was the norm rather than the exception. We were able to build such an organization, one that developed many very effective project managers and project teams, one that sustained strong project performance for several years. Recently, I have been actively consulting, teaching, and writing about the topic.

This real-world experience has been complemented by an eclectic academic background, including a degree in electrical engineering, a masters degree in business, a masters degree in Human Organization Development (HOD), and a PhD in Human and Organizational Systems (HOS). Both my HOD and HOS research focused on leadership and culture in complex organizations. Henry Mintzberg (1979),[3] describes complex organizations as those that deal with "sophisticated innovation, the kind required of a space agency, an avant-garde film company, a factory manufacturing complex prototypes, or an integrated petrochemical company…one that is able to fuse experts drawn from different disciplines into smoothly functioning ad hoc project teams." These are the sorts of organizations I have worked in and led, organizations filled with project teams that perpetually encounter new information and must adapt to it, and organizations that must be competent users of what they learn if they are to survive.

My business and industry responsibilities required close interaction with inter- and intracompany engineering development and manufacturing teams. Some of these teams collaborated with other teams on major projects including the International Space Station, the Iridium satellite constellations, aircraft navigation simulators, aviation electronic subsystems, computer development, and worldwide communications networks to name only a few. As an individual contributor, I have time and again witnessed groups of truly motivated and capable people collectively behaving as a very stupid organization while at other times behaving brilliantly. As a manager, I have successfully, and at times unsuccessfully, influenced the organizational work activities and systems to make them more efficient and to avoid recurring problems. As a leader, I have built culture and infrastructure to foster organizational and project competence. As a member of industrywide councils, I have witnessed the efforts of customers, peer companies, and suppliers as they struggle with similar challenges. I've seen just how difficult it is to build organizational project competence, and just how fragile that competence can be. Those experiences, the successes and the failures, left their mark having taught me a few lessons about how projects and project-based organizations should behave, and why they often do not behave as they should.

These parallel paths of industry and academia give me a unique and fruitful perspective about how projects work, why they tend to succeed or fail, what project team behaviors or habits most influence the likelihood of project success, and what organizational behaviors or habits enable or inhibit project performance. The lessons we learned were put into practice when we identified and developed new project managers, when we developed tools and infrastructure to support the project teams, and when we worked with customers and suppliers. Those experiences morphed into a set of notes that I thought might one day become the foundation for a book.

Several years later I found myself teaching in a graduate business program and consulting for aerospace industry businesses. At one point, I was asked by a client to quickly put together and present a two-day class on the fundamentals of project management. I decided to not focus on the traditional project life cycle or the traditional array of tools and techniques but instead to spend the time talking about the fundamental objectives of project teams and how they could accomplish those objectives. In other words, this was to be a course about what matters and why it matters rather than a course about what to do and how to do it. The course was developed around a discussion of the most important habits of effective project teams. It described the habits, explained why they were so important, and offered an introduction to the tools, techniques, and practices that teams could use to embody those habits. That first course was such a success that the client, GE Aviation Systems, subsequently commissioned me to conduct it with project managers, functional managers, and leaders across their organization in the United States and England.

That material, my personal experience, and my stimulating interactions with hundreds of managers and executives at GE became the foundation of this book. The managers who attended those sessions embraced the material and successfully put it to use. I hope the reader will find the information and insights as useful as have the people at GE Aviation Systems, Honeywell, and other businesses.

HOW THIS BOOK IS ORGANIZED

This book has a sequential flow. The experienced project professional should resist the temptation to skip Chapter 1, a foundational introduction to project management, project terminology, and the differences between project work activity and process work activity, because the chapter includes definitions and premises that are the foundation for the eight habits. Chapters two through five generally build on one another as they describe front-end project planning and monitoring activities. Chapters 6 through 9 address topics related more to the ongoing project execution efforts. The epilogue summarizes the tenets of the book and offers advice for those who would put the eight habits into practice.

This book intends to help the working project manager and project-based organization leaders benefit from my experience. Mark Twain once observed that a person who undertakes to carry a cat home by the tail learns ten times as much as the person who simply watches. Perhaps that is so. But it has been my experience that project managers and project-based organizational leaders are too-often in such a panic that they fail to learn useful lessons from their repeated attempts to carry the proverbial cat by its tail. Those of you with badly scarred bodies may find this book gives you insights and perspectives that can make the next attempt at cat-carrying less painful, perhaps even successful.

ACKNOWLEDGEMENTS

I extend a special thank you to the leaders at Honeywell, Space and Avionics Systems in Clearwater, Florida, during the 1970s and 1980s, who built and nurtured a robust project-based organization in which I was privileged to learn and grow as a novice project manager. Later, Jay Lovelace and the team he assembled at Space Systems Operations in Glendale, Arizona, including Randy Roberts, Bob Saunders, Bill Unger, myself, and others shared the rewarding experience of building such an organization. In the process we struggled, learned, and prevailed. I acknowledge the many people at GE Aviation Systems and other organizations who listened to my notions about project management, challenged those notions, then adapted and deployed them as appropriate for their situation. In the process I learned a great deal more about what I thought I already knew.

Special thanks go to Randy Roberts who took the time to critique this work and in so doing to give me both encouragement and honest critique. I also owe a special debt to Laurie Harting, my editor at Palgrave Macmillan who gently but firmly guided me through the process of converting my thoughts into the book you are now reading.

CHAPTER 1

PROJECT MANAGEMENT

"Why do so many professionals say they are project managing, when what they are actually doing is fire fighting?"
—Colin Bentley, 1997

Project management is an important, even vital, business competency. The Economist Intelligence Unit, a leading source of economic and business research, says, "90 percent of global senior executives and project management experts say good project management is key to delivering successful results and gaining a competitive edge."[1] No wonder, since trillions of dollars are spent annually to fund projects. The Standish Group, an organization that monitors software-development projects, reported that during the 1990s in the United States, more than $250 billion was spent each year across approximately 175,000 information technology (IT)–application development projects.[2] The United States Department of Defense (DOD) spent about $50 billion on research, development, and test evaluation in 2010, and most of it was controlled through project-based contracts.[3] Global construction-project spending was $5.3 trillion during the first six months of 2010.[4] If spending is an indicator of importance, then projects have been and continue to be a vital and major activity in many sectors of the world economy.

The demand for advice and training about how to conduct projects more successfully is also strong. An online search for "project management consultant" surfaced over 16 million hits, suggesting that a lot of money is being spent trying to learn how to run projects successfully. Another search uncovered 320 formal education institutions in the United States that currently offer a specialty in project management, including 122 certificate programs, 225 master's degree programs, and 23 doctorate programs. The Defense Acquisition University in Fort Belvoir, Virginia, has for several decades offered extensive instruction and certification for program/project managers throughout the DOD and its civilian contractor community. The Project Management Institute (PMI), the leading project management professional organization, offers an array of training and professional certifications to its 200,000-plus membership. Millions of dollars and hundreds of thousands of hours are spent annually on efforts to get more value from the massive amount of money and other resources that are being invested in projects.

Yet projects very often fail to deliver as promised. McManus and Harper, in a 2008 study published by the British Computer Society, reported that "statistics show that regardless of the original budgets defined by projects there is still a real issue with project overrun in terms of both cost and schedule. The study showed an average overrun of 24% on original baselined schedule and budget across all completed projects."[5] The Standish Group study mentioned earlier, based on a review of more than 10,000 global software projects, found that "only 35% of software projects are delivered on time, on budget and within requirements."[6] That means that about two-thirds of all such projects overran their budgets, took longer than planned, or delivered less capability than intended, hardly a record of which to be proud. The same study also found that nearly one-third of all projects were canceled before they could be completed, and more than half of all projects cost almost twice their original estimates, costing organizations about $140 billion in unplanned spending. It gets worse. The Standish study also found that the software projects tackled by larger firms delivered only about 40 percent of their originally specified functionality. That means that more than 90 percent of the time, software development projects in large firms delivered less than half the performance promised when the project was evaluated for approval. Dr. George Eng of the University of Calgary, in Alberta, conducted a review of twenty $1 billion-plus Canadian construction projects and found that every project overran its planned budget by 20 percent to 100 percent.[7] Assuming that Dr. Eng's findings are representative of the large-scale construction industry overall, and based on an annual global construction-project expenditure of about $10 trillion,[8] this business segment is incurring several trillion dollars a year of unplanned project-cost growth. The evidence is clear: Projects too seldom deliver on their promised results, and the consequences are expensive, traumatic, and destroy peoples careers.

To be fair, project management is inherently challenging work. Organizations and teams are often trying to develop new solutions to seemingly intractable political and technical challenges. Even simple projects often begin with daunting expectations and limited resources while facing great uncertainty. It should be no surprise that success is so elusive. Nevertheless, we must do better because we currently waste too many resources—the Standish Group study estimated that American companies spent $81 billion on canceled software projects in 1995 alone—and frustrate too many lives to allow the status quo to remain.

But, notwithstanding these grim statistics, not every project fails. Many projects do succeed in meeting their costs, schedule, and technical objectives in spite of the challenges. Some industries, organizations, and project managers have better track records than others. Industry norms and dynamics are inherently more supportive of project activity in some arenas than in others. For example, the defense industry has significantly more overall regard for a commitment to baseline project plans than does the commercial aviation industry. Some organizational cultures better understand how to foster project success, valuing learning and the free flow of knowledge over power politics that control the flow of information. Some project managers have learned through trial and error how to tease success out of what seem to others to be chaotic situations. These managers have gleaned from their experience a deep understanding of the strengths and weaknesses of various project-monitoring techniques. They have learned that some specific criteria, processes, and competencies, when plied effectively, improve the likelihood of project success. Organizations and project teams can succeed. What is more important, success does not have to be random or infrequent. Organizations and teams can take actions to improve their likelihood of success.

THE EIGHT HABITS OF SUCCESSFUL PROJECT MANAGERS

This book describes a set of eight habits that, when practiced diligently, have improved the likelihood of project success. Some projects are less challenging than others. Some projects are doomed from the start. Indeed, just like the rest of us, project managers may occasionally succeed in spite of doing everything wrong or fail in spite of doing everything right. However, the eight habits listed here have been demonstrated to be effective. Project managers who practice these habits have time and again found success more often than those who do not.

Success habit #1 – Foster and nurture a shared vision of what the project is attempting to accomplish

All project stakeholders, including external or internal customers who are paying for the endeavor, senior leadership in the project organization, strategic partners or suppliers, functional departments (e.g., marketing, distribution, sales), the project manager, and project team members have some reason to believe they have a right to influence the definition of what the project is supposed to accomplish and to determine whether it has succeeded. In an ideal world, stakeholders would have a consensus vision for the project and be able to clearly articulate that shared vision to the project manager and the project team members before the work begins. However, this is rarely the case. Instead, project teams often find themselves struggling to shape a vision from among the disparate, sketchy, and often shifting notions of various stakeholders. Successful project managers assume responsibility for understanding their various stakeholders' notions of project success, and then work with those stakeholders to shape a single vision that can be accomplished. Successful project managers develop for themselves and their team a coherent project vision to guide their efforts whether or not the other stakeholders share a single vision because they know that to do otherwise is to fail.

Success habit #2 – Translate the vision into a coherent set of performance specifications and requirements

Customers and project sponsors may not be able to correctly articulate the requirements and specifications. Requirements may also come from industry standards, company policies, or discipline best practices. Successful project managers insure that they have a coherent set of requirements and specifications that accurately reflect the stakeholders' vision and integrate other sources of requirements. Project managers use the requirements-development activity to further refine the project vision and to develop specific work-requirement activity descriptions that team members can accomplish. The requirements and specifications also form the basis for standards against which the work activity is assessed.

Success habit #3 – Create and maintain an integrated plan for accomplishing the specifications, requirements, and vision

Some projects begin with only a sketchy plan, based on the belief that immediate action is more beneficial than planning for action later, even if that early action proves later to be futile. Many projects begin with a set of disintegrated plans. That is to say, there may be a budget plan, a schedule, and a technical scope-of-work plan, but the three may have little to do with one another. The budget is often based on customer affordability or competitive pressures. The schedule is often based on an arbitrary target-completion date. The technical scope of work often contains everything the customer or sponsors think they can get, without much regard for cost or technical risk. As a result, it may be impossible to accomplish the scope of work within the desired time frame or budget—hence, a *dis*integrated plan. Successful project managers make sure they have a clearly articulated technical work scope that they believe the team can accomplish within the specified budget and time frame. Thus, the individual plans are compatible; they form a single, integrated project plan.

Success habit #4 – Monitor the project team's performance against the integrated plan and its progress toward the specifications, requirements, and vision

They develop an array of metrics and other monitoring techniques that alert them to any deviation from the mutually agreed plan. Successful project managers do not merely rely on the standard monitoring systems provided by the organization. Instead, they adapt and supplement those systems to accommodate the unique traits of each project. Certainly, plans will change as work progresses, but the project manager and the project team members are passionate about immediately recognizing the change, and the monitoring system makes that possible. The monitoring system also enables the manager to continually measure the team's performance against the plan, enabling them to quickly adjust resources in order to stay on target.

Success habit #5 – Acknowledge and accommodate both uncertainty and ignorance

The team that proposes or initially plans a project makes assumptions about technology, productivity, and resources that may or may not turn out to be true. They also inevitably uncover things they did not know about technologies, capabilities, efficiency, and other factors that influence the project's success. Successful project managers foster a learning and adaptive team culture that embraces uncertainty as a normal part of project activity. They also build in adequate margins in the budget, time, and requirements to allow the team some flexibility in dealing with the inevitable consequences of ignorance and the uncertainties that are inherent in every project.

Success habit #6 – Embrace but control change

If uncertainty and ignorance are project realities, then change is inevitable. Change comes from many directions, including but certainly not limited to, shifts in the stakeholder vision, changes in market dynamics, shifts in strategic funding priorities, and changes in resource availability. Some organizations and project managers prefer to ignore change because they do not understand how or are unwilling to deal with it. Others attempt to prevent change, foolishly pretending they can mandate a stable, unchanging environment. Successful project managers accept the inevitability of change. They develop and use a robust discipline for identifying, assessing, and implementing continual changes.

Success habit #7 – Act to influence the future

Teams often come to see themselves as victims—of fickle stakeholders, of poor supplier performance, of technological change, or perhaps just of bad luck. Successful project managers reject the victim mentality and instill that attitude in their teams. Rather than becoming overwhelmed by their environment and circumstances, successful managers and their teams anticipate and actively work to shape their environment, thereby improving their chances of success. They may not always succeed in shaping the environment, but they are always trying to do so. As a result, their odds of success improve.

Success habit #8 – Communicate

Practicing the other seven habits relies on good communication. A team must communicate effectively if it hopes to shape and build stakeholder and team-member consensus around a shared vision. A team must communicate effectively if it hopes to quickly identify, assess, and implement change. Successful project managers are passionate and effective communicators both within and outside the team. They also build a project team culture that values learning, knowledge sharing, and effective communication.

FOUNDATIONAL PREMISES

The eight habits of successful project managers are built on a set of fundamental premises about the nature of project management. Understanding those premises will help you better understand the habits and apply them appropriately in your own projects.

Premise one: Project management is general management. It has been said that project management is one of only a few general management jobs remaining in today's highly integrated and centrally controlled organizational structures. Project managers are, by the nature of their position, tasked with making the same kinds of decisions a traditional business-unit general manager makes. They must balance near-term and long-term project objectives, costs versus the schedule and technical performance, and quality versus cost and schedule. They must balance customer satisfaction and profitability, and the competing desires of various stakeholders. The eight habits are founded on the premise that project managers are in effect the general managers of their projects and must behave accordingly.

Premise two: Projects succeed or fail early in their life cycle. Project managers and their organizational leaders boast about, or confess to, the consequences of those early project decisions and investments much later in the life cycle. Product development projects pass through several phases, beginning with the concept and definition phases, when the product is visualized and then translated into specifications and requirements. This is followed by the design phase, when the product is designed to meet those requirements. The resulting design is built during the manufacture and test phases. The decisions made during the early phases have great impact on the uncertainty and risk the project team will face later. Miller and Lessard, two researchers who studied the challenges of large engineering projects said, "Projects fail not because they are complicated, but because they face dynamic complexity. Rising to the challenge of large projects calls for shaping them during a lengthy front-end period. The seeds of success or failure are planted early."[9] The seeds of project success are sewn early through vision consensus building, rigorous integrated planning, adherence to baseline control discipline, and early acceptance of the challenges the team faces and the resources necessary to address those challenges.

An important corollary to premise two is that top management's leverage for project success is greatest early in the project and declines steadily as the project evolves (see Figure 1.1) Sadly, most organizational leaders spend a great deal of time and energy pursuing new projects only to neglect them during the vital planning and early execution stage, not reengaging aggressively until late in the project's life when things have gone awry and there is little to be done to salvage the situation.

Another corollary to premise two is that resource investment is most beneficial when done early and helps project managers to identify and address or prevent problems rather than having to scramble later to overcome problems. Again, sadly, most organizations tend to understaff and underfund projects during the early phases, asserting that teams perform better when confronted with robust challenges. Instead, teams tend to ignore potential

Figure 1.1   Leadership Involvement in Projects

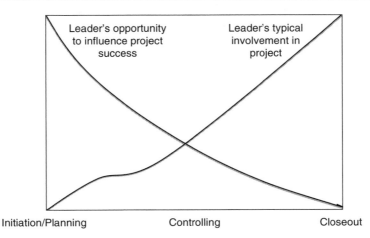

| Leader's opportunity to influence project success | Leader's typical involvement in project |

| Initiation/Planning | Controlling | Closeout |

problems because they lack the resources to deal with them. They resort to merely hoping the problems will not emerge, a recipe for disaster.

When organizations and project managers practice the eight habits, leaders get involved early in the project's life, when it matters most, and need to be engaged less later in the project's life.

Premise three: Project managers and their teams are both accountable and empowered. Many organizations hold their project managers accountable for project success or failure. Fewer organizations are willing to empower those managers and their teams to accomplish success. Organizations must provide adequate and timely resources. They must also make timely decisions about the inevitable resource conflicts. They must provide enabling processes, disciplines, and cultures. Some of the eight habits help project managers merit and gain the necessary empowerment.

Premise four: Projects are about learning efficiency rather than resource efficiency. Organizations often restrict project resources in the mistaken belief that doing so fosters more efficient use of resources. The thought is that perhaps the team will perform at its most efficient level if budgets are trimmed, schedules are aggressive, and resources are restricted. Advocates of this position assert that the resulting challenge will bring out the creativity in the team and yield the most efficient outcome. That is nonsense. Projects that are driven to meet overly aggressive goals and are also resource constrained tend to take unnecessary risks, risks that when they occur, cost the project far more than the price of a few more skilled people. A team that is worried about being unable to meet a critical product performance requirement will, if it has sufficient resources, be able to determine the extent of the concern and to address it early. On the other hand, a team faced with too few resources and too little time will simply hope that things

work out. The consequences when things do not work out
are typically far direr, even catastrophic, than if the issue
had been dealt with early. Early discovery of uncertainties and areas of ignorance makes project teams efficient.
Restricting resources does not. The eight habits encourage
truth telling, rapid learning, and the appropriate application of resources.

Premise five: Project management is about disciplined
flexibility. Project management based organizations must
walk a delicate line between adopting disciplined policies,
procedures, techniques, and practices and maintaining
essential flexibility. No two projects are alike. Thus, no specific procedure or process is suitable for every project. Each
team must have the opportunity to work with process managers to tailor or adapt the bureaucracy to fit their needs.
Certainly, teams will seek what is optimum for their projects,
and process or procedure owners will seek uniform compliance for all projects. Organizational leaders must foster an
environment wherein potential conflicts between these two
interests surface quickly and are dealt with maturely. Milton
Rosenau and Gregory Githens make this point quite clearly:
"The best organizations avoid a rigid set of step-by-step procedures for project management. Instead, the best organizations educate all stakeholders on the principles and allow
for discretion and common sense. To be sure, templates
and checklists are helpful job aids for the novice; just don't
become a slave to your tools."[10]

Premise six: Project management is "predictive"; it
uses a specific approach to understanding and managing project activity. This book assumes readers will apply
the recommendations in an environment in which predictive rather than adaptive project management is practiced. Adaptive project management emerged about ten
years ago as an approach to managing software product
development. It has since been used in a few other arenas. However, predictive project management remains as

by far the most commonly used management approach. The eight habits described herein may or may not be as effective in an adaptive project environment. Certainly, the examples and perspectives documented herein are not about adaptive project management techniques and situations.

The reader should keep these foundational premises in mind when reading about the eight habits. The habits are only relevant within the context of these foundational premises.

WHERE TO FROM HERE?

The reader who is a veteran project manager or a seasoned project organization leader may elect to skip the rest of this chapter, going directly to Chapter 2 and the discussion about project vision. Remember that the chapters should be read in sequence because subsequent habits build on, or refer to, earlier habits. The remainder of this chapter addresses three topics. First, it describes the nature of project work activity as opposed to process work activity and task work activity. This material may help the uninitiated—or the battle scarred but confused—better understand why some of the habits are so vital for project managers. Second, it describes briefly the source and structure of what we think of today as project management. The material describes how modern project management emerged as a practice, what it is intended to accomplish, and the purpose of some of the traditional project management tools. Third, it defines several terms commonly used when talking about project management. These terms are much more clearly articulated and used in academia and the project management literature than they are in practice. The material sorts out those differences. Fourth, it describes the functions of project management, explaining how the traditional plan, organize, lead, control (POLC) model applies to project management. This brief description may help the reader better understand why some of the eight habits exist and what they are intended to achieve.

A PROJECT IS A TYPE OF WORK

The work organizations perform is generally one of three types: *tasks*, *processes*, or *projects*. These are alike in that all three are done to accomplish a goal, require resources, and produce some sort of output. But, they also have important differences that influence how they should be planned, monitored, and controlled. The eight habits help project teams address the unique characteristics of project work activity.

Tasks occur throughout an organization all the time. A technician at Toyota's Georgetown, Kentucky, automobile production plant calibrates a piece of equipment used to align steering columns. A work team unloads a freight-car load of tires. A clerk fills out a purchase order to replace worn-out safety vests. These are examples of tasks: relatively short-duration work activities intended to accomplish a particular result one time. The activity is generally ad hoc, requiring little or no advanced planning or preparation. Tasks seldom involve large groups of people.

Processes are also found everywhere in an organization. The production line process at that Toyota Georgetown plant manufactures about 400,000 automobiles a year.[11] The inventory-control and distribution process assures that materials are available to support the manufacturing line. The equipment-calibration processes ensure that production and test equipment performs as intended. The training and operator-certification processes ensure that employees understand how to properly operate equipment. A process is a form of recurring work activity that attempts to produce the same product or service output over and over again. One fundamental and critical measure of process success is repeatability, making a process a fundamentally different type of work activity than a task.

Projects are also found throughout organizations. Executives at the Georgetown plant decide to build a new warehouse to replace an older, less secure facility. The production director decides to launch a project to develop, install, and train employees on a new software package that will better manage factory inventory. The organization authorizes a project to modify the production line to enable it to yield 20 percent more volume. A project is a complex, one-time work activity requiring significant resources, robust coordination, and a significant amount of time. It has a distinct beginning and end. No project is exactly like another one, just as no task is exactly like another one. A project is essentially a long-duration and complex "task," which, unlike a standard task, demands planning and sophisticated monitoring and control.

In practice, a project may also include some amount of repetitive process work as well as unique work. For example, a project team designs and develops a cockpit display for a new airplane then provides several hundred such displays over a period of time. (Some would prefer to call such work activity a program rather than a project. More will be said about this distinction later.) Initially, the work activity is unique as it focuses on creating the new design and building, then testing the prototype. Later the work becomes more process oriented as the team begins building several hundred units, although as a practical matter, each unit in such a small-volume production lot is often sufficiently different from the others to justify it being called a "project" rather than process work activity. The project also has process work activities that enable the early product-development stage of the work. For example, the team establishes a process for identifying, validating, and sharing changes to their initial design plan. The team also adopts a configuration change control process to deal with the many changes that will occur. So, like tasks, projects are unique, and they may also require a limited amount of recurring work output like a process. However, projects require more preparation and planning than tasks, and they typically do not deliver a large amount of recurring product or service output.

Just as projects may include process work, processes may also rely on projects to accomplish a one-time work activity. For example, a process team establishes a project to select and install a new, more energy-efficient, sheet metal stamping machine that will make the process more efficient. As another example, a process team learns that dipping assemblies in an acid bath before they are painted improves adherence and significantly reduces the number of units that must be repainted, so it puts together a project to design, build, install, and test a new acid-bath system.

One should not be overly concerned about a bright-line distinction between projects and processes. It is more useful to think of a spectrum of interacting work types running from the brief ad hoc task, to unique but complex project work that requires significant planning, to recurring process work, acknowledging that all three types of work may overlap. This does not, however, diminish the need to understand the different nature of each type or to manage them differently.

Projects and process work both demand planning and control. With projects, the emphasis is on planning, whereas control plays an important supporting role. With processes, the emphasis is on keeping the process under control, whereas planning plays a lesser supporting role. However, the nature of the two types of work imposes unique demands on those planning and control activities.

Efficient, productive, and relevant project and process work are essential elements of overall organizational success. Leaders must make sure that their organizations select worthy projects, provide the resources to enable project success, and monitor the performance of those projects to confirm that resources are being used effectively to accomplish the project objectives. Yet, this is much easier said than done. As the earlier examples illustrated, projects often cost and take much longer than planned, sometimes completely failing to accomplish their goals, and thus wasting precious time and resources. Leaders must also make sure their organizations understand their processes, maintain process stability, continually improve process performance, and modify or replace those processes as often as needed to keep up with new technologies and market pressures. Processes are also vulnerable to erratic performance or even collapse. Too often, they unpredictably yield poor-quality outputs that increase costs and dissatisfy customers.

Projects and processes share several important characteristics that influence how leaders deal with them. Both activities are an effort to accomplish some result, to perform work. People are actively engaged in both activities. Both project and process work activity must be planned, executed, and controlled in order to accomplish the desired outcomes. Both projects and processes must be accomplished with limited resources in terms of people, time, money, facilities, and equipment. Processes and projects may occur at any level of the organization from the individual employee to a department to the whole corporation. These similarities lead to some commonality in management and oversight. The classical functions of management (planning, organizing, staffing, controlling, and directing) certainly apply to both projects and processes. The danger is that leaders will appreciate the similarities and be unaware of, or disregard, the critical differences.

At the same time, there are important differences between projects and processes, which are at least as important as the similarities. A project has a defined beginning and a defined end. For example, a project team may be tasked to install and test a new stamping machine in a foundry. The project begins with a decision to buy the new machine and ends when the new machine is approved for use on the production line. A process, on the other hand, is a recurring activity. For example, the process for assembling 50-inch flat-screen television sets may yield 1000 sets a day. The process cycle itself has a beginning and an end—the cycle starts with the gathering of the parts and ends with an assembled set ready to be shipped—but, unlike a project, the work does not change; it is repeated over and over again. This difference means that leaders should monitor and assess projects differently than they do processes.

Project performance is measured differently than process performance. Typical project performance metrics include assessments of cost versus plan, schedule versus plan, and actual work accomplished versus planned cost and schedule. Project metrics may also include key progress milestone completions, such as product-design verification, design-document release, qualification testing, and first-article build. Many of these metrics are indicators of progress along a planned path to completion. Typical process metrics include process stability, yield, and cycle-time. These metrics are indicators of stability, consistency, and efficiency over time. Leaders must put the appropriate metrics in place and make sure that they are monitored and that appropriate actions are taken in response to the data.

Another difference between projects and processes is the nature of learning. Process activity improves as the organization iteratively learns how to most efficiently accomplish the same activity. The process team seeks to understand how to make the process more consistent, faster, and less expensive. It can observe the process over and over again. Projects, on the other hand, attempt to accomplish unique work activities that are not repeated. Project learning is focused on one-time discovery of new relevant knowledge for one-time use on a specific project. Certainly, project teams and their organizations can benefit from the learning on a particular project. In fact, they may well apply some of that learning to future projects. The distinction is that process teams are primarily focused on learning for the sake of improving a recurring activity while project teams are primarily focused on learning for the sake of accomplishing a unique activity. Any recurring leverage is potentially beneficial to the organization, but not to the active project.

Consider a process team that is working on an assembly line paint process for automobiles. It uses statistical process data to confirm that the paint is being applied precisely as intended. It also continually looks for ways to improve the process that will make the paint application more consistent, faster, less expensive, or higher quality. What the team learns is applied to a process that is performed thousands, perhaps even millions, of times. The team searches for evidence of variation and for the causes of that variation. It also looks for minute changes that can save a few cents, eliminate a few seconds of processing time, or reduce variation because saving a few cents, or a shaving a few seconds off each process cycle quickly adds up to become a significant benefit to the overall process and the organization.

Consider a project team working to install a new, automated, warehouse retrieval system. The team will be doing this work only once. It cannot make use of statistical process tools because there is nothing repetitive about what they have set out to do. Instead, it will apply project planning and control techniques to forecast how best to accomplish this unique work activity. The project team seeks to learn how the new retrieval system works, how it must be adapted to interface with existing systems, and perhaps how existing systems must be adapted to enable the interconnections. The team is searching out the major issues that may prevent the new system from being usable, that may force the team to do a great deal of unplanned work, or, alternatively, that may lead to unexpected opportunities to create new retrieval capabilities. It is not interested in small improvements. It is interested in major risks or opportunities that may imperil or enable the project's success.

The staffing activity is also different between processes and projects. Project teams assemble for the duration of the project then disband while process teams may remain in place for long periods of time. Thus team building, role definition, and day-to-day task assignments differ greatly. Each project team member's role must be defined uniquely for each new project and may change over the course of the project because each project involves a unique combination of stakeholders, technologies, resources, capabilities, and requirements all of which may change as the project evolves and the team learns. On the other hand, a process team may redefine roles infrequently, perhaps when a major process change occurs. Project teams are assembled using temporary labor and resources, assets that are moved from project to project or process to project for the duration of the work activity, while process teams are assembled and remain relatively stable for a long period of time. It is true that some long-running project teams may also have relatively stable core teams. The Space Shuttle Program, initially authorized by President Nixon in 1972, flew its final mission in July 2011. The 40-year old program was around long enough for some engineers to have begun and ended their career on the same initiative. However, programs and projects typically last for several months to a few years. As a result project managers are frequently faced with the challenge of rapidly gathering individuals and developing them into a cohesive team focused on the new project and its agenda, something process managers face less often.

Projects typically use borrowed resources while processes typically use dedicated resources, another broad generalization that communicates an important distinction. Projects are commissioned, accomplish their work, and then disband. Thus, the project team members and their resources are generally assembled from various areas then dispersed after the project ends. Processes on the other hand are generally ongoing operations to which staff and resources are often permanently assigned. Project teams find themselves struggling more often and harder than do process teams to gather and retain resources.

The eight habits acknowledge and accommodate these unique attributes of project work activity. Managers who practice these habits will more often find project success.

MODERN PROJECT MANAGEMENT

Projects, project managers and project management techniques of some sort have been around virtually forever. Neanderthals did project work when they planned a hunt to drive herds of beasts over cliffs. The construction of the great Egyptian pyramid at Giza about 2500 B.C. was a massive project involving tens of thousands of people, millions of pounds of stone, and decades of effort. The Channel Tunnel project, begun in 1988 and finished in 1994, connected France and England via a 31-mile undersea rail tunnel. The completed tunnel was identified by the American Society of Civil Engineers as one of the Seven Wonders of the Modern World. Every custom home that has ever been built, from a log cabin on the Appalachian frontier to that most recent "McMansion" in a subdivision near you, has been a project.

Project management as we think of it today first emerged in the late 1950s. One of the earliest comprehensive articles on the subject was "The Project Manager" written by Paul Gaddis in 1959.[12] This Harvard Business Review paper focused on the project manager's role, his or her competencies, and the training and skills necessary to be successful. Bechtel, the global construction firm, first used the term "project manager" in the 1950s when referring to a manager located in a remote environment with an autonomous team. By the early 1960s Bechtel had embraced the notion of a project manager for each job.[13]

It was about this time that the American government began to make a "project management system" a condition for the consideration for research and development contracts. The government representatives had become frustrated about having to deal with several different contacts within the contractor's firm. The contractor's functional organization structure caused government agents to have to deal with design engineering leaders, production leaders, test leaders, procurement leaders, finance leaders, and others in order to track the progress of the project. The government's demand for a project management system was nothing more than a desire to have the contractor name a single individual as a liaison between the contractor and the government. Such a liaison would coordinate within the contractor's organization across the various functional departments and management hierarchies, and then represent the organization when communicating with the government customer.

Firms seeking government contracts had two choices. They could completely reorganize themselves around projects rather than functional departments or they could superimpose some sort of matrix leadership structure with designated project managers who would have authority across the established functional departments.

The former was a radical change while the latter, although expensive and awkward, was less radical and therefore often adopted.

A few organizations have attempted to establish "projectized" structures rather than matrix structures, but none lasted more than a few years, and they all appeared to fail for similar reasons. Initially, the project performance improved, customers were delighted, and organizational leaders were delighted. However, within a couple of years the organizations began to falter. First, they became less competitive as they began to bog down under the weight of redundant capabilities across each project. Each team had insisted on having independent capabilities, which were not fully utilized. Second, project teams adopted their own approaches to tools, disciplines, and techniques, making it difficult to shift people from project to project. This independence also made it necessary to maintain several different policies, procedures, and processes for accomplishing similar work.

Project independence was efficient for the project in the short run but terribly inefficient for the organization in the long run. Each of the powerful and independent project teams insisted on making decisions that were optimal for their particular projects. Teams often refused to share their carefully chosen cadre of experts with other project teams. Each team established its own test labs, ordered its own equipment, used its own design tools, and on and on. Within a year or so it became difficult to move people from one project to another and to efficiently create new project teams because the employees were coming off different projects with their own unique ways of doing things. Before long, each organization collapsed under the weight of all these inefficiencies. Although the matrix (project management) structure is costly and inefficient, experience demonstrates that it is better than the alternative.

Several massive government projects, including the Manhattan Project, the Navy Polaris Missile Program, and NASA's Apollo Program, got under way about the time the government issued its decree that contractors establish a matrix system. (The reader will notice the use of the separate terms "project" and "program" from time to time. These are sometimes not the same thing, and their differences will be described later. For now, assume there is no difference between the terms.) These massive ventures represented the ultimate of two common attributes of projects: schedule urgency and great technical uncertainty. The projects demanded innovative approaches to planning, monitoring, and control. That demand led to more aggressive development and use of a number of project management tools, such as the program evaluation review technique (PERT) and the critical path method (CPM). PERT was specifically devised in 1958 for the Polaris Program by an office of the U.S. Navy, the prime contractor Lockheed Missile Systems, and the consulting firm Booz Allen & Hamilton. CPM was first used the same year on the construction of a new chemical plant but was subsequently adopted and adapted for the Polaris and Apollo programs.[14]

The CPM/PERT techniques have been a core part of nearly all of the traditional project management training and tool kits since then. The techniques are essentially a six-step activity, as follows:

1. Define the project and all of its significant activities or tasks.
2. Decide what activities must precede and what must follow others.
3. Draw the network connecting all the activities.
4. Assign time and/or cost estimates to each activity.
5. Compute the longest time path (the critical path) through the network.

6. Use the network to help plan, schedule, monitor, and control the project.

Indeed, these six steps are embedded in some of the eight habits advocated in this book.

As a side note, this enthusiasm for planning and management systems occurred during a period when management principles such as operations research and systems theory were at their zenith. President Kennedy's Secretary of Defense, Robert McNamara, was the prime exemplar of this enthusiasm and his work to bring integration and systems rigor to the DOD made a great impact on the entire aerospace and defense industry, spilling over into other industries as well.

The government and the research and development (R&D) contractors originally intended the project management structure to address a specific problem, the need for a single-point contractor interface with whom the government representatives could deal. It was quickly learned that the project management structure not only provides that single point interface for the government customer, but also does much more. It provides a single-point interface between the project and the contractor's leadership team, between leadership and the project team members, between the project and the functional departments, and between the contractor and the project's subcontractors. The project management structure also more efficiently uses what the organization knows, enabling it to better learn on the fly and to solve problems. Finally, the structure enables the organization to more efficiently use its resources and adjust those resources as each project learns.

Of course, the project management structure also introduces new challenges. There is the obvious added management overhead that comes with having an additional management chain (project managers as well as

functional managers). There is the confusion and coordination that arises because individuals report to two or
more bosses, their functional manager and the project
manager or managers. There is the inevitable conflict
and competition as the project teams vie for resources to
accomplish their particular work activity. There are the
blurred lines of authority as project managers and teams
work across functions and departments to accomplish
their goals. Finally, the project management structure is
one that many organizational leaders may not understand
and thus may not manage appropriately.

In closing this topic, I am reminded of Peter Drucker's
comment on the reporting structure for new-product development and other innovation projects. He said, "innovative
efforts should never report to line managers charged with
responsibility for ongoing operations....The new project
is an infant and will remain one for the foreseeable future,
and infants belong in the nursery. The "adults," that is, the
executives in charge of existing businesses or products will
have neither the time nor understanding for the infant."[15]
Project managers are responsible for nurturing and pro-
tecting the project work activity.

A FEW DEFINITIONS TO EASE UNDERSTANDING

This section begins with definitions of three constructs:
project, project management, and program. There are in
practice many entirely different definitions or interpretations of these particular terms. For example, it is quite
common in the aerospace industry to use the term *program management* rather than *project management.* In the
construction industry, the term *project manager* is more
commonly used than *program manager,* no matter what the
size of the program/project. Firms are also not consistent
in their interpretation of what a program manager or a
project manager does. Some firms use program manager

as the job title for planning and control staff, the people who develop and maintain the earned-value management system (EVMS). They are essentially the project schedule and cost accountants. In these firms the project or program management function as it is described in this book is often the responsibility of an engineering department manager. In other firms the project manager is their designated customer-contact person for a particular program or project; he or she may have very little decision-making authority inside the firm and exercises little influence over the project activity. Some aerospace firms use the term "program" to denote an externally funded initiative and "project" to denote an internally funded initiative, naming the managers accordingly. GE Aviation Systems currently describes the program manager as the senior customer and management interface responsible for the nonrecurring development and recurring build of a product or service. They also assign an engineering program manager to be responsible for the nonrecurring development activity who reports to both an engineering department head and the program manager for that activity. From time to time GE may assign the same person to both roles, further confusing the uninitiated—and sometimes the initiated as well. The point is that one must be aware that local conventions do not always follow the established academic and business literature doctrine. The PMI acknowledges that local interpretations are rampant, stating "The diversity of meaning makes it imperative any discussion of program management versus project management be preceded by a clear and consistent definition of each term."[16]

Within the past several years the academic and business literature has settled on "project management" as the preferred term, a preference that has not yet found its way into the operational world. The material in this book is targeted at programs or projects, program or project managers, and leaders of program-or project-based organizations.

Thus the terms "project" and "program" may be used interchangeably throughout the book. However, the conventional description of each is offered below.

A *project* is, according to the PMI Book of Knowledge (PMBOK), "a temporary endeavor undertaken to create a unique product, service, or result."[17] The PMBOK describes a project as having three specific attributes. First, it is a temporary endeavor with a definite beginning and end. Second, a project aims to accomplish something that has not been done before (a prior team may have built a similar office building but no team has ever built this particular office building under these specific conditions). Third, the requirements and specifications for the product or service created by the project are "progressively elaborated." That is to say, they are made more specific and refined as the work progresses.

Project management is, according to the PMBOK, "the application of knowledge, skills, tools, and techniques to project activities to meet the project requirements."[18] The management task includes dealing with competing demands. The work scope, time available, target cost, project risks and opportunities, and quality expectations all compete with one another. The various stakeholders also have differing and perhaps competing needs and expectations. The project manager and project team must referee those competitions thereby establishing, communicating, and controlling the initial requirements and their elaboration as the work progresses.

Norman Augustine, retired CEO of Lockheed Martin Corporation said, "Unlike the life of a pilot, which has been described as long periods of utter boredom interspersed with moments of sheer terror, the life of a project manager might more aptly be said to be one of long periods of sheer terror interspersed with rare moments of utter boredom. It is a life willed with risk, hard work, and career exposure."[19] The "terror" a project manager experiences may vary greatly from organization to organization. The PMI tells us the project manager is "the individual responsible for managing the project," a definition that holds up in most project-based organizations. The issue arises when one begins to explore whether the project manager has the authority and influence to accomplish that responsibility. Some organizations bestow great responsibility, great authority, and appropriate resources on their project managers while others bestow great responsibility but no authority, thus declaring them the designated "blame-takers" when the project gets into trouble or fails.

A *program* is, according to the PMBOK, "a group of projects managed in a coordinated way to obtain benefits not available from managing them individually."[20] The literature also often describes a program as work activity that includes both nonrecurring development and recurring build or delivery of a product or service; refer to the GE Aviation Systems example cited earlier.

Customer is a term that may be applied in at least two distinctly different ways. First, a customer may be the external funding authority for a project. Bechtel Construction may build a new airport for the city of Denver—the city is the customer. The city government, and/or the legal entity established by the city, fund the work, establish the requirements, and monitor the progress. A customer may be internal rather than external. For example, Able Engineering Services (AES) may commission a project to upgrade the local area network throughout its engineering facility. The AES management team authorizes, funds, and monitors the work activity, and the AES senior leadership is the customer. Second, customers may instead be the end users of a product or service. Using this definition the traveling public, especially the citizens of Denver are the customers, or the "primary user community," for the new airport. The engineers working at AES are the customers, or the primary user community, for the new local area network. Thus a customer may be the funding authority, or the user community, or perhaps both.

Stakeholders are those parties that have an acknowledged interest in project success and who believe they have a right to participate in defining project success criteria. A project many have many stakeholders, including the customers who will use the project product or service, the individual or entity that funds the project, senior leadership in the organization managing the project, functional departments interacting with or supporting the project, the project manager, project team members, key subcontractors and strategic partners, or others.

A *matrix* is an organizational structure having more than one hierarchy. Typically, the structure overlays project management across a functional-department hierarchy. Traditional organizational structures are generally one of three types. "Functional structures" are those with hierarchies built around functional departments. The directors of engineering, production, quality, finance, and so forth, report to a general manager. "Divisional or product structures" are those with hierarchies built around product or service offerings. The directors of product lines, such as soaps, detergents, polishes, and abrasives, report to a general manager. Each director may have within his or her organization engineering, production, quality, and finance activity. Matrix structures group employees by both function and product, or by function and project. Thus, employees find themselves reporting to two bosses, one in the functional chain of authority and another in the product or project chain of authority.

Predictive project management is the most commonly used approach for initiating, planning, and controlling projects. It is the foundational approach advocated by the PMI and is the core philosophy behind the material in the PMBOK. The PRojects IN Controlled Environments (PRINCE) scheme of project management, advocated in the United Kingdom by the Office of Government Commerce, is also founded on this approach. Predictive project management assumes one can reasonably predict how a project will unfold. That is to say that one can with some confidence reasonably predict the project scope, schedule, and cost well enough to develop a plan and monitor progress against that plan. The points herein are related particularly to the predictive project management approach.

Adaptive project management, also sometimes referred to as "agile project management," takes a fundamentally different approach. Adaptive project management is more often used for iterative software development and rapid commercial product development (cell phones, and personal digital assistants for example), although it is currently being used experimentally in other fields. The approach acknowledges the uncertainty of the path from requirements to finished product. Rather than drawing a detailed roadmap from start to finish, the project team focuses on understanding requirements and features, and then works to rapidly develop each feature once its requirements are fully defined. The team accomplishes as much as possible between project start and a predetermined product-design release date. This book does not directly address adaptive project management, and the eight habits described herein are not directly applicable to agile or adaptive project management principles, although some of them may apply.

THE FUNCTIONS OF PROJECT MANAGEMENT

Nearly 40 years ago Peter Drucker described "five basic operations in the work of the manager. Together they result in the integration of resources into a viable growing organism."[21] He said that the manager sets objectives; organizes the work activity; motivates and communicates to make the team a cohesive unit; measures performance to assure progress and trigger corrective actions; and develops people, including himself. Drucker's five management operations or responsibilities still resonate in today's literature, which often describes the functions of management as planning, organizing, leading, and controlling resources and activities in order to achieve the organization's stated purpose. Planning includes defining the strategy and goals and then developing a plan to accomplish those goals. Organizing involves determining what activities need to be done, how they will be done, and who will do them. Leading involves the coordination and motivation of the people doing the work. Controlling involves monitoring activities and adapting the plan as necessary to achieve success.

Rosenau and Githens offer a complementary model specifically for project management that includes five functions: defining, planning, leading, controlling, and completing.[22] They assert that project management begins with a clear definition of what the project is intended to accomplish and stakeholder concurrence with that definition. The project manager then must develop a plan for accomplishing that vision and goal, just as any manager would. Rosenau and Githen's description includes organizing within this definition of the planning function. They describe leading and controlling in much the same way they would be accomplished by a traditional manager. Finally, they describe the function of completing as assuring the project results conform to the product requirements and the stakeholder expectations.

The PMBOK describes five project management "process groups" including "initiating," "planning," "executing," "closing," and "controlling."[23] Each group could be considered a project management function. Initiation occurs when the project is authorized. It is essentially a milestone event, the project start authorization, rather than an activity. Planning includes both the definition function and the planning functions described by Rosenau and Githens. "Executing" is the effort of implementing the plan to accomplish the defined result. "Closing" is comparable to their version of project closure. It includes the final deliveries and the administrative closeout of activity, including disposition of assets, archiving of records, and so on. "Controlling" includes their version of that term as well as Drucker's notion of measuring performance and accomplishments.

So far, we have recognized two management functions that are somewhat unique to project management. The first is the defining of the project vision and goals. The second is the closing of the project in compliance with expectations. Both these functions arise because of the one-time nature of projects. Projects are created to accomplish a specific result, and then they are disbanded. Thus, project managers must attend more frequently and more carefully to the start-up and the ending stages of the activity. Project management also involves two other unique activities, perhaps not functions or process groups as described above, but certainly fundamental activities that project teams must attend to. They are *progressive elaboration* and the *triple constraint*.

The progressive elaboration challenge arises in many complex product development projects. It may also arise when stakeholders have vague or conflicting perspectives about what the project is intended to accomplish. That confusion or vagueness then levies on the project team the expectation that they will help resolve the unknown or unresolved requirements.

This activity is as much socio-political as it is technical. The technical dimension includes determining and adapting to interfaces between systems and subsystems. It includes the selection of appropriate design architectures, determination of what functions will be implemented in hardware and what in software, how the requirements will be articulated and then verified, and a host of other technical factors. The socio-political dimension includes such activities as helping the customer or customers articulate their expectations (requirements), helping various stakeholders understand and negotiate their expectations, maintaining group commitment to those expectations and requirements, and facilitating consensus change as the situation evolves and the understanding about requirements changes.

Project managers often must lead their teams and the stakeholders in the initial definition and progressive elaboration of the project requirements and specifications. Success or failure in this endeavor often means the difference between project success and failure. A few of the eight habits directly address this activity.

The project triple constraint is a traditional framework used to describe the other basic project management activity. Conventional project wisdom contends that a project involves the relationship among three parameters: cost, schedule, and technical. The technical parameter is sometimes renamed the requirements parameter, shifting the definition to address the description of the technical performance expectations rather than to address the technical development scope of work. The technical parameter is also sometimes described as the "scope" parameter, a broader term that includes all work activity not just the technical work. No matter what term-of-art is used, and no matter what relative amount of technical activity is included in the use of the selected term-of-art, the underlying philosophy is the same. The triple constraint argues that teams begin their work with a baseline project wherein the technical requirements can be accomplished within the established time period and for the agreed cost. The three constraints of cost, schedule, and technical/requirements/scope are thus said to be "in balance." Over time, stakeholders may change one of the three parameters, perhaps to incorporate new technical features. The project team would then adjust the cost and schedule plan to accommodate the revised technical requirements.

Traditional project management lore rarely discusses how it is that the triple constraint comes to be balanced in the beginning. Instead, the literature takes as a given that the project begins "in balance", and it is the project team's responsibility to defend or adjust that balance in response to stakeholder demands. After almost 50 years of that traditional lore, the initial creation and preservation of a balanced project triple constraint is in practice widely, ignored or completely misunderstood, as is discussed further in Chapter 4.

CHAPTER 2

HABIT # 1—FOSTER AND NURTURE A SHARED PROJECT VISION

"Vision without action is a daydream. Action without vision is a nightmare."

—Japanese proverb

What is it about a clear, compelling, and consistent vision that enables project team success? Why are teams with such a vision more likely to find success? Christenson and Walker, writing in *Project Management Journal*, assert that "a significant driver of project management success is effective and intelligent leadership communicated through an inspiring vision of what the project is meant to accomplish."[1] But just what is a project vision and how does that inspiring vision manifest itself as a driver of project success?

A project vision has four distinct attributes (see Table 2.1). It is a single coherent description of why the project matters. The vision describes what the project

Table 2.1   Project Vision Attributes

- It is a single, coherent description of why the project matters.
- It is easy to understand.
- It is behavioral and actionable.
- It is challenging.

team will try to accomplish, what difference will be made when they succeed. A project vision is easy to understand. The vision must be articulated in such a way that all the team members can see what their roles will be. It must also be articulated in such a way that stakeholders outside the project team can embrace and retain their commitment to the vision. A project vision is behavioral and actionable. It must show the team how the vision can be translated into a set of specifications and requirements that it believes can be accomplished and verified. It must also be able to see how the vision can be turned into an integrated cost, schedule, resource, and technical plan. A project vision is challenging. The team must see the vision as something worthy of its effort and sacrifice. It must perceive that its extraordinary effort and creativity can result in an outcome of which it can be proud.

This chapter describes why the project vision is so important. It also explores why project visions are too often absent entirely, vague and poorly articulated, or conflicting. It describes the difficulties this creates for project teams. Finally, it describes the project manager's role in fostering and then maintaining a clear and coherent vision for the team and offers guidance for accomplishing that role.

THE PROJECT VISION MATTERS

The clear, agreed, and achievable project vision is the cornerstone of project success. It stabilizes the project environment and enables the project team (see Table 2.2).

Table 2.2   Project Vision Enables Success

- It facilitates a positive culture that emboldens and empowers the project team.
- It clarifies purpose, fostering a shared understanding of what is to be accomplished.
- It aligns goals and thus aligns efforts.
- It maintains the team's sense of direction in a dynamic project environment.
- It provides a framework for prioritization and decision making.
- It enables decision making at lower levels, making the team more agile.

A shared vision facilitates a positive culture that emboldens and empowers the project team. Peter Senge describes the discipline of creating and maintaining a shared vision in his book *The Fifth Discipline*,[2] arguing that effective learning organizations embrace the notion of shared vision as a core discipline: "Visions are exhilarating. They create the spark, the excitement that lifts an organization out of the mundane." He goes on to describe several other ways a shared vision impacts organizations positively, stating that, "A shared vision is the first step in allowing people who mistrusted each other to begin to work together. It creates a common identity. In fact, an organization's shared sense of purpose, vision and operating values establish the most basic level of commonality." Senge also asserts that shared visions compel the courage that empowers teams to take risks and experiment, to search for new understanding, and to focus on long-term goals rather than immediate pressures.

A clear and shared project vision clarifies purpose. This shared understanding of intent—the vision—helps them bond as a team, just as a shared vision helps young athletes bond as a team. Athletes who adopt the team vision, rather than a personal vision, are eager to make personal sacrifices to further the team's goals. Project team members are also more apt to make personal sacrifice to further the project team goals.

A project vision aligns goals and thus aligns effort. Project team members may have unique individual roles within the overall project. A small group may be designing the software while another small group is designing the electronic circuitry, and yet another group is developing test equipment to verify product performance. These groups constantly make decisions about their piece of the overall project, which influence the work of other team members. The efforts of these small groups and individuals are better aligned when they share a common vision. Individual efforts are less likely to conflict with other team member's efforts.

A project vision maintains the team's sense of direction in the midst of what can be a challenging, even chaotic, project environment. The team must constantly resolve uncertainties, often exposing its ignorance about technology, suppliers, previous work, and a host of other factors. These learning and discovery dynamics create an environment of perpetual adaptation and change, both of which can be quite confusing. As mentioned earlier, project stakeholders may have conflicting interpretations of the project vision that can shift over time. This can create confusion and conflict for a project team; but a coherent internal project vision can help it remain focused on what it is trying to accomplish. Day in and day out, team members are challenged to decide whether to focus on task A or task B, how best to use limited resources, what technical compromises are the most appropriate to make, whether they need additional help to remain on schedule, and a host of other important matters. Those decisions are more difficult to resolve when members of the team hold different, even opposing, visions about what they are as a group trying to accomplish. Indeed, astute project leaders know that frequent, recurring debates over project decisions may well be a symptom of conflicting visions. The same prioritization and decision-making dilemmas can arise when the organization is deciding how to allocate resources across various projects and processes. A clear and shared vision of each project enables the organization to make appropriate, timely resource-allocation decisions. A project vision enables decision making to take place at lower levels, making the team both quicker and more agile. Individual team members can make appropriate decisions themselves rather than elevate them for the project manager to decide, if they understand and agree on the project vision. As a result, there is less decision-making delay because questions do not have to be elevated for higher-level review, scheduled on busy calendars, described to a supervisor who may be less well informed about the relevant issues, debated, and then, maybe, resolved. Weick said, "the real trick in highly reliable systems is somehow to achieve simultaneous centralization and decentralization."[3] A shared project vision helps facilitate the blend of centralization because all the team members are working toward a common objective while it also facilitates decentralization because the shared understanding enables the lower level decision making.

PROJECTS INVOLVE MULTIPLE STAKEHOLDERS WITH UNIQUE VISIONS

In an ideal world every project would begin with a single, coherent, achievable, and agreed-by-all-stakeholders vision. But of course the real world is rarely ideal. Projects often have multiple stakeholders, who each may claim the right to determine or at least influence the project vision. Some may have only a vague notion of what the project is supposed to accomplish while others may have a clear vision for it. They may or may not acknowledge one another. Nonetheless, their collective perspectives determine whether the project can have a single coherent vision and influence the shape of that vision.

Every project has a customer who funds the effort and expects to benefit from the results. The project customer, the entity funding the project effort, may be internal or external. An internal customer is often called a *project sponsor*. Examples include the Bechtel Corporation, which wanted to develop and deploy a new software tool to help capture and recover labor and equipment costs for construction projects around the world; or Toyota, which decided to reconfigure its Camry production line in Georgetown, Kentucky. Examples of projects with external customers include Boeing, which won the contract to build the International Space Station (ISS) for the National Aeronautics and Space Administration (NASA); a general contractor hired to build a new house for a couple; or a contractor hired to construct a new classroom building for a local college. The customer or customers, whether they are internal or external to the organization within which the project is accomplished, are clearly important stakeholders with a legitimate claim to shape the project vision.

A project for an external customer also reports to internal company executives who lay claim to shaping the project vision. The Boeing ISS internal project team certainly considers the people at NASA overseeing their project as the customer and thus a legitimate project stakeholder. But they also report to Boeing executives, who may share the NASA customer vision but also have their own priorities, such as Boeing's profitability and growth, which NASA executives will not care about. Internal management may also have as a goal that they will be able to apply the results of a project to other customers, meeting internal needs in addition to satisfying external customer's expectations, something else that is not a priority for NASA management.

Of course, internal senior leadership is not a monolith. Individuals on the leadership team may have different visions for the project or visions that may not be openly stated. The marketing leaders may envision a very capable product that sells for a low cost. The engineers on the management team may envision a product that is technically superior to the company's current model. The chief financial officer may envision a project that is completed on time and within budget. As a result, this stakeholder group is often evaluating project success against disparate, even opposing, criteria for success, which may translate into contradictory or confusing messages being sent to the project team.

The result may be conflict and delay in making resource and priority decisions that may lead to major problems. In short, a fuzzy or conflicting project vision among senior management increases the likelihood of project failure.

The project manager and the members of the team are also legitimate stakeholders. They may have their own personal views about what the project is. One team member may consider a project that ends quickly, so he can return to his normal work routine, to be successful. Another may believe the project's budget to be entirely unrealistic, and so tacitly decide to ignore it. This adds to the likelihood of project failure. Yet, every team member has a powerful vested interest in a coherent, achievable, shared vision because they are the ones who must bring the project from vision to reality. They are being held accountable for doing so.

However, it may be very difficult or even impossible to initially align all these parties around a shared vision. For example, one firm started a project to design a new software system for tracking the financial contributions of university alumni. The marketing team presold the software to three different universities. Although their needs were similar, each university requested specific capabilities to make the software compatible with their existing systems. The marketing team didn't fully understand these technical requests and as a result they did not communicate them to the project team. Thus each customer had a different vision of project success and the project team had yet another vision. The project team attempted to fulfill the version of the vision they understood, delivering a project outcome that did not satisfy any of the different customer visions; thus the project was deemed to have failed. The point is that it is easy enough to say that a project vision must be customer- or stakeholder-focused, but it is not always so easy to identify just who the customer(s) or stakeholder(s) are, much less reconcile their disparate visions. The complexity of the project stakeholder community can significantly complicate creation of that customer-focused vision.

Sometimes the environment does not permit a consensus stakeholder vision. Perhaps customer executives are locked in a battle over a high-technology versus a low-risk solution for, say, a new aircraft. Perhaps the subcontractor company that is developing the cockpit displays wants to incorporate some of their features into its own new product line. Perhaps that subcontractor has a partner that is providing the glass and electronics for those displays, who wants to use this project as the rationale for building a new state-of-the-art manufacturing facility. These disparate stakeholders may well never be willing to compromise enough to agree on an integrated and shared vision of project success. Stakeholders, including customers, are not always competent either. Miller and Lessard, writing about the challenges of large engineering projects (LEPs) commented that, "Sponsors are not equal in their competencies to shape projects. Shaping and anchoring LEPs, just like shaping and anchoring movies or operas, depends not only on the quality of the story (i.e., the project) but also on the talents of the players and the context in which they work."[4] Despite these challenges, the disparate visions must be shaped into a single project vision.

Project sponsors, whether they are external customers or internal business unit leaders, should have a vision for their projects. just as an artist has a vision for her art. Project sponsors should carefully articulate the vision so that all stakeholders and the project team members can understand, embrace, and act on it. Project managers must help the project sponsors overcome the hurdles that discourage the emergence of a single, coherent, achievable project vision.

Teams occasionally find themselves operating in an environment where there is no vision of project success, not even an abstract or conflicting vision (see Figure 2.1). Teams that find themselves without a vision inevitably discover that team members and stakeholders are moving in various directions without a plan or coordination. As a result their work is nonproductive or even counterproductive. For example, during a risk assessment workshop, a few members of a project team were struggling with an assignment to generate a list of potential risks and opportunities. After failing to answer several basic questions about the project, they admitted they had no idea what their new project was about. Even so, upper management was urging them to begin working right away to maintain the schedule that had been promised to the customer. It seems that immediately after the contract was awarded, the customer had reassigned their main point of contact to another project and a replacement had not yet been named. Additionally, the main point of contact within the project team organization, the project manager who had negotiated the contract with the customer, had several months ago accepted a promotion at another facility. A new project manager had been assigned after an eight-week delay, but he was already working on two other projects as well as helping to pull together a bid on a new project. As a result he had not yet read the contract for this particular project, had not yet met with the project team, and had not yet visited the customer.

Figure 2.1 Project Visions

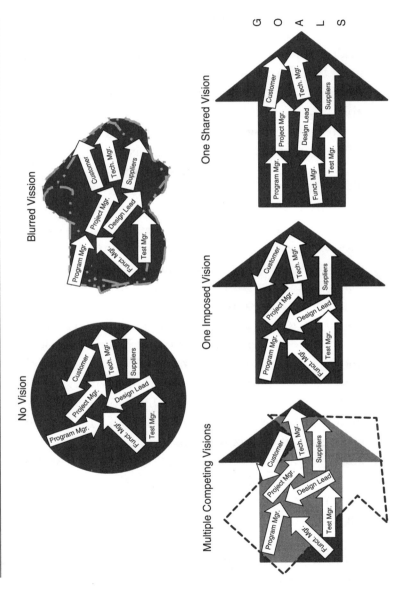

The project contract and related specifications were vague or incomplete on several key points, but the agreed-upon schedule was clearly documented. A preliminary design review (PDR) had been scheduled for only six weeks from the date of our conversation with the frustrated team members. The team was attempting to make progress without the benefit of knowing its destination—without a vision. Project success seemed highly unlikely and customer dissatisfaction seemed assured. Project managers must work with the sponsors to create a viable vision about which all will agree. Failing that. the project manager must create a vision for the team, even if it lacks outside stakeholder support.

Teams may find themselves operating in an environment where one or more project visions exists but is unclear and subject to significantly different interpretations. Consider the case of a typical married couple that hires a contractor to build them a new house. The husband and wife each has a vision of the perfect house. He has in mind a home office, a media room, a three-car garage, and perhaps a workshop as well. She has in mind a large eat-in kitchen, a large garden tub in the master bathroom, lots of storage space, and her own home office. They both want an open floor plan suitable for entertaining, three bedrooms, two full bathrooms, and a powder room. They also want the house to be under 3000 square feet in size, agreeing that anything larger would be "a waste of space" for the empty nesters that they are. They also agree on the budget. They want to pay no more than $450,000 because they believe they can get that when they sell their current house. Notice that their shared vision of the price has nothing to do with an assessment of the costs of building their dream house. Their separate visions for the house are not necessarily logical or consistent; they overlap in some areas, differ in some areas, and conflict in some areas. Worse, the husband and wife may not know what the other considers important. In fact, they may not consciously understand what features of the house they themselves consider most important. Nonetheless, when asked, they say they have discussed the plans and have reached general agreement about their shared vision for the new house.

So, what is their building contractor to do? The contractor cannot build a house that satisfies both of their individual visions because the price and floor space requirements preclude putting in all the items they both want, and may even preclude everything each one wants. He cannot build a house that satisfies their mutual vision because it is vague, contradictory, and entirely fails to address some important areas of disagreement, which the couple still has but tacitly decides to not discuss. Certainly, the contractor cannot build a house that satisfies the subconscious visions the couple may have because he does not know what they are. The contractor, if he has any hope of satisfying the clients, must help them come to terms with their individual visions and reconcile themselves to agree on a more specific and clear vision that the he can accomplish. This shared vision becomes the contractor's project vision, the vision he can translate into specifications and requirements that enable him, his crew, and his subcontractors to build a house the couple will be happy with. The contractor and his team face a difficult, frustrating, and likely futile challenge if he fails to recognize and bring to the surface the husband and wife's independent subconscious visions and then reconcile those different visions into a single achievable vision.

To take another example, a regional freight carrier put together a team to replace a manual routing system with a software-based system that had already been successfully implemented by other freight carriers. The project team was also tasked to buy and install new office computers to host the system and to connect them via an improved computer network. A project manager was selected and several employees were assigned to work on the project with an outside consultant and a technical advisor. One might assume that because this project was clearly defined, its vision was well understood, but that was not the case.

The owner of this freight carrier was not a friend of technology, believing that the manual systems were reliable, less expensive, and quite good enough to meet the company's needs. But he was not around much, having turned day-to-day operations of the company over to his son, who was anxious to move the business out of the technological "dark ages." Dad had reluctantly approved the project but warned that he would close it down if it became too expensive. Still believing that the new system was probably unnecessary and wasteful, he was poised to kill it at the first opportunity.

The son was only a bit more technology savvy than his dad, but he saw the project as an opportunity to declare his independence and to wrest a bit more control of the company from his dad. He did not appreciate the inherent risks, and he desperately wanted the project to move along quickly without technical or cost problems.

The routing-system supervisor was currently overseeing a team of ten individuals but, according to the software vendor's proposal, her group would be reduced to four if the new system proved successful. She was therefore worried that her department would be merged with another one and that she would be demoted. She was equally concerned about being unable to accomplish the routing activities during the transition to the new system. She was in favor of a slow careful transition but would have been secretly pleased if the project was cancelled.

Meanwhile, the IT coordinator saw the potential to expand his authority by increasing the size and relevance of the activities for which he was responsible. He saw this project as the first of several initiatives to add IT systems and infrastructure within the company, resulting in a bigger IT department budget, more staff, and a more central role in the organization. He was highly motivated to see the project get under way and to have it declared a success.

Notice that none of the stakeholders, except perhaps the current routing-system supervisor, had much interest in the specific features and functionality of the new system. To make matters worse, work on the project began without any serious analysis of how long it would take, how much it would cost, or what the standard for measuring completion or success would be. There seemed little likelihood this project team would be able to find success. At least some of the several important stakeholders were going to be disappointed no matter what the outcome.

In fact, the project suffered delays and cost increases because the sponsors continually argued about nearly every resource and priority decision as they tried to jockey to drive the project outcome toward their individual vision of success. The project was eventually canceled, but only after a lot of money had been spent. The project had failed not because the technology was too challenging or for a lack of funding, and not because of a lack of a sound deployment plan. (The consultant had provided a detailed and entirely achievable deployment plan for buying, installing, and testing the new system.). It failed because of the unreconciled competing and even incompatible visions that led the participants to fight over every decision. That perpetual conflict, rooted in the lack of a shared vision, was what doomed the project to failure.

Sometimes teams are forced to work with a clearly articulated but disagreeable vision, one that is imposed on them rather than one they embrace. They may, for example, find themselves working to accomplish plans that were developed with too little appreciation for local issues that might require unique responses. They may also find themselves attempting to accomplish tasks for which they lack technical skills or resources. Such teams may work diligently and expend a great deal of energy but make little progress. The following example is typical.

During the past decade many large corporations have taken steps to expand IT systems as part of a broad initiative to integrate all parts of their businesses, including engineering, procurement, and production. The desire for higher levels of functional integration has been one factor in a trend toward making site-based organizations obsolete. For example, a company may have a 2000-person site devoted to defense department business, and a different 1,000-person chemical processing facility that develops and manufactures specialty chemicals for the cosmetics industry. Each site/facility likely has its own IT system, developed to best support the site's activities; now the IT services will be provided by a centralized IT organization serving all sites.

One major corporation, let's call them Alpha, adopted this strategy of replacing existing site-based IT organizations and systems with centrally managed systems. Local teams, under the guidance of central managers, were created to implement the new systems. The site leaders and the local members of the IT conversion teams were unhappy about the transition, resenting the loss of local control. They were unhappy about having to use remote call-center support rather than local support, convinced that response time would be longer and problem resolutions more difficult—and that turned out to be true at many sites. They were worried about losing local jobs. They found themselves working on a project whose vision was clearly articulated, but which they and their local supervisors did not embrace. Predictably, those teams found it difficult to be enthused and creative in the execution of the projects. The result was implementation problems, delays, cost growth, and less than optimal systems being deployed.

Change is always discomforting and sometimes the members of a project team will be unhappy about what they have been asked to do. Such is a reality of business life. Leaders must recognize the inevitable consequences and take steps to minimize them by working hard to create and gain acceptance of a single shared vision. Failing that, leaders must build in sufficient cost, schedule, and staffing contingency to cope with the inevitable conflict and delay.

Teams do sometimes find themselves engaged in a project with a clear and compelling vision that team members can fully embrace. All the affected parties are involved in the development of plans; and thus find themselves acting in concert rather than opposition. Intergroup communication is open and frequent. There is a shared sense of progress and accomplishment.

For example, in the mid-1980s the Air Force Space Technology Center (AFSTC) launched a competitive project to develop a new generation of computer chips for military satellites, the customer's vision was clear. The AFSTC wanted to make available to various DOD satellite development projects a computer that would survive the radiation effects of a nuclear explosion. It was the end of the cold war era and the DOD community was afraid the Russians might attempt to blind U.S. military communications by exploding nuclear devices in the vicinity of orbiting satellites, disabling them and in so doing disabling military communications and intelligence gathering. The AFSTC intended to fund and oversee two contractors who would race to develop the computer. The technology at the time was such that a computer chip containing about 100,000 gates[5] typically required three sequential design iterations, or cycles. The first design cycle included the initial design of the circuitry, design verification, implementation of the design in silicon, putting the silicon into packages so it could be tested, and testing of the devices. Engineers typically found a few significant errors that had to be corrected. The second design cycle usually included correction of the errors found in the first cycle and perhaps a few design modifications or enhancements, then design verification, implementation in silicon, packaging, and testing. Engineers would then verify the previous errors had been corrected, and also identify a few more subtle errors that the errors discovered during the first cycle had masked. The third design cycle included the correction of the remaining errors, design verification, implementation in silicon, packaging, and testing. With luck, the third pass chips would be fully functional and usable for assembling prototype computers.

The AFSTC selected Honeywell and IBM as the two contractors because both companies were operating at the cutting edge of very high-speed integrated circuit (VHSIC) technology, the leading electronic component technology at that time, and because they each submitted price-competitive and technically feasible bids. Both contractors were delighted to win this new project, the Generic VHISIC Spacebourne Computer (GVSC) Program, because it provided government funding to further advance their technologies and because project success would likely lead to several government contracts to provide computers for various satellites that were planned for development over the next decade. Thus the AFSTC's (the immediate customer), Honeywell's, and IBM's (the two contractors) visions were aligned in that they all wanted to offer future DOD satellite projects a robust and capable radiation-hardened computer solution.

The Honeywell and IBM project teams even had similar visions of success. Each wanted to beat the other to the marketplace. This strong desire to be first to market with a robust solution was well founded. The DOD satellite development community is often reputed to behave much like lemmings. The lemming is a 3- to 6-inch long rodent found in or near the Arctic. Like many other rodents, they tend to have boom and bust cycles of population growth.

During boom periods, the lemmings migrate in large groups and have been known to attempt to swim en masse across large bodies of water in search of a new habitat. This behavior was often mistakenly believed to be mass suicide by those who saw thousands of them dive into the Arctic Ocean and swim away from shore, and thus was born the myth of one lemming following another to certain death. DOD satellite development also goes through periodic boom and bust cycles that are, relatively speaking, as dramatic as those of the lemmings, and they do often display common group behaviors, not unlike the lemmings. Satellite development teams tackle extremely risky technical and political challenges, yet in some respects they are very risk adverse. The consequences of a technical mistake may be severe—perhaps loss of a billion dollar satellite. So, technical adventurism is infrequent. They often try to select designs and components that other design teams have already selected because those are considered to be technically, and politically, lower risk decisions. Thus, the mythical lemming effect is often attributed to the DOD satellite development teams who tend to follow the decisions of other teams rather than take unique technical risks.

Both Honeywell and IBM appreciated the value of being the first to market with their computer-chip set because the first to market would likely be the first to be selected for the next DOD satellite project and would therefore likely be the preferred choice of subsequent DOD satellite projects. The first to market with a good solution would likely capture a major share of the market for years to come.

The Honeywell team decided that to beat IBM to the marketplace, they needed to accomplish the design in two rather than three design cycles. To increase the odds of success, they decided to attempt to achieve first-pass success of all five of the computer chips necessary for their computer architecture. They had little confidence that they could actually do this, but they believed that embracing such a vision would assure the best possible first-pass results and better their chances of coming up with a successful design after two cycles.

The first-pass success vision drove the team to seek every possible means to analyze and verify the accuracy of their initial chip designs. They came up with innovative analysis and verification approaches. They checked and rechecked their work. They sought out independent reviews of what they had done. All this effort caused the first cycle to last for nearly a year and a half, rather than the typical year. As a result, their first-pass chips were available nearly six months after IBM's first-pass chips were completed, a fact that gave IBM a public relations advantage and drew interest from several DOD satellite-development teams even though the IBM chips had several typical first-pass errors and could not demonstrate functionality. However, when the first-pass Honeywell chips were finally completed, three of their five chips had no errors or design flaws and the remaining two chips had only minor errors. This performance success wowed the marketplace, and the DOD satellite developers descended on the Honeywell team. The Honeywell team quickly completed the second pass redesigns and delivered a fully functional computer chip set after only two cycles, nearly one year ahead of IBM. The first- and second-pass successes won Honeywell the first DOD satellite computer opportunities and led to further marketplace success in ensuing years.

The clear, consistent, and stable Honeywell GVSC Program vision enabled the team to focus its energy on a challenging but achievable strategy, leading to project success. That vision of first-pass success was the catalyst for creativity, innovation, effort, and teamwork that propelled the Honeywell team to a remarkable achievement.

PROJECT MANAGERS MUST SHAPE THE VISION

Few project are fortunate enough to be handed a single, coherent, achievable vision for their work. Nonetheless, the project team must create for itself a vision or glean one from the disparate visions being thrust upon it. The project manager must understand each stakeholder's unique vision and find among them a single project vision that the team can embrace and work to achieve (see Figure 2.2). The project manager, who holds primary responsibility for fostering or creating a single project vision, must work tirelessly to build a level of consensus among the stakeholders, a consensus that acknowledges the different stakeholder visions, but one that reaches agreement on what the project team must accomplish. That single vision, derived from all the competing and conflicting stakeholder visions, becomes the foundation for the specifications and

Figure 2.2   Visual Mapping of Project Vision

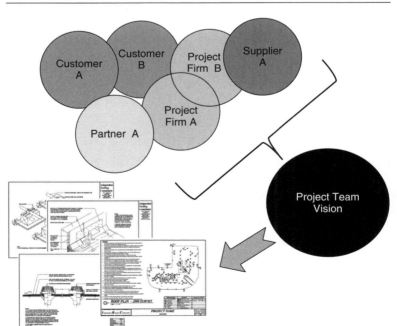

requirements around which the project activity will be planned and executed.

The challenge of building such a consensus is a massive one. Yet, failure to do so has a massive effect on the chances of project success. If left to their own devices the project stakeholders, who may not even acknowledge one another, will not come together to negotiate a single project vision. The project manager is uniquely positioned to bring those stakeholders together and to help them reach agreement on the project vision.

Project managers should ask themselves a series of questions about their project's vision, questions that when answered will bring to light the actions necessary to create and sell a vision of project success:

- Who is affected by the project and who affects the direction the project might take? Who will judge whether or not the project has succeeded?
- Who are the various project stakeholders?
- Do I understand their visions, or lack of vision, for this project?
- Can the stakeholder visions be aligned or compromised into a single vision?
- Do the project team members already have a vision or visions of what this project is about?
- What single project vision can be distilled from the stakeholder visions?
- Has that project vision been clearly articulated?
- Is the vision simple and straightforward?
- Is the vision motivating and energizing?
- Is the vision understood and shared by customer(s), business, suppliers, and the team?
- Is the vision actionable and measurable?
- How aligned is the team around the vision?
- How aligned is the vision with the key business values and initiatives in which the project is being accomplished?

The project manager has four distinct responsibilities with regard to shaping project stakeholder's visions. The project manager is uniquely positioned to identify all the important stakeholders, decide which ones should be acknowledged, and to learn what the stakeholder expectations are. Second, she must accept the responsibility for helping key stakeholders form and/or adopt a vision if they do not have one. Third, she must accept responsibility for working with the various stakeholders to adapt their independent visions into a single vision for the project. The first two responsibilities involve situation analysis, facilitation, and perhaps creativity while the third responsibility also demands negotiation skills and political savvy to get the stakeholders to find common ground and persuade some of them to compromise their expectations. Fourth, the project manager must uncover or create, articulate, sell, and nurture this vision. Peter Senge says, "Shared visions emerge from personal visions. This is how they derive their energy and how they foster commitment."[6] He is describing how important it is that organizations build a shared vision by encouraging individuals to develop their own visions then integrate those individual visions into a collective vision that everyone can embrace. Senge argues that leaders must guide their organizations toward such a collective vision, allowing it to evolve and mature rather than delivering that vision as part of some corporate guidance or strategic plan.

Senge's advice is sound, especially for the leader of an ongoing enterprise and perhaps even for some major long duration projects. The Space Shuttle Program has been active for 40 years. The Big Dig project(discussed in more detail in Chapter 7, the most expensive highway project ever conducted in the United States, rerouted Interstate 93 through a tunnel that runs under downtown Boston. It, too, began in the 1970s and did not end until 2008, at a cost of over $22 billion versus an original estimate of about $6 billion (in same-year dollars). These two projects were in the planning stages for a decade or so before they got under way. Certainly some projects take a while to start and to complete. Certainly, there is time to allow the stakeholder vision(s) to evolve and to allow the project team members to develop personal visions that become a shared vision.

However, project managers often find themselves in a situation where time is a vicious enemy. They may have inherited a new project that is already getting under way, that is planned to last for only a year or so, and that is currently in desperate need of context. The project manager cannot wait for a shared vision to evolve from the bottom up. A modest IT project may last six months or even less. A commercial electronics device such as a cell phone or laptop computer may go from project start, to prototype, to first production in less than a year. A typical aerospace electronic product development project may last for one to three years. As a result, project managers find they must move very quickly to identify stakeholders, understand and integrate their expectations into a single project vision, then help their project team embrace that vision as their own—no mean feat!

The project manager faces additional challenges. Christenson and Walker[7] contend that, "both a project vision and an organizational vision share many common characteristics. However, a project vision is more complex because projects use multiple temporary organizations each with their own cultures and subcultures." Even so, it is a necessary feat. Christenson and Walker said, "Rigorous applications of project management methodologies are responsible, though only partially, for project success. We argue—that a significant driver of project management success is effective and intelligent leadership communicated through an inspiring vision of what the project is meant to achieve and how it can make a significant positive impact."

Christenson and Walker also said, "We argue that much of the skill of project management leadership is about ensuring that the project need is adequately articulated into a project vision statement that facilitates enthusiasm and commitment for its successful realization. In this way a deep understanding of the value of the project, its motivational potential for those involved and its credibility as a worthwhile endeavour that aspires to achieve a best-in-class outcome can be encompassed through the artifact of the vision."[8]

CAPTURING THE VISION

Let us assume for a minute that the customer(s), internal senior management, and the project team have a shared vision of project success. That shared vision must be clearly documented in an approved "project mission and goals charter statement." First, the act of documenting, reviewing, and approving the statement is a way to verify that all stakeholders share the assumed common vision. Second, people come and go. As time passes some of individuals who were not party to the original understandings may replace the key stakeholders. The project mission and goals statement helps encourage consistency over time. Third, relative power and influence changes over time. Individuals who failed to get their way in the past may later have more influence and be in a position to "reinterpret" the project vision. Again the documented vision provides stability and a basis for dealing with change. Fourth, visions sometimes must change; customer needs shift, technical learning occurs, or new competitive forces emerge. The mission and goals statement provides a baseline from which to understand the extent and impact of a changed vision. It enables all stakeholders to move to a new consensus.

The project mission and goals charter statement documents what is *not* included within the project scope, as well as what is included. For example the statement may assert that the new warehouse construction project includes the structure and basic utilities but excludes any security or access control systems. These exclusions help further define the project limits and deliverables.

The project vision, as captured in the mission and goals statement, also describes the deliverable work product and results. Stakeholders should discuss, agree on, and document the specific results that should emerge from the project activity. This will help assure a shared vision. It will also help the project team understand what tangible outcomes will constitute project success.

The project vision must be monitored and nurtured after it has been defined, articulated, and embraced. Later as the project unfolds managers must continually test the vision to confirm it is still appropriate or to determine how it should change. Appropriate questions include:

- Is the goal of project still important to the customer and the company, and have any of the key stakeholders visions changed?
- Does the project team understand and embrace the vision? Are they acting in concert with the vision?
- Would we have the same project vision if we were beginning this project today?
- Is the project on track to accomplishing the vision as stated and, if not, what are the stakeholder implications?
- Can the project vision be adjusted to meet the different stakeholder needs?

A PROJECT VISION CONTINUALLY EVOLVES

The challenge of fostering and maintaining a shared vision is even greater because stakeholder visions are not static. They may shift for any number of legitimate reasons including marketplaces change, financial changes, organizational priority shifts, or the emergence of new technologies. For example, some aviation electronics firms may have begun a series of new product developments to position themselves for a next-generation air traffic management system but a surge in political conservatism may spark a congressional enthusiasm for balancing the federal budget, which may result in a loss of government funding for the aviation infrastructure funding essential to making the new system feasible. The firms would appropriately find themselves slowing, delaying, or even canceling product development projects.

Stakeholders may also adjust their project visions for more mundane reasons. Several years ago the 76-year-old president of a successful but small engineering firm provided small-volume special equipment for a variety of needs, including a few unique assemblies for use on the Space Shuttle. A project team within the firm was currently working to develop an improved Space Shuttle assembly. The Space Shuttle work was not profitable. In fact, supporting NASA was often far more demanding than any of the other work done by the firm, and at times the demands put a severe strain on the firm's ability to satisfy other customer commitments. Nonetheless, the president felt it was his civic duty, even his privilege, to support NASA and the Space Shuttle program. One day the president had a health scare that caused him to suddenly decide to retire, leaving control of the business to his son. Within less than thirty days the son had canceled all project work related to the Space Shuttle and informed NASA that the firm would cease supporting the current products in 24 months. A critical project stakeholder had been replaced and the new stakeholder had an entirely different perspective than his predecessor. Nothing about the marketplace, the technologies, or the profitability had changed. Instead, someone who had a different perspective and priorities, had replaced a key stakeholder.

A project vision may change for other reasons. As a project progresses the team inevitably makes discoveries and resolves uncertainties that may well affect outside stakeholder or project team member visions for the project. Preliminary testing may reveal that the selected technical approach is not feasible and that the only alternate approach will be both more expensive and less capable than expected. Or, a team may find that the performance requirements and the power consumption requirements are incompatible, making the product less attractive than expected versus competitor's products. Thus, the team may uncover new information or insights that cause stakeholders or team members to reassess what the project can accomplish, thereby altering the project vision.

Environmental forces may drive a project vision to change. Certainly the British Petroleum oil well platform disaster and the subsequent environmental damage in the Gulf of Mexico in 2010 altered the visions of many projects in the oil industry, the fishing industry, the tourist industry, and other industries in that region of the United States, or around the world.

Project visions may be thought of as existing on a two-dimensional grid. In Figure 2.3, we see along the horizontal axis that one stable and coherent vision, like the GVSC project vision described earlier, provides a guiding beacon that enables teams to steer a path toward success. But as described above, not all project visions remain stable throughout a project's life. Sometimes a project vision changes chaotically. Such dynamics can lead to dramatically changing interpretations of what the project is intended to achieve. With regard to the vertical axis, notice that a blurry project vision, or even no vision at all, may be less detrimental to project success than are multiple visions

Figure 2.3   Vision Management Arena

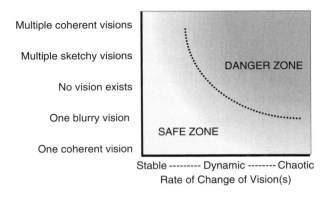

because multiple conflicting visions encourage project conflict, contradictory and wasted effort, and indecision. Another reason is that a project manager may have more success creating, garnering support for, and maintaining a vision where none exists or where stakeholders have only fuzzy notions about the project vision. The project manager has a much greater challenge when stakeholders are individually attached to conflicting visions.

Although project visions may change, the project team's consensus must not change. Visions may change for many legitimate reasons. The BP oil spill would certainly be a legitimate reason for a fish processing company to slow down the construction of a new processing plant. The introduction of the iPhone was a legitimate reason for several companies to speed up their efforts to develop more advanced phones. The completion of Boeing's new Dreamliner airplane and its success in the marketplace was a legitimate reason for Airbus to rethink its vision for their next new airplane projects. What must not change is team consensus. Teams operating in unison are capable of shifting quickly to adopt a new or altered vision but teams operating without a mutually agreed vision will likely falter when the environment imposes a shift in the project vision.

SUMMARY

Project managers should keep in mind the following vision management tools, techniques, and practices:

- Express visions—Project managers should understand that their projects have multiple sponsors and stakeholders who may have various visions of what it means for a particular project to succeed. They should work to understand those various visions and distill from them a few vision alternatives the stakeholders and sponsors may be able to agree on. Then they should express candidate visions starting a dialogue toward arriving at a consensus vision.

- Invest in consensus building exercises—Project managers should sponsor them and participate in them. Project success is more likely when sponsors and stakeholders are more aligned and less likely when they are less aligned.

- Champion a vision—The project manager can be a catalyst for achieving a project vision that can be shared by all parties. The project manager is uniquely well positioned to be able to discern what vision is most appropriate for the project team and to convince the stakeholders and sponsors to embrace, or at least to accept that vision for the project.

- Force the issue—The project manager must be willing to go higher if necessary. Consensus around the project vision is a vital first step toward project success and lack of consensus is a powerful inhibitor of success. Resist the pressure to begin work prematurely. The project manager is obligated to work toward a coherent project vision before work begins.

- Deliver a vision to the team—The stakeholders and sponsors may be unable or unwilling to deliver a coherent consensus vision to the team. If so the project manager must create and deliver such a vision to the team, one that the team can embrace and that has the best chance of satisfying, or at least appeasing, the stakeholders and sponsors.
- Sell the vision to the team—Project managers should work to help the team members understand and embrace the project vision, a vision that will help them find success.
- Make the vision statement a part of the project management plan—The vision statement provides a continual reminder to all parties about why the project exists and what it is supposed to accomplish. It also serves to educate new members about the teams' purpose.
- Monitor vision commitment—Commitments waiver and visions shift over time. Project managers must continually monitor stakeholders, sponsors, and team members communicate, listen, test, communicate, and listen.
- Continually state the vision—Leaders may choose to begin every meeting or discussion with stakeholders, sponsors, suppliers, partners, subcontractors, or team members with a summary reminder about the project vision. Such reminders help nurture continued support.

Birner, Hastings, and Geddes said, "The most significant success factor for project teams is that they have a common and shared idea of what difference they are trying to make as a result of the project."[9] A shared vision is perhaps the foundation of foundations for a successful project while disparate visions will without doubt destine a

project to failure. Disparate visions cause misunderstandings and disagreements about priorities and they in turn
lead to confusion and conflict about resource allocations.
Disparate visions also assure that at least some, perhaps
all, of the stakeholders who care about the project will be
dissatisfied with its outcome. On the other hand a shared
vision that is clearly documented, communicated, and
maintained give the project team a good start toward success because at least then everyone knows what is to be
accomplished. Stakeholders are also more likely to make
resource and priority decisions that will enable project
success rather than make decisions that conflict with one
another and thus impede success. The project manager is
more responsible than anyone else for the creation, articulation, selling, and nurturing of that shared vision.

CHAPTER 3

HABIT # 2—TRANSLATE THE PROJECT VISION INTO COHERENT REQUIREMENTS

"Would you tell me please, which way I ought to go from here? That depends a good deal on where you want to get to, said the cat. I don't much care where, said Alice. Then it doesn't matter which way you go, said the cat."
—Lewis Carrol, *Alice in Wonderland*

Leonardo Da Vinci is frequently credited with having the first vision of a helicopter, what he called the Helical Air Screw in 1490 A.D. He wrote, "I have discovered that a screw-shaped device such as this, if it is well made from starched linen, will rise in the air if turned quickly." However, Da Vinci was not the first to have the idea. A book written in China in the fourth century A.D. describes "flying cars with wood from the inner part of the jujube tree with ox-leather straps fastened to returning blades as to set the machine in motion." The Chinese may have been describing a toy, whereas Da Vinci likely had in mind a more substantive application. Nonetheless, the concept for a helicopter existed as long as 1800 years, and certainly no less than 300 years, before the first working models were built by several different European experimenters between 1750 and 1850. Progress toward a viable design concept continued until the early 1900s when a working prototype was finally demonstrated.[1]

The helicopter was destined to remain only a vision until the technology advanced sufficiently (i.e., the development of the internal combustion engine for power and cyclic controls for stability). Nearly 400 years after Da Vinci sketched his vision of a helicopter, engineers were able to document the technical requirements and performance specifications that would enable a project team to make a helicopter a reality.

Project visions are rarely as exotic or as far ahead of the state of the technology as was Da Vinci's Helical Air Screw. Today, it is rarely the case that technology is hundreds of years, or even decades, after the vision that causes a project to be proposed—we usually label such notions science fiction. Projects are nearly always founded on more pragmatic and feasible visions that must be appropriately translated into a coherent and consistent set of requirements and specifications.

Translation of a viable project vision into a work scope definition has always been a challenge. In 1907, less than five years after the Wright brothers' historic flight at Kitty Hawk, North Carolina, the U. S. War Department awarded them a contract to build one working airplane. The competition had been fierce, "Theirs was one of 41 bids, ranging from $850 to $1 million, and the Wright's proposal of $25,000 was not the lowest." but the Wright brothers' were deemed to have a less risky proposal and were selected.[2]

The Wright brothers had to deal with a work-definition package, in particular a two-page contract and a one-page list of specifications (see Figure 3.1). Specification No. 10 of

Figure 3.1   Signal Corps Specification No. 486

Donor	Original Source	PIMA ID	Donor ID	Category
Ed Erslev	Frank A Dobbe	NA	G-RP.2217	OCR-G-RP
	John O. Moench			

SIGNAL CORPS SPECIFICATION, NO. 486.

ADVERTISEMENT AND SPECIFICATION FOR A HEAVIER THAN-AIR FLYING MACHINE

To the Public:

Sealed proposals, in duplicate, will be received at this office until 12 O'clock noon on February 1, 1908, on behalf of the Board of Ordnance and Fortification for furnishing the Signal Corps with a heavier-than-air flying machine. All proposals received will be turned over to the Board of Ordnance and Fortification at its first meeting after February 1 for its official action.

Persons wishing to submit proposals under this specification can obtain the necessary forms and envelopes by application to the Chief Signal Officer, United States Army, War Department, Washington, D.C. The United States reserves the right to reject any and all proposals.

Unless the bidders are also the manufacturers of the flying machine they must state the name and place of the maker.

Preliminary, – This specification covers the construction of a flying machine supported entirely by the dynamic reaction of the atmosphere and having, no gas bag.

Acceptance. – The flying machine will be accepted only after a successful trial flight, during which it will comply with all requirements of this specification. No payments on account will be made until after the trial flight and acceptance.

Inspection, – The Government reserves the right to inspect any and all processes of manufacture.

GENERAL REQUIREMENTS

The general dimensions of the flying machine will tic determined by the manufacturer, subject to the following conditions:

1. Bidders must submit with their proposals the following:
    (a)   Drawings to scale showing the general dimensions and shape of the flying machine which they propose to build under this specification.
    (b)   Statement of the speed for which it is designed.
    (c)   Statement of the total surface area of the supporting planes.
    (d)   Statement of the total weight.
    (e)   Description of the engine which will be used for motive power.
    (f)   The material of which the frame, planes, and propellers will be constructed.

Plans received will not be shown to other bidders.

Continued

Figure 3.1—Continued

2. It is desirable that the flying machine should be designed so that it may be quickly and easily assembled and taken apart and packed for transportation in army wagons. It should be capable of being assembled and put in operating condition in about one hour.
3. The flying machine must be designed to carry two persons having a combined weight of about 350 pounds, also sufficient fuel for a flight of 125 miles.
4. The flying machine should be designed to have a speed of at least forty miles per hour in still air, but bidders must submit quotations in their proposals for cost depending upon the speed attained during the trial flight, according to the following scale:

   40 miles per hour, 100 per cent.
   39 miles per hour, 90 per cent.
   38 miles per hour, 80 per cent.
   37 miles per hour, 70 per cent.
   36 miles per hour, 60 per cent
   Less than 36 miles per hour rejected.
   41 mi les per hour, 110 per cent.
   42 miles per hour, 120 per cent.
   43 miles per hour, 130 per cent.
   44 miles per hour, 140 per cent.

5. The speed accomplished during the trial flight will be determined by taking an average of the time over a measured course of more than five miles, against and with the wind. The time will be taken by a flying start, passing the starting point at full speed at both ends of the course. This test subject to such additional details as the Chief Signal Officer of the Army may prescribe at the time.
6. Before acceptance a trial endurance flight will be- required of at least one hour during which time the flying machine must remain continuously in the air without landing. It shall return to the starting point and land without any damage that would prevent it immediately starting upon another flight. During this trial flight of one hour it must be steered in all directions without difficulty and at all times under perfect control and equilibrium.
7. Three trials will be allowed for speed as provided for in paragraphs 4 and 5. *Three* trials for endurance as provided for in paragraph 6, and both tests must be completed within a period of thirty days from the date of delivery. The expense of the tests to be borne by the manufacturer. The place of delivery to the Government and **trial flights will** be at Fort Myer, Virginia.
8. It should be so designed as to ascend in any country which may be encountered in field service. The starting device must be simple and transportable. It should also land in a

Source: Edwards, Vernon (2002). "The True Story of the Wright Brothers' Contract (It's Not What You Think.)" WIFCON.COM http://www.wifcon.com /anal/analwright.htm, accessed Jan. 5, 2011.

their contract stipulated that the airplane "should be sufficiently simple in its construction and operation to permit an intelligent man to become proficient in its use within a reasonable length of time." Anyone with project management experience will immediately react to the vagueness of such phrases as "sufficiently simple," "intelligent man," "become proficient in its use," and "reasonable length of time." The loosely worded specifications no doubt created problems as soon as the Wright brothers began to design the airplane. They had to come up with a physical design that would comply with the specifications. How would they interpret these subjective phrases? Was a month a reasonable period of time for an intelligent person to become proficient in using the airplane? How about one week? How about an hour? What does "proficient in its use" mean to the Army customer? Does "use" include just operation or does it also include maintenance? Does proficiency include the ability to make routine repairs? How does one define an "intelligent person"? Each different interpretation of these requirements translates into a different approach to starting the engine, takeoff and landing techniques, flight controls, and maintenance, and each alternative translates into unique design constraints. No doubt the Wright brothers had lively conversations between themselves and with the Army customer representatives about how to interpret these phrases during the airplane design phase and later when testing began, on September 1, 1908.

The first two weeks of flight-testing were relatively successful. Orville Wright made several flights of up to an hour and even carried a passenger on a couple of trips. But on September 17, he took off, carrying U.S. Army Lieutenant Thomas Selfridge. Something went wrong. The plane began to shake, and Orville killed the engine, after which the plane dived and crashed. Both men were injured, and Lieutenant Selfridge subsequently died from his head injuries, making him the first passenger to be killed in an airplane accident. A broken propeller blade that cut a control line had caused the crash. The Wright brothers had defaulted on their contract but, despite the tragedy, they were granted several extensions as they continued to work on design modifications.[3]

Today, every project team struggles to develop or to cope with its customer-provided requirements and specifications definition. Recall the regional freight carrier that established a project team to replace its manual routing system with an automated system. The customer in this case was the organization itself, more specifically the son who wanted to prove his independence. The requirements and specifications developed by the consultant were a poor reflection of the vision of the customer and other stakeholders.

The project requirements, specifications, and scope of work definition is accomplished using a variety of tools such as the Statement-of-Work (SOW), the Work Breakdown Structure (WBS), and techniques that help a customer or a project team define, agree on, communicate, and track the project work. Sometimes customers provide a detailed work definition, although they will never cover all the specifics a team must consider. As we will see later, the project team always adds some additional work definition. Sometimes the project team is tasked with developing its own work definition, and then reviewing and negotiating it with the customer. Regardless of who develops the work definition, the most commonly used tools and techniques include the project scope statement, the statement of work, the requirements and the specifications documents, a list of project deliverables, and a list of key event milestones.

The *project scope statement* is a summary of the overall project intent, goals, and objectives. This big picture overview articulates the project vision, thus establishing the parameters within which the more specific work activity can be understood. The scope statement is usually the preamble to the overall project description and requirements document package. For many projects, this is the only place one finds a documented project vision statement.

The *SOW* describes in some detail the work that will be done to accomplish the project objectives. The SOW describes work activities, referring to the requirements and specifications the work activities are intended to address. It is a common assertion that the customer should describe what is to be done and the project team should decide how it is to be done. One often hears the same assertion used to differentiate what the project manager is responsible for, the "what," versus what the functional project team members are responsible for, the "how." In practice, the SOW too often contains a mixture of what is to be done and how the work is to be accomplished, another point we will address in more detail later. In the case of the Wright brothers' contract, the Army provided very little in the way of a SOW. They did state that the supplier must deliver a finished airplane and that the supplier must participate in the testing of the airplane. But, the Army was determined not to pay for research and development work, so they specifically asked for the delivery of a finished vehicle, choosing not to direct the design and production process. Customers do not always practice such self-restraint.

The *requirements document* describes attributes of the deliverable products, systems, or services that embody the project vision. It often becomes part of the contract. The requirements are also used by the project team as a source for understanding the work activities to be accomplished and the standards against which the project outcomes should be measured.

The *specifications document* lists the metrics associated with the requirements. For example, in the Wright brothers contract, we find clear and easily understood specifications: "The flying machine must be designed to carry two persons having a combined weight of about 350 pounds, also sufficient fuel for a flight of 125 miles." (paragraph 3 of the requirements and specification document in Figure 3.1 above). Of course, it also included vague and subject-to-wide-interpretation specifications, as in paragraph 10 of the same document as described earlier. Project teams must negotiate the unambiguous and clarify the ambiguous in order to establish a foundation for project success.

In practice, the terms "requirement" and "specification" are not always used properly. For example, the 14 "general requirements" the Army gave the Wright brothers were contained within a document titled "Signal Corps Specification, No. 486." In other words, the requirements were a subset of the specification rather than the other way around. One quite often finds project documentation containing requirements and specifications intermingled under either heading, creating another challenge for project teams to sort through.

Specifications are generally one of three types. *Design specifications* describe the physical characteristics of the product, system, or service. For example, paragraph two of the Wright brothers contract states that, "it is desirable that the flying machine should be designed so that it may be quickly and easily assembled and taken apart and packed for transportation in Army wagons. It should be capable of being assembled and put in operation in about one hour." This is, however, a somewhat vague description ("quickly and easily assembled and taken apart") of the desired physical characteristics of the airplane. *Performance specifications* describe key operational characteristics of the end product, system, or service. Paragraph nine states, "It should be provided with some device to permit of a safe descent in case of an accident to the propelling machinery." This operational characteristic imposed design constraints and thus created or defined work scope activity the Wright brothers project team had to accomplish, work activity that was not otherwise documented. *Functional specifications* describe how the end item will be used. Paragraph four states: "The flying machine should be designed to have a speed of at least forty miles per hour in still air." This performance specification may have indirectly imposed physical constraints on the airplane design, but the Army cared only about the performance aspects. Note also that this specification is worded as a goal ("should be designed") rather than as a requirement, a common mistake that often leads to subsequent disputes about whether a project has met the requirements. The three types of specifications are not always articulated separately. The Wright brothers contract demonstrates an overlap among design, performance, and functional specifications, as well as a mix of requirements and goals. The discipline of requirements and specifications development has not improved much in the past 100 years.

The *list of deliverables* specifies the tangible outcomes the customer expects from the project activity. It may include deliverable documents such as plans, progress reports, test results, analyses findings, review packages, schedules, and so forth. The list will nearly always include the key deliverable hardware, software, and system delivery expectations, perhaps including prototypes, test articles, and final deliveries.

The *list of key milestones* identifies the critical project events and project deadlines for each. It may include project start and end dates, formal review events (such as preliminary design review, critical design review, and production readiness review), key interface events (such as customer delivery of essential components to be integrated into the project system), and key test and verification events (such as product testing, system qualification testing, or operational field testing). Sometimes the list includes dates for the delivery of key documents or products, thus overlapping with the deliverables list.

These project work definition tools and techniques help the project team translate the vision into actionable work and work product descriptions around which they can build a project plan. The work definition narrative is helpful, even essential, in several ways.

WHY DO WE NEED CLEAR WORK DEFINITION?

The work definition package is the foundation for project planning. As asserted in Chapter 2, one cannot gather resources for and execute a plan to accomplish a vision. A project team must have more specific descriptions that tell it what resources are needed, what the time lines are , what skills are required, what support is needed or expected, and so on, all of which is derived from a mutually agreed work definition package. Assuming the vision is clear, the project work scope is achievable, and resources are available, one can develop a plan to accomplish the agreed SOW, requirements, and specifications. A vision describes an end state and leaves open how one will arrive at that end state. It also often leaves open to interpretation just what that end state is, how the team should go about reaching that end state, and how one may verify it has been reached. A work definition package provides the specificity that enables a project team to lay out a roadmap to make that vision a reality and to unequivocally demonstrate it has been made real.

The project scope statement, SOW, requirements, and specifications help clarify and stabilize the vision. The documents provide a formal and detailed elaboration of the customer's vision statement. If the vision statement is concise, coherent, and achievable, the scope of work definition package provides the specificity that will enable other stakeholders to understand the vision and its implications for them. If the vision statement is feeble or missing. the work definition package offers insights to the customer's vision or lack thereof that may enable the team to bring the customer and other stakeholders closer to embracing a shared vision through a dialogue about the meaning and consequences of the work defined. The mere existence of the work definition package provides some assurance of at least some level of agreement among at least some of the stakeholders about what is to be done. It also provides a starting point for a dialogue with the other stakeholders about their expectations. The "stray" stakeholders find it more difficult to cling to their independent perspectives when a formal work definition package is in place, communicated widely, and followed. The mere presence of such a reference point is a project stabilizer.

The work definition package also provides the elaboration that helps team members interpret the vision in terms of their individual responsibilities. It reduces the likelihood that each individual team member will make separate decisions about how to interpret the implications of the vision or how to go about implementing the intent of the vision. Without it they may find themselves adjusting their perspectives, priorities, and focus away from the project agenda and toward their functional department agenda, the one that is easiest to accomplish with the available resources, or toward their personal agenda rather than the project interests. The work definition package helps build initial understanding and ongoing consensus.

The package also reinforces the tendency of individual team members and work groups to make complementary rather than contradictory tactical decisions. As the work on the project progresses each team member makes dozens of independent decisions daily. For example, a specific test activity may have grown complicated and time consuming. Some members of the test team believe the test must be completed tonight in order to move on to the next testing stage that will use a very expensive and in-great-demand test chamber. Missing the test window tomorrow will force a several week delay until the chamber can again be scheduled. Other members of the test team may not be aware of the consequences of delaying the current test. So, an appropriate decision about working late may or may not be made. Many such decisions are made daily by many members of the project team. A mutually agreed and comprehensive work definition package can help steer those decisions so that the right ones are made. Those decisions are more aligned when the work definition package exists, is comprehensive, is communicated, and is embraced by the stakeholders. They are less aligned, or in conflict, when no such package exists.

It also provides a reference point for addressing the consequences and adaptations resulting from new insights and priorities as the work progresses. Project teams must adapt to new technological developments, capability, priority changes and a host of other factors as the work progresses. The work definition package helps make it evident that change is occurring and brings to light the consequences of that change because it provides a baseline against which potential change can be measured. It is difficult for the team to recognize changes to the work activity if it has no clear definition of that work.

Two parts of the work definition package, the SOW and the requirements/specifications deserve additional discussion. Each is prone to misuse and abuse by those who create them and by those who use them. Each deserves special attention by all the stakeholders, especially the project team, in order to avoid unnecessary difficulties.

The SOW is generally defined as the document that describes the requested work activity. However, in practice the entire work definition package may be referred to as the SOW, in which case it may contain within it something referred to as the "scope of work." In other cases this sub-document is referred to as the SOW. We will use the latter definition, considering the SOW to be a subset of the work definition package, the subset that describes the scope of work activity. Many organizations use the SOW as a general catchall for many types of information they want to communicate to the project team. They may include a mix of work scope, requirements, specifications, delivery expectations, support to be provided, cost expectations, or any number of other items. On the other hand, many organizations also fail to include the specific work that they expect to have done within the scope of the project as it is, or should be, captured in the work definition. So, while this kind of SOW contains useful information, it is often also missing some critical information.

Even the most complete and detailed customer-generated SOW will not address some key project activity, activity that should be captured in the work definition. Customers may be disciplined enough to detail all of their expectations but they will certainly not address work mandated from other sources. For example, the customer may not include Environmental Protection Agency or Occupational Safety and Health Administration regulations in the SOW. Industry or professional norms and conventions may need to be followed, items also not included in the work activities in the customer's SOW. Different sorts of work activity may be imposed as a result of the unique expertise or resources made available to the project team, insights the customer may not have or may not care to address. The team may also have made choices about how they will accomplish the project that will impose unique work activity. So, even the best customer-provided SOWs are always incomplete descriptions of the project work scope activity.

Project teams must hold themselves accountable for developing an appropriately detailed and unambiguous SOW to guide their activities. They must understand what the customer SOW provides, if one exists, and if necessary, engage the customer to clarify, negotiate, and revise the instructions. They must add the activities that customers may not be aware of or not care about and so do not provide, but that are necessary to accomplish the work.

Teams that fail to do so will by default leave it to each work group or individual to sort out for themselves what work must be done, a path that leads to contradictory assumptions, project team frustration, and likely project failure.

In summary, requirements and specifications come from many directions and encompass many dimensions. Ideally, the customer or project sponsor would provide a complete, concise, nonconflicting, and subject-to-only-one-interpretation set of requirements and specifications. Do not count on it. In fact, it almost never happens. Instead, teams must sort through a mixture of formal and informal communications from multiple sources, piecing together what they believe to be an initial set of requirements.

The project management and engineering development field is awash in various types of requirements and associated specifications. The admittedly partial list below hints at the variety:

- System design requirements
- Performance requirements
- Interface requirements
- Test requirements
- Reliability requirements
- Supportability requirements
- Maintenance requirements
- Life-cycle requirements
- Environmental requirements
- Design-to-target cost requirements
- Design-for-producibility requirements
- Product evolution requirements

Forsberg, Mooz, and Cotterman,[4] internationally known project management consultants, offer another perspective on the variety of versions of requirements, prefacing the following list with the statement "requirements—only half a word":

- user
- customer
- stakeholder
- contract
- internal
- baselined
- unbaselined
- concept independent
- concept dependent
- allocated
- derived
- functional
- performance
- design
- verification
- requirements musts
- requirements wants
- requirements weights

Of course, not all these requirements are essential, or even useful, on every project. Project teams and leaders must determine those that are useful and assure they are provided or developed.

As we have seen, some projects begin with a distinct lack of requirements while others begin with many requirements from many sources. Some of those sources and requirements are worthy and some less so, but they come nonetheless. Requirements may come from customers. Some customers, especially those working in the government-contract arena, provide extensive work definition packages, including page after page of SOW description, requirements, and specifications. Customers also communicate requirements in the proposal and negotiation process, in formal and informal reviews, and through ad hoc communications at all levels. Requirements also come from internal sources. Organizational policies and procedures impose requirements on a project team. The functional departments that support the team often add their own requirements as well. Formal requirements and work direction may invoke requirements indirectly by reference to supporting documents, policies, and so forth. Requirements also come in the form of industry and professional standards and norms, simply because it is expected that some activities will be accomplished and demonstrated in a generally accepted "best practices" (within that particular community) manner. Too, every organization has a unique history, resources, capabilities, and culture, and thus many unique habits, routines, and expectations about how things should be done. Project requirements arrive from many directions and in many forms. Project teams must sort from among these diverse inputs a set of mutually agreed requirements and associated specifications that will drive their effort. Failure to do so leaves each project work group and individual to fend for themselves in determining what requirements to consider, another path to frustration and project failure.

Project teams put themselves at risk when they assume initially that the only requirements that matter are the ones documented in their contract or project charter. Initially undocumented requirements may nonetheless be quite real. Teams must take the precautionary action of searching out, openly discussing, negotiating, and then either eliminating or embracing all the stakeholder requirements at the front end of a project rather than later. The teams may then be able to enforce some level or discipline when stakeholders attempt later to introduce new or revised requirements. Teams that fail to practice the appropriate discipline up front will spend the rest of their project life in running skirmishes about the validity of requirements and their interpretation.

DEALING WITH SIX REQUIREMENTS CHALLENGES

Project teams face six types of challenges when attempting to develop, document, and embrace a set of project requirements and specifications to guide their work. The first four are relatively straightforward: vision problems, articulation problems, translation problems, and quality problems. The other two, dealing with "desirements" and "to-be-determined" requirements, are more insidious and are described in detail below.

First, as already described in some detail, vision problems create requirements and specifications problems. Second, requirements and specifications are often poorly articulated. Customers that develop some version of the requirements and specifications tend to fall short of their obligation in similar ways. They may specify the design or the methodology (the "how") rather than the requirements and specifications (the "what"), perhaps because they do not know what they truly want, which means that they may issue requirements and specifications that may be conflicting, confusing, and full of gaps. For example, a customer may state that a mechanical assembly is to be manufactured from titanium rather than aluminium. Titanium is much more expensive and more difficult to work with, but it weighs less than aluminium. What the customer really wants is a light-weight assembly but rather than specify that, it has instead specified how to achieve that (unnamed) result. Customers may have a clear and agreed vision but are unable to accurately articulate the requirements and specifications that embody that vision. Perhaps, they do not fully understand the vernacular and conventions of the appropriate technological arenas. Perhaps their haste to make the requirements and specifications available causes them to make mistakes. Perhaps they are sorely understaffed and provide sketchy information intending to provide more clarity later. Whatever the cause, the result is a poor translation of vision into requirements.

Project teams proceed at their peril when they accept such requirements and specifications. Accepting the customer's "how" may make the project team blind to better "hows"—approaches the customer has not thought of or does not fully understand—for achieving the "what." Thus, the team may find itself being compliant because it is following the customer's direction, but it is headed for project failure because it is taking unnecessary risks. Additionally, accomplishing the "how" may not satisfy the "what." The customer's prescribed approach may be technically infeasible or may demand resources and skills the project team does not possess, or, it may be perfectly doable but does not lead to the expected outcome. The team will in the end be held accountable for project failure. Its only defense is to do the necessary work up front to assure the requirements are comprehensive, accurate, and achievable.

Third, requirements and specifications may also fall victim to "translation" problems. Sometimes the project team errs when it incorrectly interprets customer's vague instructions. It may be sure that it "knows" what the customer means by a particular standard reference, but it may not, and that misunderstanding can result in a mistranslation of the customer's requirement. Requirements and specifications can be large, multifaceted documents, and contradictions are almost inevitable. Team members may think they know how to resolve a contradiction, but the customer may have a different interpretation and may not agree that a conflict exists. Every organization, even every work team, has its own slang and terminology. Sometimes the project teams thinks the customer's requirements are perfectly clear, not understanding the customer's slang or giving it a different meaning. Sometimes customers purposefully make their initial requirements vague, planning to revise them as the work progresses and the appropriate interpretation becomes evident. This may be a strategic choice; they hope to force the project team to accept the evolving requirement without compensation. As a result, the project team finds itself facing ever-changing requirements interpretations that result in overall project risk. Sometimes customers deliver clear, concise, and flawless requirements and specifications but project teams simply misunderstand them, thus creating their own issues. In all cases the solution is essentially the same. Project teams must be passionate about critiquing and validating their interpretations of the requirements and specifications. Doing this tedious work early and often will pay big dividends in avoiding unnecessary work, cost, schedule, and technical risk.

Fourth, requirements and specifications may also be flawed because of quality problems. Let us set aside all the challenges of missing or conflicting visions, of customer articulation problems, and of translation problems. Let us assume the project team has managed to sort through all the noise and now understands the project requirements it will embrace. There is an art, discipline, and skill to capturing, translating, and communicating those mutually agreed requirements and associated specifications into something the project team can understand and effectively use. The project manager and the project systems engineer are jointly responsible for ensuring that a comprehensive, yet clear set of requirements are communicated to the project team members.

Fifth, project teams sometimes fail to recognize and respond appropriately to "desirements" masking as requirements. Sometimes individuals within the customer community may find themselves negotiating with one another about what requirements and specifications will be communicated. Such internal negotiations may be as much about company politics and jockeying for power as about technology and need, resulting in items that are not truly required finding their way into the requirements document. Sometimes, customers may collectively assert they need specific features and functions but also agree privately they could do without them if necessary. They see no harm in including such items, hoping the project team can accommodate them without great difficulty— after all, if you don't ask you don't get. For example, the customer marketing team may think it would be great to have the new iPad include a phone, and they want to challenge the project team to develop such a capability for the next generation iPad. The marketing team may not realize that this added feature creates significant complexity, compromises other features, and may delay completion of the next-generation design. They just think it would be a great feature, and so they make it a requirement. Such "desirements" often creep into the list of requirements.

There is certainly nothing wrong with customers asking for what they would like as well as what they truly need, or with a project team trying to accommodate them. A problem arises when the customer and the project team do not agree about what are true requirements and what are desirements. A desirement that adds unacceptable cost growth, schedule delay, technical risk, or quality compromise must be recognized, discussed, and eliminated before rather than after the team has spent precious resources in implementing it. A desirement that adds acceptable cost, schedule delay, technical risk, or quality compromise must be recognized and the appropriate adjustments made to the project plan. All project stakeholders must embrace the true requirements and maintain a proper perspective about anything not a true requirement. The agile project management consulting firm 3Back[5] maintains a blog that posted a query about project requirements: "When is a requirement truly required?" They offered six potential answers:

1. A customer would like it.
2. An engineer decides it would be good.
3. The development team creates a spec.
4. The product owner says it is.
5. The business asks for it.
6. There is a test which actually requires it to be there and fails when it is not.

The 3Back team argued, "When there is a test that makes it required with a pass/fail, then it is a requirement, until then it's just a *desirement* [their usage of the word, but commonly used by others]."[6]

Perhaps their position is a bit too strong. One can certainly imagine instances where a requirement is real but somewhat subjective. For example, the project team working on the replacement displays for the Space Shuttle Orbiter (see Chapter 2) was challenged to develop display screens that could be read clearly when exposed to direct sunlight through the windows and that could also be clearly legible when viewed from off-angles. Both requirements were important and necessary. The sun's glare can be intense in space, and yet astronauts must be able to read the displays. Astronauts in orbit may also be floating about the cabin and find it necessary to read the screens while positioned away from the central line of sight. NASA was able to define a specific off-axis viewing requirement, but they found it quite a challenge to translate the glare requirement into a specification because every person's eyes react uniquely to the screen, the glare, and the data displayed. In the end this "subjective" requirement (subjective because different individuals may have different notions of whether the amount of glare is "acceptable") was no less a requirement because of its inherent subjectivity. Although every project team should strive to achieve the standard of testability for each requirement, it is not always possible to do so. Project teams must know however that these subjective requirements are prone to frequent reinterpretation and thus represent a serious project risk.

So-called desirements are sometimes articulated as goals. Recall that the Wright brothers project requirements included a few items stated as a "should" rather than a "shall." Today most contract managers, and their contractors, understand that a "should" is a goal but not a requirement. No matter how they are labeled, project teams must distinguish between what requirements they must meet and what goals the customer would appreciate them also trying to accomplish. Teams must then understand just how important those goals are to the customer. Will the customer tolerate cost growth, schedule delay, or technical compromise in order to see the goal achieved or are they only interested in the goal if it can be achieved with no added cost, delay, or technical risk? That determination influences the type of work activity the team will embrace and defines degrees of project success or failure. Project teams will eventually have to deal with the issue of customer desirements. Doing so early is painful, but much less painful than being forced to deal with them later.

Sixth, requirements and specifications often contain items that are not fully defined. These so-called to-be-determined, or TBD, requirements may appear when the requirements developers have not yet gathered enough information or made key decisions that will determine how to correctly state the requirement. Perhaps some larger systems decisions that will influence a requirement for the subsystem being developed by the project team have not yet been made. Perhaps some analysis has not yet been completed. In any event, the requirements developer has elected to not yet convey it to the project team. TBDs represent great risk and should be resolved as quickly as possible. TBDs usually cause the idling of resources and cost growth because some team members find themselves delaying their work or doing less important work while they wait for the customer to resolve the requirement issue This ties up systems engineering resources because the engineers must do unplanned work, either helping to resolve the TBD requirement or analyzing the implications of various potential resolutions. For example, a customer may be unsure whether a piece of equipment will be located in a cockpit adjacent to the electronics cabinet or in a cabinet in the cargo hold. They have elected to leave the location requirement TBD at this time, planning to determine the answer at a later date. Meanwhile, the project team assigned to develop the equipment does not know whether it will be installed in the relatively benign temperature and pressure environment of the cockpit or the relatively harsher environment of the cargo hold. That decision influences how the chassis must be designed, whether some less expensive components can be used, and how the equipment will be tested. The equipment project team will fall behind schedule if it waits for a decision. The team will waste a lot of time and strain the budget if it makes an assumption that proves to be wrong. Assuming the team does make an assumption about the requirement they will then be saddled with managing the consequences of that interim assumption. At some point in the future they may have to reverse several related decisions, cancel material orders, revise drawings, revise documents, and deal with several other consequences of a subsequent change to the assumption. All this adds risk which the customer imposed by making a late decision about the requirement; this is risk that the customer typically refuses to bear responsibility for, having successfully transferred it to the equipment project team because the project team allowed it to do so. The

TBD also causes delayed learning. Project team efficiency is measured in terms of how rapidly it can learn what it does not know and then adjust to that new knowledge. A delay in resolving a TBD leads to a delay in deciding how to accomplish the related work activity, it leads to a delay in understanding the implications of the finally decided resolution, and it leads to a delay in the accomplishment of the related work activity, all of which delays project team learning. In short, TBDs add risk to a project; whereas the timely resolution of TBDs results in a more efficient use of resources, improved schedule performance, efficient subsequent technical decision making, and a product that is more likely to meet the specifications and vision.

Project teams must be passionate about identifying and then quickly resolving TBDs. It is the team's responsibility to steer the stakeholders away from TBDs. It may elect to proceed without resolution if it deems the risks to be manageable and the consequences acceptable, but it must refuse to proceed if not. In the end, the responsibility lies with the project team to accept or refuse the added risk of project failure inherent in unresolved TBDs.

Some projects do not lend themselves to early determination of all requirements and specifications. In fact, some projects make such early resolution impossible. Boeing engineers cannot determine what every subsystem and component requirement and specification will be for a new airplane immediately upon starting the project. Their major subsystem partners usually agree to work cooperatively with the Boeing team to determine those requirements as the airplane design matures. The overall aircraft and the various subsystems evolve through a series of progressively more detailed design iterations. Each design iteration brings to light more detailed design insight and thus more mature requirements and specifications. Large complex projects of this sort will naturally start with many TBDs and preliminary requirements.

Customers and project managers often use these iterative design situations as their alibi when they have disregarded the risks inherent in open requirements and specifications. However, reality of the progressive design iteration and progressive maturation of requirements and specifications cannot be an excuse to disregard the consequences of open requirements and cavalier assumptions. It is even more important for project teams to understand that the timely, but technically sound, resolution of open requirements is essential to project success. Doing so may require the team to defer some work until requirements are clearly understood. In other instances the team may proceed based on interim assumptions that can later be reversed with acceptable consequences. In every case, teams must be passionate about managing the identification and resolution of TBDs.

REQUIREMENTS MARGIN

Chapter 6 describes the reality that projects exist in an environment of ignorance and uncertainty. Chapter 7 describes the obvious corollary that change is a constant occurrence for project teams. One way to cope with such uncertainty and the consequential change is to maintain adequate margins: cost margin, schedule margin, and technical margin, to name a few. Each project is a unique blend of challenges, and therefore needs a unique balance of margins in different areas of the project plan. Nearly every project needs some amount of requirements margins.

Technical uncertainties and risks spring from several sources. First, requirements are always uncertain and vulnerable to being changed as the team learns more about its challenge. Second, technology performance is often uncertain; electronic components may not perform as expected, or software algorithms may not work for a specific application, or the manufacturing process may be unstable. Third, systems may have interface peculiarities not fully described in the technical documents. Fourth, new designs may not perform as robustly as planned. The list goes on. Therefore, project teams should always strive to establish initial design requirements and specifications that allow appropriate margin.

Project teams should immediately establish a preliminary list of key project requirements and associated specifications along with a current understanding of the perceived margins for each requirement (see Table 3.1). A few points should be made about the table. First, it does not show every requirement and specification. Instead, it is a summary of the relatively few critical requirements deemed most important to the stakeholders. Systems engineers and design teams may be working to satisfy many more requirements, but the few selected for this summary should be the ones sure to draw attention because they are most critical. Second, early in the project the immature design may cause margin estimates to be relatively crude. This summary table provides a way to monitor progress toward closure as the design matures. It also provides the data that should spark corrective actions (see Table 3.1 notes). Third, this summary may be used to communicate with stakeholders about critical trade-off decisions. Certainly there is no magic about this particular table or format but project teams that understand and manage their requirements margins from project start to project finish have a better chance of success than those who do not.

SUMMARY

Requirements definition is one of the most crucial parts of a project. Incorrect, inaccurate, excessively defined, or a lack of requirements will nearly always result in cost growth, schedule delays, wasted resources, and customer

Table 3.1 Key Requirements Margin

Requirement	Specification	Current estimate	Margin goal	Current margin	Status
Weight	10 lb.	9.7 lb. ± 0.2	0.25 lb.	0.3 lb.	Green – No action
Power					
Peak	12 W	13 ± 0.2 W	0.5 W	– 1 W	Red – Note 1
SS	5 W	4 ± 0.2 W	0.25 W	1.0 W	Green – No action
Spare					
memory %	30%	35% ±2%	5%	5%	Yellow – Note 2
CPU clock speed					
Nominal temperature	2.0 mhz	2.2 ± 0.3 mhz	0.1 mhz	0.2 mhz	Green – No action
High temperature	1.6 mhz	1.85 ± 0.3 mhz	0.1 mhz	0.25 mhz	Green – No action
Unit price (2010 $)					
Required	≤ $100,000	$ 97,000 ± 5,000	$25,000	$3,000	Green
Goal ($250,000 Incentive)	<$ 80,000				Red – Note 3

Note 1. Customer considering requirement change to 14 watts peak. Current design solutions add to unit price.
Note 2. Current memory margin is okay, but pending design change may consume 20% of margin. Decision 12/15.
Note 3. Tiger team assigned to come up with ideas to get below $80,000. No good solutions yet. Must freeze design within 130 days.

dissatisfaction. Project teams that hope to succeed have no choice but to do the vital up-front work of embracing, assembling, reviewing, negotiating, revising, documenting, and faithfully managing the project requirements and specifications as well as the other parts of the project work. The requirements analysis must cover the entire scope of the project, considering the views and needs of all the project stakeholders. Unreasonable, inappropriate, or vague requirements must be negotiated into something the project team can achieve.

The basic points are simple, albeit not easy. Nonetheless, they are essential. Project teams that hope to find success must:

- establish a clear statement of overall objectives, the project vision;
- conduct a thorough and comprehensive analysis of the work necessary to accomplish the vision;
- negotiate the requirements and specifications with the customer and explain them to all key stakeholders;
- be eager to create the requirements and specifications for the customer—surely, they can pass the exam they create for themselves;
- negotiate requirements margin as a way to mitigate risk;
- know the difference between *desirements* and requirements;
- deal with TBDs—be willing to make assumptions but also be absolutely unwilling to make assumptions, as appropriate;
- document the results and communicate them to all stakeholders;
- assure the project team understands and embraces the agreed requirements and specifications;
- put the documents under revision control;

- accept that just as visions will shift, so to will requirements shift—manage changes aggressively; and
- continually test for requirement consent among the stakeholders—commitment drifts over time.

Currently, there are a number of requirements-management tools available. Some are tailored for specific activities and environments. Some have extensive capabilities and interface with state-of-the-art design tools. However, as with many tools, project teams must understand and remember what they are trying to accomplish with the tool rather than becoming slave to it. Some of these tools are quite complex and require extensive user training. Some have rigid user constraints that benefit the tool and its algorithms but may make it difficult for the project team to accomplish some unique objective. Teams are advised to remember that they should adapt these tools to help them prosecute their project rather than adapt their project to suit the tools. Project teams will also find that the risk and opportunity techniques and disciplines (see Chapter 8), can help them identify requirement and specification issues and find ways to address them. Teams need not be victims of poor requirements and specifications. They can take action to lessen the challenges and to deal with any that remain. In fact, they must do so if they hope to succeed.

Do not start work without clear requirements. Translating the vision into a coherent set of performance specifications/requirements is vital, but it takes time and effort. Do the work early, diligently, and persistently, or do much more work dealing with the consequences.

CHAPTER 4

HABIT # 3—BUILD AN INTEGRATED PLAN FOR ACCOMPLISHING THE VISION

"A goal without a plan is just a wish."
—Antoine de Saint-Exupery
(1900–1944)

PLANNING IS ABOUT PREDICTIONS AND LIKELIHOODS

Planning requires us to make assumptions about the efficiency of future efforts, about the outcomes of decisions we have yet to make, about the performance of technologies we may not fully understand, about our individual and team competencies, and about a host of other factors. Those predictions are the foundation on which our often multiyear project plans are based. Project success is significantly influenced, perhaps even determined, by the accuracy of some of those many predictions and likelihood assessments. For example, a corporate team may plan to install a single software program that will be used by every business unit to purchase materials and supplies. The system will replace the various unique software programs or manual processes currently in use at each business unit. The team planning this activity must make many predictions and assumptions, including:

- The new software will provide all the essential functions currently provided by the existing software products and manual processes.
- The new software interfaces are compatible with all the existing software products, computer platforms, and manual processes.
- The current procurement department and IT department personnel will cooperate in the transition from the old systems to the single new system.

These and many other predictions define the challenge the project team faces and influence the likelihood of project success. They should also influence the project plan.

But, as any prognosticator knows, predictions can be humbling. Many respected authorities have made what turned out to be colossally bad predictions. Just a few examples include[1]:

- "Heavier-than-air flying machines are impossible"—Lord Kelvin, president of the British Royal Society and a nineteenth-century expert on thermodynamics, circa 1900.
- "Who the hell wants to hear actors talk?"—Harry M. Warner, cofounder of Warner Brothers, 1927.
- "I think there is a world market for maybe five computers."—Thomas Watson, IBM president, 1943.
- "Television won't last because people will soon get tired of staring at a plywood box every

night."—Darryl Zanuck, cofounder Twentieth-Century Fox, 1946.

- "You ain't going nowhere son, you ought to go back to driving a truck."—Grand Ole Opry's Jim Denny to Elvis Presley, 1954.
- "It will be years—not in my time—before a woman will become Prime Minister." – Margaret Thatcher, 1974.
- "So we went to Atari and said, 'Hey, we've got this amazing thing, even built with some of your parts, and what do you think about funding us? Or we'll give it to you. We just want to do it. Pay our salary, we'll come work for you.' And they said, 'No.' So then we went to Hewlett-Packard, and they said, 'Hey, we don't need you. You haven't got through college yet.' "—Apple Computer Inc. founder Steve Jobs on attempts to get Atari and HP interested in his and Steve Wozniak's personal computer, 1975.
- "Six-hundred-forty-k ought to be enough memory for anybody."—Microsoft founder Bill Gates, 1988.

Clearly, even experts tread on thin ice when making predictions. However, those of us who use the predictive project management model must take that perilous step of predicting the future. Project planning teams must predict how technology will perform. They must predict what tasks must be accomplished in what sequence. They must predict what staff will be made available and how competent and efficient that staff will be. They must predict how long it will take to complete complex tasks. They must predict the labor rate for the staff that will accomplish those complex tasks. They must predict the intricate interdependencies among the multiple tasks to be accomplished. The list goes on and on. Just as Thomas Watson or Bill Gates may have misjudged the future of computers, so too, a project team may misjudge just exactly how their project will unfold. Nonetheless, they must build a plan, create a roadmap describing how they intend to accomplish the project specifications, requirements, and vision. That plan must be built on a foundation of many predictions and assumptions, great and small.

As described in Chapter 2, customers sometimes hold visions that not only foster project uncertainty but are actually founded on massive uncertainty.

SO, WHY BOTHER TO PLAN?

If plans are so vulnerable to inaccurate predictions and misestimating, why develop a plan? Why should the winning bidder for the Army's project described in Chapter 3 bother to plan when so much is unknown and perhaps unknowable? The answer is that project planning is unavoidable despite such uncertainties because it is at the heart of the predictive project-management model. It is the foundation of the principles that guide how project work is managed. Even the agile project management approach, described in Chapter 1, relies heavily on a broad-brush plan and rigorous, tightly controlled short-term plans. If a team rejects planning because of the uncertainty of predicting the future, then they must also reject any disciplined approach to managing the work. They must cast themselves into the darkness and stumble awkwardly toward what they hope is the destination—a perilous, expensive, and often futile approach. Sadly, it is also an approach that is too often employed.

We have acknowledged that project planning is uncertain. Yet, in spite of its uncertainty planning is worthwhile, even necessary, for several reasons:

1. It helps us discover the things we don't know about the details. The act of planning causes

us to probe and bring to light critical interde-pendencies, unrecognized prerequisites, essen-tial resources, and other factors that we might otherwise not be aware of. It lays bare the holes in our project business model, our team, and our implementation approach. It allows us to discover important points of disagreement or incompatibility before it is too late. Discovering these constraints at the last minute, when they must be immediately overcome, rather than ahead of time when alternate approaches can be evaluated, is usually more expensive, causes delays, and jeopardize the project. Planning helps us avoid these expensive and traumatic last-minute discoveries.

2. It helps determine if all potential participants understand their roles, the commitment required, and the risks. These misunderstand-ing or disagreements about roles can then be resolved before, rather than after, they create major problems.

3. It provides di ection. A new product design team may be ı elying on support from various functional groups including software design, hardware design, systems engineering, testing, and support. The individual team members must also understand the tasks for which they will be held accountable, the schedule they are expected to meet, and the budget for their work. The plan spells out for team members and stakeholders just what their jobs are.

4. It reduces the uncertainty that is inherent in making the necessary planning predictions. The integrated project plan captures an agree-ment between the customer(s) and the team about what will be done, when it will be done,

and how much it will cost. That shared agreement brings a degree of certainty to all parties. The plan provides the organization wherein the project resides with a description of what resources will potentially be needed and when they likely will be needed. The plan also provides functional groups with an estimate of when the product will be ready to go on the market and enables these groups to plan their own activities. Even though the plan may not unfold just as it was first envisioned, it provides a mutually understood initial basis for coordinating activities.

5. It minimizes waste and redundancy. Individual team members, functional groups, and critical suppliers working without a coordinating plan will find that at least some of their effort will be wasted because it turns out to be unneeded, incorrect, conflicting to some extent with the efforts of others, or overlapping with the efforts of others. The task interdependencies identified during the planning activity make clear what information or results are necessary before a specific task should be started, thus avoiding wasted or unnecessarily difficult work.

6. It establishes the goals or standards used in controlling project activity. The plan is the yardstick against which progress is measured. One cannot determine whether the team is making cost, schedule, or technical progress unless there is a preexisting plan against which to assess that progress. One must start with a plan in order to determine the important metrics or factors to monitor as an indicator of team progress.

7. It provides a baseline from which to determine that change has occurred and to assess the

impact of that change. Without a plan everything is change and nothing is change. Teams
are unable to adjust because they do not know
from what baseline they should make the adjustments. Cost and schedule growth become entirely
unpredictable and technical risk becomes inde-
finable when there is no baseline plan.

ORGANIZATIONS TOO OFTEN
DISCOURAGE PLANNING

Many organizational practices and cultures discourage
disciplined and thorough planning in spite of the fact
that these same organizations may have in place policies
that mandate that same rigorous planning, policies that
are routinely ignored. Project managers report that many
organizational and customer forces discourage them from
planning their projects before they get under way.

Project managers often cite schedule pressures due
to delays in getting started as a force that drives them to
start work right away. One university took twice as long as
planned to get approval to install a computer network in a
new classroom building. Then the process for selecting a
contractor was delayed when one of the bidders protested
the process, prompting an independent review of the decision. A contractor was finally selected nearly six months
later than planned. The university then asked the selected
contractor to make several technical and performance
changes, changes that significantly altered the contractor's
plan for doing the work. Even so, the university urged the
contractor to begin work immediately in order to be done
before the students arrived on campus in only three months.
The contractor found himself pressured to begin work on
a project that was not yet accurately defined or negotiated.
He risked cost and schedule problems if he rushed ahead
with the work. Yet, he would almost certainly be unable to

get the system installed and tested before students arrived if he insisted on negotiating a firm work scope and plan before starting to order equipment. The contractor elected to appease the customer by starting immediately. Three months later the university was unhappy that the system did not perform as they had hoped (although they never formally agreed on just what performance they were seeking), that it had not been fully tested before the students arrived, and that the contractor was asking for additional compensation for changes that had been requested along the way. The customer made front-end planning difficult but was unhappy about the consequences of failure to adequately plan before starting.

Project managers also cite staff availability as a factor: They often worry that personnel available at the time may be reassigned unless they are quickly put to work. Perhaps, the company has recently won several similar jobs and finds that it has too few experienced displays software engineers to do all the work that is coming in. The project manager knows she must immediately put the software engineers assigned to her team to work or risk having them reassigned to one of the other new projects. She knows that those other project managers are scrambling to get their teams in place and that she may well lose some of the most capable people if she does not get them started right away. She feels she cannot afford to wait for the plan to be developed.

Project managers also often complain that their senior management does not appreciate the importance of up-front planning, preferring to see activity. They feel they are not appreciated for taking the time to plan first and may even be criticized for doing so.

Project managers also often comment that the planning process and tools are cumbersome. They say the planning tools provided by their organization are poorly deployed, poorly supported, wrapped in cumbersome bureaucracy, and inflexible. This makes the mechanics of planning frustrating, and that frustration discourages teams from making the effort.

Sometimes project managers confess that they believe plans have little value. This belief occurs more often in organizations with dynamic projects that require frequent changes to the plans. The difficulty of changing plans, perhaps because of cumbersome processes and tools, discourages teams from making all the revisions, causing the project plans to quickly become obsolete. It is also common that the lack of disciplined change management causes plans to unravel. Teams that allow unauthorized scope changes rarely fold those changes into the plan. Plans are further eroded when team members are allowed to do work that falls outside the current formal plan. Project managers working in these environments soon come to see little value in building a plan to begin with, and so they resist the activity. The point is that systemic disregard for planning is frequently a symptom of systemic, poor project management discipline.

It is also an aspect of human nature that people would simply rather work than plan for work. Many people would much rather dive right into assembling their child's new bicycle than stop to read the directions. Similarly, many people would rather immediately begin work on a new project than take the time to build plans for doing that work. Even the most disciplined project managers find they must persuade their team members to take the time to plan.

In short, there are many powerful procedural and cultural forces encouraging teams to begin working immediately rather than plan the work before beginning. Some of these forces can be dampened or offset, but others are an inherent part of the environment in which projects are created and accomplished. The forces must be recognized and overcome.

Project managers offer a much smaller list when asked what forces in their environment encourage disciplined planning before work begins. Some say there are no such forces, that in fact they are systematically discouraged from planning. A few point to organizational policies or procedures that mandate front-end planning, a mandate they say is often disregarded in practice. Occasionally, a project manager says that the only incentive for good planning is his or her own personal experience that planning has fostered project success. Only occasionally, does someone say that the organization actively encourages disciplined front-end planning, provides useful resources to enable such planning, and then verifies the quality of that planning.

In most organizations it is the project managers who decide whether to charge ahead without a plan or to develop robust project plans. Project managers are usually selected for their ability to get things done, sometimes in spite of organizational impediments. Effective planning can happen when project managers value it, whether or not the organization values it. Conversely, planning tends to not happen, or to be done poorly, when project managers do not value it. Having said this, organizations that have a negative or laissez faire attitude about planning tend to end up with project managers who have a similar attitude.

Successful organizations learn to appreciate, value, encourage, facilitate, and even demand the development and maintenance of integrated project plans if their projects are to be successful. The environmental forces opposing disciplined planning must be offset in order to make planning an activity in which project managers and project teams will willingly engage. However, project managers are responsible for the success or failure of their project, they must develop and manage to an effective project plan whether or not organizations provide support.

PROJECT TEAMS OFTEN
PLAN POORLY

We have just described why project teams tend to leap into action before carefully planning their project activity. But even when project managers drive hard to develop project plans, they can encounter organizational obstacles that result in plans being poorly developed. The root cause is often due to a systemic misunderstanding of the fundamental nature of project planning.

Many readers will recall the traditional project management triangle (see Figure 4.1), often called the "triple constraint." The triple constraint asserts that a project, any project, strives to accomplish three conflicting and delicately balanced objectives—cost within a predetermined budget, completion on or before specified schedule milestones, and product or service performance that meets technical objectives. The assumption is that every project starts with a cost target, a schedule completion date, and a scope of work that are in balance. That is to say, the agreed-to work scope can be accomplished within the agreed-to budget and time frame. And any effort to modify one of the triangle elements will disturb the balance unless appropriate adjustments are made to the others. Hence, the old saw that the customer may "pick two," but not all three, because the project team

Figure 4.1   The Project Management Triple Constraint

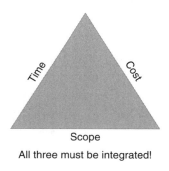

Scope

All three must be integrated!

must be free to adjust the third element to keep the triangle balanced.

In the real world, this ideal state of balance, or "integration," among the three project constraints is seldom initially established and is rarely maintained if it is established. A project team will find that it has been given a budget based on affordability, a schedule based on need or whim, and a work scope or technical target based on neither. Thus, there is no so-called balanced triple constraint going in, a fact that is often tacitly understood but rarely acknowledged. Instead, teams press ahead until the inherent initial conflicts between cost, schedule, and scope becomes undeniable, a point where resolution of those disconnects is often difficult, expensive, and even traumatic to overcome. These project plans begin out of balance, never find their balance, are therefore quickly discounted or ignored, and so lead to disappointing project outcomes. They also lead to a discrediting of the value of project planning.

The following paragraphs briefly describe a typical planning exercise for an internal company project. The freight carrier IT project described earlier is a good example.

Someone in authority, the son who has begun running the business his father built, thinks that a particular initiative may have merit and begins to explore the idea. He decides that the manual routing system should be replaced—with something less arcane, something different than what his father created, something he can take credit for. Our eager and aspiring young boss really does not know much about the details of the current routing system, and he knows even less about the capabilities of the various software systems that might be available to replace it. He relies on the routing system supervisor, the IT coordinator, and the various candidate vendors to sort that out. What he does know is that his dad will never agree to the project unless it can be done for less than $100,000.

He also knows that he wants the project done quickly so that he can brag about how much better it is (he hopes)—within six months should be enough time.

The routing supervisor and the IT coordinator have different attitudes about the project, one hopes the project will fail and the other hopes it will succeed. The routing supervisor sees the complexity and risk of the project while the IT coordinator sees it as a straightforward IT installation project. They understand the technicalities of their own areas of responsibility but not how their area affects the others' area. The resulting technical requirements are never formally documented but the ones that are identified turn out to be contradictory, confusing, and incomplete.

The various software vendors recognize some of the shortcomings of the requirements provided by the potential customer but are only concerned about the specific requirements that might affect their ability to win the contract. They can sort out the other requirements afterward. One vendor has a fine software solution that requires very little change but his price of $75,000 is deemed unacceptable. The winning vendor has offered a bid of $60,000 because its salesman, in his zeal to book an order, disregards a couple of the requirements. Never mind that the software will have to be significantly modified for this application; also never mind that the winning software solution is not directly compatible with some of the interfaces and processes the customer currently uses. This vendor knows that changes will have to be made to existing systems and that the customer has not considered those costs—that fact can be brought up after the vendor gets the project under way.

The IT supervisor determines that the computer and network equipment can be purchased for about $30,000 and decides that he and his assistants can do the installation themselves. He does not bother to plan how long it will take to get the equipment ordered and delivered, and assumes he has ample time to install it before the holiday season. He does not know that the network equipment he chose has a 40-week delivery lead-time due to supplier shortages, something he could have learned by placing a call to the local distributer.

So, our project gets underway with an external budget of $90,000 ($60,000 for the winning contractor and $30,000 for IT equipment) plus an internal budget of $10,000. The internal budget was determined by the fact that is what is left of the politically acceptable $100,000 overall budget, not because it has any relationship to the estimated cost or scope of internal work to be done. The project is scheduled to last for eight months because the son thinks that should be long enough and because the winning bidder said it could do it within that time limit (the vendor was too desperate for a win to say otherwise). No one actually bothered to validate the schedule against the scope of work. The project scope and technical requirements are a mishmash of disjointed specifics that the software vendor intends to interpret to his advantage.

Clearly, this project has not begun with a balanced project triple constraint—in that regard it is a too-typical project. The project cost plan is itself flawed. The cost ceiling has been determined by what is politically acceptable. The planned cost includes a desperate vendor bid and excludes any analysis of the internal costs. The cost plan does not consider the likelihood of the vendors' strategy to charge more for the technical requirements flaws. The schedule end date has been determined by whim. The schedule plan fails to consider procurement lead times and makes vague assumptions about installation times. The technical baseline is in some state of disarray in part because the motivations for the project have little to do with system performance. Finally, no effort has been made to determine if the nebulous technical objectives can be accomplished within the time and cost targets. Thus, there is no initial balanced triple constraint and there is no integrated project plan. There seldom is.

Poor up-front planning has set this project up to fail. Inadequate or improper front-end planning has led this team to miss, misunderstand, or ignore some important work activity and several key risks that might have been better handled. Poor planning has also created some otherwise avoidable risks that put the project in jeopardy. The lack of planning integration has assured the team will be unable to follow the cost, schedule, and technical plans. As a result they will quickly find themselves ignoring the plans altogether. Quoting Michael Schrage,[2] a research fellow at MIT, "The most important problem facing this community (referring to the software development project community) is rampant dishonesty. We lie about schedules; we lie about features; we lie about functionality; we lie about budgets; we lie about costs; we lie about measurements and then we lie about how much we are lying. To be sure we often lie with the best of intentions—to protect and please—but let's not kid ourselves: Dishonesty has become a management ethic. We lie and then complain we aren't perceived as credible." Schrage was addressing, among other things, the fact that we often begin projects knowing, but refusing to admit, that our project plans are disconnected and unachievable. We press ahead with the project until denial is no longer possible. There is a better way, a way that begins by building an integrated plan from the start.

Many organizations, organizational leaders, project managers, and project teams do not understand how to plan projects; they do not understand the need to initially balance the triple constraints, they do not understand that it is their task to do so, and they do not understand how to go about it. Never mind the assortment of planning tools (e.g., Microsoft Project, Open Plan, HO Project & Portfolio, and BrightWork). Never mind the policies, procedures, and processes deployed within an organization. Leaders and teams seldom fully understand what they should be trying to accomplish with those resources and so they misuse or ignore them.

Some organizations do make an effort to develop integrated baseline plans for their new project bids. They recognize that disconnected cost, schedule, and technical scope plans like the ones described above can be a very expensive experience, one that disappoints customers and senior management alike. Their efforts are often thwarted by their eagerness to submit a winning bid, the uncertainty of the project requirements, and the lack of sufficient time. However, these same organizations that try to build a balanced triple constraint plan as a foundation for their bids often fail to practice that discipline when planning the actual project activity after they have won the competition or when project changes occur. Their experience has taught them to strive for that discipline when bidding new projects but it has not taught them to remain disciplined after they win.

Integrated project planning is an attempt to establish some proximity of initial project cost, schedule, and scope balance, a balance that must be roughly maintained throughout the project life. Integrated project planning does not presume perfect balance can be achieved or maintained. It does presume that approximate balance can be achieved and maintained, and that such balance is vital for project success. The following section describes how to establish an integrated plan.

INTEGRATED PROJECT PLANNING
HAS A SEQUENCE

So, how does one go about developing and maintaining an integrated project plan? How does one achieve a balance of the triple constraints and then hold that delicate but vital balance intact?

Mark Twain once observed that a person who undertakes to carry a cat home by the tail learns ten times as much as the person who simply watches. I first learned about integrated planning many years ago when I was managing a few active projects while also bidding on various new projects. The project teams were constantly developing plans from which to bid potential project scope changes, plans from which to bid new projects, and modifications to existing plans in order to accommodate new learning. We would typically gather all the available information from the customer or internal sources and then distribute it to the team members selected to estimate the cost, schedule, and scope impacts for the potential change or the new opportunity. Those team members would submit their responses to a small team that would review the submitted material to identify inconsistencies, conflicts, omissions, and so forth. It was nearly always the case that the estimators had made conflicting assumptions or interpretations about the work scope and how it was to be accomplished. Those conflicts and inconsistencies led to errors in the proposed plans, which had to be rooted out, discussed, negotiated, and resolved, and then the plans had to be revised.

As a side note, this is when I also learned that once a person has documented the rationale for a technical decision, cost estimate, or schedule assumption, he or she will defend that rationale with great vigor and persistence. However, the estimator is much more open to alternate rationales and approaches if the alternatives are presented and discussed before any specific assumption is documented. In short, we all love our own perspective, and once we have documented it we will aggressively defend that perspective against all other alternatives.

Our planning activity was frustrating because we were using an approach that enabled—almost mandated—each participant to make his or her own critical assumptions about many dimensions of the work scope, cost, and schedule. Our planning was also thwarted because we were attempting to deal with work scope, cost, and schedule definitions all at once. Then, natural human nature, the bias to defend what we had asserted, acted to thwart any effort to reconcile, adapt, or alter those assumptions. In short, we were causing many of our own problems.

What I learned was that successful, integrated project planning should follow a specific sequence, a sequence which helps the planning team move closer to consistent assumptions and to integration of the triple constraints (see Figure 4.2, Integrated Planning Has a Sequence, below). Planning teams should focus first on what work is to be done, the scope of the project. Then they should focus on the time required to accomplish that agreed scope of work and thrash that time plan against the scope of work to integrate the two. Finally, they should focus on the resources required to accomplish the scope of work within the agreed schedule and thrash that resource plan against the previously agreed work scope and schedule.

The sequence matters. The planning team must reach mutual agreement about (1) scope; then (2) schedule; and then (3) cost. Of course there are exceptions, of a sort. A project team tasked to accomplish as many product-feature improvements as possible in a year within a specific budget, say $1 million, starts with that given constraint but immediately proceeds to determining how many features can be incorporated within that time limit. Teams should begin by establishing a mutually agreed scope of work, then establishing a schedule, and then adjusting the agreed scope of work to align with the agreed schedule.

Group participation matters. The core planning team must build consensus around the assumptions that allow cost, schedule, and scope to be integrated into a single

Figure 4.2   Integrated Planning Has a Sequence

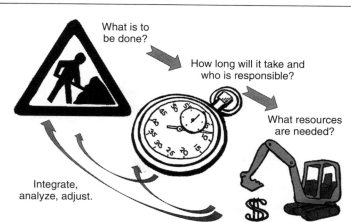

plan. These individuals become the disciples who help the rest of the project team and other stakeholders understand and embrace those critical integrating assumptions.

One effective approach is to convene a meeting of the core team, perhaps six to twelve members who have experience relevant to the pending activity. The team begins by sketching a WBS (work breakdown structure) on a whiteboard while asking those present to describe their understanding of the scope of the work. Someone may open the conversation by referring to the customer-provided WBS or SOW, but the group will soon find itself discussing different interpretations of those documents, what issues were not addressed in them, how to approach the work, and so on. After an hour or two the group should have a very rough agreement about the major components of the work scope and the key assumptions that everyone present has agreed to. The whiteboard should contain a rough WBS that captures the essence of what was agreed.

At that point, the team should begin a discussion about how long it will take to do that mutually agreed scope of work. Those present may make suggestions about how long each major element of the WBS will take, and what tasks are dependent on other work being done. In essence, the team is sketching out a first draft of a constraints-driven schedule for the agreed work scope. Inevitably, that schedule will be much too long to meet customer needs. The team might initially develop a 100-month schedule as opposed to the customer-expressed desire that the work to be accomplished within 60 months. Rather than simply hope that the team will be able to work faster, the group should begin discussing what work scope and schedule assumptions are driving the schedule. They can then come up with alternate interpretations of the work and alternate viable assumptions, eventually agreeing on a roughly integrated work scope and schedule, that is, a schedule compatible with the agreed scope of work.

Then the group should shift to a discussion about how much that scope of work should cost. Inevitably, the first estimates will exceed the affordability for the activity. The group can then revisit the work-scope interpretations and assumptions yet again to find alternate approaches compatible with a lower cost estimate. Eventually, the group should be able to develop a roughly integrated work scope, schedule, and cost estimate, a foundation that could be distributed to other team members for review and concurrence.

This iterative face-to-face process helps teams avoid major mistakes, establish viable roughly integrated plans that can be achieved, or helps the team build an argument to convince customers that the work scope, schedule, and cost needs are simply incompatible. Project lives become less chaotic and teams find project success more often.

Not all project activity can be planned using this relatively brief, real-time, face-to-face session to build consensus and force integration. Sometimes, the work scope is far too large or complex . However, these sessions can be effectively used to build a preliminary understanding that initiates a more formal and structured planning activity across a large or complex project.

The following narrative describes this iterative integrated project planning process in more detail.

THE FIRST STEP IN INTEGRATED PLAN DEVELOPMENT: DETERMINE WHAT IS TO BE DONE

Integrated project planning begins with the development of a clear and shared definition of what is to be done. Sometimes the project sponsors or customers provide a version of that definition in the form of an RFP, SOW, task order description (TOD), or other documents. Other times sponsors or customers provide confusing, conflicting, incomplete, or virtually no guidance, as described in several examples above. Even so, the project manager must ensure that her or his team has a clear definition of the project scope of work whether or not sponsors and customers provide clear and consistent guidance. The reader will notice that some of the points made in Chapters 2 and 3 are repeated below. This is done purposefully to emphasize the interrelationship among the eight habits.

In order to understand what is to be done, the project team must determine and agree on how it will interpret any guidance the sponsors or customers provide. Perhaps the customer uses vernacular that is foreign to the project team. Perhaps their guidance contains contradictions that must be resolved. Perhaps the team has failed to address some critical work scope. Perhaps they have left open some critical requirements. The project team must work with the sponsors or customers to resolve these gaps and conflicts, and it may or may not initially succeed. Even so, the team must decide how it will deal with any remaining gaps and conflicts, decisions that will influence what work is to be done.

Contradictions abound. Customers and sponsors often do not articulate what they want consistently. Reasons for this vary from the customer's lack of an overall project vision, to conflict between visions, to confusion about how to articulate the vision in terms of requirements and specifications, to poor articulation of the vision and requirements. These contradictions must be identified and resolved so that the project team is clear about the work scope. Otherwise, the individual project team members will interpret unresolved contradictions in unique and contradictory ways. Those different interpretations will cause team members to make subsequent conflicting decisions, will cause the individuals to do work that thwarts the efforts of other team members, and will create an arena wherein decision making becomes more difficult because individuals are working with different assumptions about what is to be done.

Customers and sponsors often have difficulty resolving all the important requirements and specifications at the start of a project. Sometimes they need to better understand the trade-offs between technical performance and project risk. Sometimes they need to better understand the trade-offs between alternate technical approaches. Sometimes they need to better understand the relative importance of end users' needs and desires. These and many other factors may cause a customer or sponsor to delay critical decisions hoping to be better informed later. Thus, they often leave some important specifications and requirements open or unresolved. These so-called TBDs make it difficult for a project team to fully understand what work scope is to be accomplished. Nonetheless, the team members must reach agreement among themselves about how to deal with those TBDs. Failing to do so will jeopardize project success.

Project teams must build a work-scope plan that copes with TBDs. Perhaps the team can include work scope that will quickly resolve the uncertainty, helping the customer or sponsor make appropriate decisions. The extra cost this entails will be much less than the cost of coping with the unresolved TBDs for several more months. Perhaps the team can defer a work scope that is dependent on the TBD decisions until they are resolved. Perhaps the team can plan work scope that is minimally impacted by the resolution of the TBDs while deferring other pieces of the work. Perhaps the team can establish an assumption for the TBD and plan work scope consistent with that assumption, knowing that they can readily adapt the work if their assumption turns out to be incorrect.

As we have seen, industry regulations or norms may impose a specific work scope or influence how work is accomplished. Occupational, Safety, and Health Administration (OSHA), EPA, or other government regulations may determine or influence work scope. Organizational policies may also mandate internal reviews, reporting requirements, or process disciplines that require the project team to do work that the customer or sponsor does not require. All this work must be captured in the project team's overall plan for what is to be done.

Customers and sponsors may not provide any work scope guidance. Recall the couple in Chapter 2 who had different visions of their new house and the contractor who was struggling to help them agree on a shared vision that would be compatible with their constraints. In this case, the customer, our couple, had no idea what goes into building a house. They did not know anything about the need for a set of blueprints approved by a structural engineer, or the prerequisite soil percolation test to verify that a septic system would work correctly on their rural lot, or the temporary electrical service connection that had to be installed for the construction crew, or the local requirements for installation of a radon detector and venting system as well as a residential fire detection and sprinkler system. Clearly, this customer could not define the project work scope. They were certainly not going to develop a set of specifications and requirements. They were incapable of developing a statement of work to guide the contractor and his project team. It was up to the contractor, the project team leader, to define the work scope required to build the house.

Teams must also address, clarify, and document what is *not* to be done. Our building contractor may have worked out an agreement with the couple that they would do all the interior painting, and so he must make sure the project team knows not to do the painting or buy the materials. Embraer, the Brazilian aircraft manufacturer, may have agreed with one the suppliers that their product would not be fully tested until it had been installed, along with other equipment on the aircraft, because the supplier could then avoid building expensive special test equipment. Both Embraer's and the supplier's project teams need to know about this agreement, so they factor it into their respective work scopes.

So far, I have argued that project teams need to understand what work is to be done, as well as what work is to not be done. The point has been made that project customers and sponsors may or may not be helpful in identifying, clarifying, and documenting that work scope. So, what are teams to do? How does a project team go about developing that project work scope?

Customers, stakeholders, and project teams may use any of several established tools and templates to help them capture and document their work scope. Many project environments, including construction, product development, and consulting, have adopted their own set of preferred tools and techniques to assure that project teams understand what work they are expected to accomplish. Even so, too many of the organizations operating in those environments do not understand or elect to not use those tools and techniques.

The SOW is supposed to define the work activities, deliverable work products, and set up the schedule for task completion or work-products delivery. It may also refer to industry standards, quality requirements, or regulations that may impact the work activity. The SOW format and specific content varies from industry to industry and may even be unique to each firm.

The WBS (see Figure 4.3) depicts graphically the discrete work elements and something about their inter-relationships. The WBS also provides a framework for developing the resource needs, including cost estimates, for the identified work scope.

Companies sometimes mandate a "standard" WBS hoping to use it to collect actual cost performance from projects then use that information to determine what to bid for similar work in the future. However, this standardization can create accounting, communications, and coordination complications if the customer imposes its standard

Figure 4.3   Work Breakdown Structure (WBS) and Responsibility Assignment Matrix (RAM)

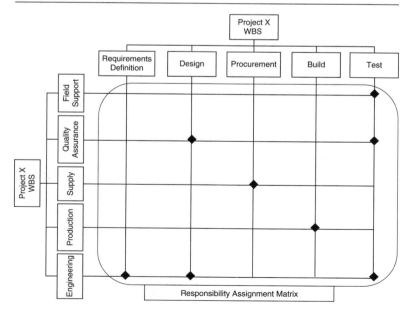

WBS, while the project team's organization also imposes its own, but different, standard WBS, which forces the team to depict and manage work scope in compliance with both so-called standards. So while standard WBS templates may be helpful in aggregating costs from various projects, they are not necessarily helpful, and are perhaps even detrimental, for teams trying to determine and document their work scope. Organizations need to allow project teams the flexibility to use the WBS tool to best advantage for its intended purpose, structuring each project's work performance.

The "WBS dictionary" is the narrative description of the work scope within each WBS element. It describes what is, and what is not, to be accomplished. A WBS and WBS dictionary traditionally strives to satisfy three fundamental principles. First, they include 100 percent of the work defined for the project. Second, since the various elements of the WBS must not overlap, it clarifies the distinctions and separations between the work elements. Third, the WBS and WBS dictionary capture the planned work-scope outcomes, not the work-scope activities.

The responsibility assignment matrix (RAM) describes the roles and responsibilities of each member of the project team or the functional organization in completing the work activities captured by the WBS and WBS dictionary. The intersections between WBS work elements and individuals or departments become the fundamental work elements with which to best measure cost, schedule, and technical/scope performance.

These tools and templates can help a project team identify, clarify, document, and communicate its work scope; however, they are not in themselves sufficient to get the job done. The project team must adapt the tools to fit the unique needs of their project. In fact, the social interactions surrounding the use of these tools and templates are far more important than the selection of a particular tool set. For example, a geographically dispersed team tasked to design a new commercial air conditioning system may find that members of the team working at locations in Czechoslovakia, Michigan, and Kentucky are each working within different local organizational structures and thus with work activity traditionally partitioned in different ways at each location. The team may discover some of these differences as they work to develop and document the agreed project work scope, thus avoiding the confusion, delay, wasted work, and project risk that would ensue if the differences were not recognized at the start of the project. They may also find that no traditional tool accommodates the site-specific differences and so elect to adapt a tool to their unique needs. So one sees that, as is true with many such tools, it is the process of using them that matters far more than the specific tool outcomes themselves. Teams that work hard to develop, flesh out, debate and agree on, then document their work scope are the ones that more often find success, no matter what tools they employ while doing it.

THE SECOND STEP IN INTEGRATED PROJECT PLAN DEVELOPMENT: DETERMINE HOW LONG THE WORK WILL TAKE

Once the scope of work is established the team can begin to determine the time required to accomplish that work. Failure to do so inevitably leads to otherwise avoidable problems. For example, some members of the team may assume that the work scope includes the reuse of some specific software with only minor interface modifications while other members of the team may assume the software is to be developed with no reuse of existing code. Thus each group will make entirely different assumptions about how long the software work will take, who must be involved, and what coordination is required between other groups. The team must identify, discuss, negotiate, and resolve such differences in understanding of the work scope before, rather than after, they attempt to build project schedules.

The mutually agreed work-scope baseline enables the team to begin to develop preliminary estimates of the time required to accomplish that particular work scope. The team can begin to sketch out a preliminary *top-level schedule*, sometimes called the "integrated master schedule" (IMS). A formal IMS typically includes a master program schedule (MPS), sometimes called the "integrated master plan" or the "master milestone chart." It is the highest summary-level project or program schedule. The IMS very often also includes a detail schedule that captures the lowest-level work activity within the project. This detail schedule includes all the milestones and activities that are monitored by the project team as it tracks its performance against the plan. The IMS for large and complex projects may also include one or more intermediate schedules that depict some level of detail between the MPS and the detail schedule. These intermediate schedules can be useful when the team is discussing major parts of the project plan, but it is not beneficial for the team to start by developing schedules at the lowest detailed level. The project team's first attempt at a preliminary schedule is typically at the MPS level. Teams should initially disregard these various formal labels and hierarchies, instead staying at the highest level of conceptual schedule planning. There will be ample time for detail once the overall schedule is established.

The work-scope baseline enables the team to begin to identify the schedule interdependencies among the different work scopes and participants. Team members can begin to identify the interfaces between:

- groups within the team (systems engineering, design, design analysis, and testing, etc.);

- groups within the business but outside the team (functional departments and facilities managers, etc.);
- their team and other project teams (relying on the work of other teams or delivering work to other teams);
- the team and suppliers (component and material providers, subcontractors developing subsystems, specialists providing critical expertise when required, etc.); and
- the customer and the project team (resolution of critical TBDs, key customer milestones requiring project team contribution, etc.)

Each of these interface points creates a constraint on the overall project schedule because the team is dependent on cooperation or coordination between the parties, and that necessary cooperation is outside the team's control. Teams must identify these intersections, perhaps further clarify which parties are responsible for what work scope and the specific work product needed, mutually agree on the form and format of the finished work product, and then mutually agree on the date when that work will be completed. That date becomes one of the key milestone events in the overall project schedule.

The team must also determine the *critical path* in the overall project schedule. The critical path identifies the shortest possible time in which the project can be finished using the current schedule plan. Any attempts to complete the work scope earlier will require adjustments to the tasks along the critical path, adjustments which may include work redefinition to shorten the effort, additional resources to get the work done faster, or modification of the start and completion constraints that limit when the work task can be started or finished.

A project schedule is generally considered to have only one critical path, although in practice, more than one critical path may emerge. Occasionally, a project plan will develop with a couple of paths of nearly equal length; perhaps software development is planned to take about as long as hardware development, for example. Additionally, multiple critical paths may emerge as project activity unfolds. Teams may focus a great deal of energy on keeping to the schedule on the initially identified critical path, at the expense of effort on non-critical-path work scope. The result may be that noncritical activities are started or finished increasingly later, causing those paths to overtake the original critical path.

The project team must collectively understand and cooperate to identify and manage the critical path. First, team members who are working on tasks off the critical path may be asked to provide resources or to make accommodations to maintain or accelerate work-scope progress along the critical path. Such sacrifices are easier to accept when everyone on the team agrees about the critical path work scope and the need to focus on it. Second, team members will be more sensitive to the potential that non-critical-path work scope changes may influence the critical path. As a result, such issues can be identified, communicated, and addressed more quickly. Third, the entire project team is more apt to apply its collective energy and creativity to finding ways to accelerate the critical path work scope or to mitigate any risks to that work scope. Thus, just as teams must have a joint understanding about the work scope; so too, must they have a joint understanding about the time required to accomplish that work scope.

Defining how long it will take to accomplish the agreed scope of work enables the team to determine an appropriate *schedule reserve* and then build that reserve into the integrated plan. The notion of schedule reserve is less familiar than the notion of financial reserve, often called "project management reserve," although a project management reserve should include more than just money, as is discussed later. Project sponsors and team leaders usually appreciate the value of having an appropriately sized financial reserve pool to deal with surprises and uncertainties as well as to offset unplanned cost growth. Of course, materialized surprises and uncertainties often impact the project schedule as much or more than they impact the project budget. Thus teams should establish integrated baseline plans with an appropriate level of financial and schedule reserves.

Inevitably, the first attempt yields a schedule that is unacceptably long. Team members usually request ample time to accomplish their specific tasks, and that conservatism adds up. The key interface points are often first identified as occurring when they are mutually convenient for all parties, which stretches the overall schedule. It is not unusual to find that the first draft schedule is 25 percent to 50 percent longer than the customer or sponsors are willing to allow. The team then must scrub these initial estimates to get rid of undue conservatism and optimism, but the resulting schedules are often still too long. This is the point in the integrated planning process at which the team members must adjust the work scope in order to accommodate the desired schedule. In other words, the team begins to tie together the work scope and the schedule into an integrated project plan.

Project teams now have a choice. Typically, they choose to shorten the schedule, inserting more optimistic or hopeful estimates to depict an end date that meets the customer and stakeholders needs. However, this "success-oriented schedule" approach merely adds risk to the project. Team members may feel the more aggressive dates are unachievable, so they no longer feel committed to accomplishing those dates. Or the team proceeds, telling itself and others that the work can be done on time, and then at the last minute has to confess that schedules will not be met after all, something everyone tacitly knew from the beginning but that no one explicitly stated. Such late admissions lead to crisis management of resources, unplanned shortcuts, and therefore greater-than-necessary project risk, in addition to the schedule slip and cost growth.

There is an alternative, however. Project teams can elect to revisit the work-scope baseline, searching out different technical approaches, modified requirements, or different task sequences that may take less time. For example, a project team was planning a project to redesign the electronics box of an existing commercial airplane to replace obsolete parts that were no longer being made and would soon be unavailable. The work scope included verifying which parts were obsolete; identifying replacement parts or redesigning the circuitry to eliminate the need for the obsolete parts; documenting the new or revised design; procuring parts; building a new electronic box; formal testing to verify performance; and then the building, testing, and delivery of 100 such boxes. The first schedule was 112 weeks long. However, the available working electronics boxes and the few remaining obsolete parts would support aircraft operations for only another eighteen months, or 78 weeks, based on current average annual flight hours and equipment failure rates. To keep aircraft flying, the work had to be accomplished in less than 78 weeks.

This team chose not to build a more aggressive schedule by assuming work could be accomplished faster. Instead, it revisited the work scope and found that some tasks could be conducted in parallel without adding unacceptable risk to the activity, thus cutting about ten weeks from the 112-week schedule. They also found a few tasks that had been conservatively estimated, and as a result concluded they could cut another four weeks from the schedule, reducing it to 98 weeks.

The team still needed to find another 20 weeks of schedule improvement. It also understood that the 78-week estimate was just that, an estimate. The team felt it should

try to build a schedule containing some slack to accommodate project surprises and inefficiencies. It also felt a
need to be able to support aircraft operations in the event
the 18-month estimate was itself too optimistic. The team
agreed it needed to have a plan it could rationally expect
to accomplish in 68 weeks, allowing an additional ten
weeks of slack for problem resolution. Still, their scrubbed
and revised plan was 30 weeks too long.

While scouring the work scope and schedule in search
of alternatives, one team member pointed out that an
identified replacement part for an obsolete connector
had a 50-week lead time—the supplier would deliver parts
50 weeks after receiving the order. Two other parts had
40-week lead times. She wondered if they could place
those orders earlier or persuade the supplier to speed up
its delivery time. After a few phone calls and a supplier
visit, the team concluded it could place the orders for
those three parts 20 weeks sooner than currently planned.
That meant releasing the purchase order for those parts
separately from the other parts, adding modestly to the
overall procurement cost estimate, but it would significantly shorten the project schedule without adding inappropriate risk. The team also found that a modest change
to a particular connector specification (this connector was
one of the three so-called long-lead parts), one that would
not hurt product performance, would allow them to order
a different connector with a nominal 30-week lead time
rather than a 50-week lead time. The vendor was willing to
deliver in 20 weeks rather than 30 weeks, for a 20 percent
price premium. These changes enabled the team to redefine work scope and requirements to remove 40 weeks
from the schedule critical path. The lead design engineer
also came up with an approach that replaced the other two
long-lead components with a few readily available components. At this point the team had successfully modified
the work scope and requirements to further reduce the

schedule from 98 weeks to 58 weeks. Unfortunately, while the team members were searching out these improvements they also uncovered an mistake in the original schedule that added 6 weeks to the schedule. They ended up with a 64-week schedule, allowing 14 weeks of slack to deal with unexpected challenges. But their hard up-front work had paid off. They had developed an integrated work scope and schedule that gave them a real opportunity to succeed—a plan in which they believed, which had an appropriate margin to deal with inevitable surprises, and which would likely meet customer needs.

THE THIRD STEP IN INTEGRATED PROJECT PLAN DEVELOPMENT: DETERMINE WHAT RESOURCES ARE REQUIRED

Traditional scheduling approaches operate on a false assumption that the organization has available an infinite supply of resources, whether equipment, facilities, or staff. Essentially, teams build a schedule that appears to meet the customer desires, and then demand the requisite resources to accomplish the work scope within that time period. Their work scope and schedule is fixed and they build the resource around it. Sometimes they get most of what they need and sometimes, quite often in fact, they do not. Schedules begin to slip, and the balanced triple constraint becomes instantly unbalanced, or perhaps more unbalanced.

Some organizations, recognizing the fallacy of this planning approach, adopt *resource-constraints scheduling* techniques. When doing resource-constraints scheduling, project teams determine their work scope and the amount of resources available to them. Then, they adjust the schedule to be consistent with how long it should take to do the work with those resources. In other words, scope and resources are fixed but schedule is flexible. This approach can more easily be used on internal projects than on projects with external customers because external customers expect the contracted organization to make the necessary resources available, no matter what conflicts the contracted organization may have.

In either scheduling approach, whether it be an assumption of infinite resources or of constrained resources, the work scope plan and the schedule plan should be synchronized with the resources plan to achieve an integrated project plan. The resource-constraints scheduling approach accomplishes this integration by allowing the schedule to slip out to accommodate the available resources. The traditional scheduling approach does not often allow such schedule flexibility. Instead, the project team must revisit the work scope and schedule baseline seeking out yet another round of alternative scope and schedule assumptions that may be more compatible with the available resources.

The integrated work scope, schedule, and resource plan can only be successfully developed by coordinating with the various stakeholders. Resource planning requires tight coordination of the functional groups within the organization, groups that must balance the demands of ongoing operations, other projects demanding resources at the same time, new business pursuit activities, and personnel issues.

Sometimes the organization finds itself unable to meet all the competing needs. Recall from Chapter 2 the business unit that had several engineers with expertise in developing software for aircraft cockpit displays. The business used that expertise to compete for and win several new cockpit design projects. In fact, it was so successful that it found itself with more than twice as much work than it could reasonably accomplish with the available staff. The project teams found themselves competing aggressively for the same few lead design engineers. As a result every project fell behind schedule as the engineering department scrambled madly to locate and hire additional experienced displays software engineers.

More up-front resource planning, and more truth telling about the challenges, would have mitigated the resource problems. For example, new project teams could have developed resource-constraints schedules determined by the number of displays-engineering time made available to them. The impacts could have been thrashed against the overall project schedule to search out alternate work-scope approaches that would mitigate the impact. Or, new teams could have elected to use subcontractor design teams rather than internal staff, a more expensive solution but one that would make the schedule achievable and in the end be less expensive than continuing to fight over too few resources. The point is that project teams and their organizations need to invest time and energy in developing practical and achievable resources plans that are synchronized with the work scope and schedule plans.

This section has described a sequential yet iterative approach to developing integrated project plans. The approach calls for project teams to first develop a mutually agreed work scope, develop a schedule for accomplishing that agreed scope of work, revise the work scope as necessary to achieve a schedule that meets the customer need, and then develop a resource plan that is compatible with the integrated work scope and schedule, and finally, if necessary, further revise the work scope and/or schedule and/or resource plan until a fully integrated plan is established.

That said, let us close this section with a note of caution. Groups using this approach may fall into the "precision" trap, trying too hard to exactly follow the work scope, schedule, and resource plans, a futile and nonproductive effort that may eventually cause them to abandon the effort completely. Recall that predictive project management is founded on predictions and that many of them will be incorrect. Teams cannot accurately predict all the factors that will affect scope, schedule, and resources. They should be delighted to relatively quickly achieve approximately integrated plans, rather than take forever to achieve precisely integrated plans that ultimately are no more accurate. The goal is to achieve a reasonable degree of accuracy, not precision.

THE PROJECT MANAGEMENT PLAN

The integrated work scope, schedule, and resource plan (including the cost) makes up what we have been calling the integrated project plan. The integrated project plan is the very necessary heart of an overall project plan, but it is not sufficient. This section will address the additional elements of a robust project plan. It will also address the *project management plan* (PMP), a formal document used to capture the overall project plan.

PMPs are widely ignored, misused, made bureaucratic, and disliked, except in situations when project management is practiced effectively. There is a correlation between frequent project success and consistent development of robust project management plans. Of course, correlation does not prove causation. Organizations that frequently have project success also invest in healthy project management processes and tools, understand and believe in project management disciplines, and have a culture of knowledge sharing and problem solving rather than blaming. Such organizations also appreciate the value of planning, whether it is project planning or process planning. In short, robust PMPs are not necessarily a cause of successful projects but they certainly seem to be positively correlated with such success, perhaps because they are the artifacts that demonstrate the appropriate disciplines are being practiced.

The PMP can be an intimidating document. Table 4.1 contains an example. Note that it identifies 34 topics to

Table 4.1   Project Management Plan (PMP) Checklist

Project name		
PMP checklist		
Date	**Revision**	
	Date	
Description	**Completed**	**Remarks**
1 Project Summary		
2 Project Funds Release (PFR)		
3 Work Breakdown Structure (WBS)		
4 WBS Dictionary		
5 WBS/SOW Reconciliation Matrix		
6 Responsibility Assignment Matrix (RAM)		
7 Project Organization Structure		
8 Internal Administrative Plan (IAP)		
9 Tier I Master Schedule		
10 Tier II Intermediate Schedule		
11 Summary of Deliverable Items		
12 PBB Log established		
13 MR Log established		
14 UB Log established		
15 Dollarized RAM		
16 Preliminary PWAAs		
17 Rolling Wave Plan		
18 Time-Phased PMB @ TCL		
19 Billing Milestone Listing		
20 Working Capital Plan		
21 Communications Plan		
22 Subcontract Management Plan		
23 Risk/Opportunity (R/O) Management Plan		
24 Capital Equipment Acquisition Plan		
25 Quality Assurance Plan		
26 Configuration Management Plan		
27 Material Acquisition Plan		
28 Manufacturing Plan		
29 Make-or-Buy Plan		
30 Data Management Plan		
31 Design-to-Target Cost		
32 Technical Data Plan		
33 Design Requirements Checklist		
34 Systems Engineering Management Plan		
35 PMP Revision Plan		

be addressed, including several references to supplementary plans, which may themselves become several chapters long. Indeed, PMPs often turn into tomes, responding to bureaucracy interests rather than project need. Those tomes then become the justification for no longer developing PMPs. This devolution of a potentially useful project-planning instrument, to a bureaucratic tome, to the scrap heap is typical in less successful organizations.

The PMP serves five purposes. First, the table of contents serves as a checklist, reminding project teams and the organization of topics the team may need to address as well as what baseline and planning work should be accomplished before the team begins the project work itself. Second, the development of the PMP content helps project teams better understand their challenge and develop a viable plan of attack. Third, the act of capturing the project plan within the PMP facilitates team member buy-in for that plan. Fourth, reviewing the PMP contents with the customer(s) and stakeholders facilitates a shared project vision and community buy-in to the project plan of attack. Fifth, the PMP document is a record for all parties of what was agreed, their commitments and obligations, and the rationale for the plan. It also serves as a reference point when the plan must change to adapt to new learning and new situations.

The PMP described here represents only one of several formats and content lists. There is nothing sacred about this specific set of items. In fact, each organization should establish and continually adapt a unique set of contents that will help their teams succeed in their organizational environment. Keep these objectives in mind as each PMP content item is briefly described below:

1. **Project Summary**. The project summary contains a brief overview of the contract, scope of work, customer(s), project vision, goals, and so

on. The primary emphasis should be to capture the project vision in a single paragraph. The summary may be a few paragraphs or several pages long depending on just how complex the environment, vision, and objectives are. Senior leadership should consider this section the philosophic agreement of project intent between themselves and the project team.

2. **Project Funds Release (PFR)**. The project funds release, also often called the "contract funds release," is a document issued by the finance or contracts organization informing the project manager that the funding has been released and a cost account opened, and it is now permissible to charge activity to that cost account. Note that the PFR does not have to be included in the PMP. The team may elect to put all, or most, formal documents in the plan to make them available in one place, but it may also elect to simply include a link or directions to where the document may be found. Either way, the team should include in the PMP any unique, unusual, or significant exceptions, interpretations, cautions, and so forth, about these documents. Senior leadership should consider this section the top-level "contractual" agreement of intent between themselves and the project team.

3. **Work Breakdown Structure**. This section may contain more than one WBS. External customers may mandate reporting against a WBS that reflects their own reporting needs or desires. The project team's organization may mandate a standard WBS, as described earlier. Sometimes neither format meets the needs of a particular project plan. In those cases the team may elect

to adapt one of the mandated structures, or it may elect to create yet a third WBS. If teams elect to not use the standard WBS, they should explain any exceptions, deviations, interpretations, or other differences between it their WBS. They should also explain the relationship between the various WBSs, how they plan to manage the multiple WBS formats, what formats they will not use, and what format they will use in reviews with internal management.

4. **WBS Dictionary**. Customers, especially government customers, may provide both a WBS and a WBS dictionary. It should be completely unacceptable for the program team to merely refer to that dictionary or to merely reproduce it in the PMP. As discussed earlier, the customer WBS contains nothing about the scope of work implications of internal process and procedure demands on the WBS task descriptions. Teams must demonstrate in this section that they have critiqued any provided WBS dictionary, modifying or supplementing it to reflect how the project manager has chosen to interpret, clarify, or limit the customer-provided descriptions, as well as how they have incorporated work-scope mandates from other sources. If the customer has not provided a WBS dictionary, then the team must demonstrate that it has developed its own rigorous description of the work to be done and not done under each element and subelement of the WBS, all the way down to the lowest control account and work package. The project team may elect to include the entire WBS dictionary in the PMP document. It may also elect to refer to the document, including in the PMP only the important assumptions, clarifications,

and so on. The WBS dictionary is the narrative demonstrating that the "what" part of the integrated planning has been accomplished.

5. **WBS/SOW Reconciliation**. Sometimes the contents of the customer's WBS dictionary are inconsistent with its SOW contents. The WBS/SOW reconciliaton section demonstrates that the team has reconciled or resolved any such conflicts before letting work begin. Occasionally the team may have to document its approach for dealing with any still unresolved inconsistencies. Senior leadership should view the WBS/SOW reconciliation as a demonstration that the team understands the requirements risks and has a plan for resolving them.

6. **Responsibility Assignment Matrix (RAM)**. This document shows who is responsible for each item and subitem in the WBS. It demonstrates that the "who" part of integrated planning has been accomplished.

7. **Project Organization Structure**. This section demonstrates that the team has determined what organization structure it will use to manage the program. For example, it shows whether the project manager will have a flat structure or one with several layers, whether any special positions (risk/opportunity manager, customer service manager, and so on) have been created, or what tasks have been merged. Senior leaders should determine whether the structure is appropriate for the particular project situation.

8. **Internal Administrative Plan (IAP)**. This section describes how the project manager and immediate staff intend to manage the program: frequency of reviews, change control process,

communication with key suppliers, and so forth. It is essentially the narrative description of how critical parts of the project organization structure will operate. Senior leaders should be especially careful to assess whether they think the IAP is appropriate for the particular project situation and whether it addresses the unique aspects of the project.

9. **Tier I Master Schedule**. Teams may refer to the schedules residing within their schedule management system (e.g., Open Plan, Microsoft Project) rather than including them within the PMP document, but they should include at least a summary of the master schedule in the PMP. They should also include a description of such key points about the schedules as the amount of planned slack, critical path(s), and special focus concerns. This section, and the Tier II intermediate schedule discussed next confirm the "how long" of integrated planning has been accomplished.

10. **Tier II Intermediate Schedule**. This section of the PMP typically refers to the lower-level schedules that are in the schedule management system but does not duplicate them in the PMP. Instead, the project team should confirm that the schedules have been developed and document key assumptions, areas of special concern, critical-risk or opportunity areas, summaries of schedule reserve allocations, and so forth. Senior leaders should confirm that the project team has developed a viable schedule plan compatible with its work scope plan.

11. **Summary of Deliverable Items**. This section should itemize every key contract-specified deliverable and the date it is due, including a

description of potential specific challenges or concerns.. Each entry should also indicate who is responsible for assuring those items are delivered as well as how the team intends to monitor and report on progress toward those deliveries.

12. **Project Budget Baseline (PBB) Log**. This section confirms that the PBB has been established. It shows how funding has been budgeted for the planned work scope as well as how much of the work scope is currently unbudgeted. It is also where the team describes how it will manage changes to the PBB baseline. This section, along with sections 13, 14, 15, and 16, confirms the "resource plan" of the integrated planning has been accomplished.

13. **Management Reserve (MR) Log**. This section confirms that the team has established a financial MR appropriate for the uncertainty outlook of this specific program. It is also where the team describes how it will manage MR transactions. Senior leaders should confirm that the MR is appropriately sized, especially considering the risks and opportunities described in section 23 below.

14. **Undistributed Budget (UB) Log**. This section describes whether a UB pool exists and how it will be administered. A UB pool may be used to temporarily hold allocated but not currently planned funding for future work. For example, perhaps the project team has allocated budget for all the hardware work scope but is holding the software development funding until that work scope has been more fully negotiated with the customer.

15. **Dollarized RAM**. This section demonstrates that the team has allocated budget to specific

control accounts and allows reviewers to understand which activities are the perceived cost drivers. This section is one piece of evidence demonstrating that the team has integrated the "what", "how long", and "how much" to achieve an integrated plan.

16. **Project Work Authorization Accounts (PWAAs).** Each PWAA is essentially a formal signed agreement between the project manager and a control account (also called "work package account") manager that confirms they agree on the scope, schedule, and budget for each control account. Senior leadership should confirm that every work package has been negotiated, agreed to, and signed off by the project manager and each work package manager.

17. **Rolling Wave Plan.** The rolling wave concept will be discussed in more detail in Chapter 6. This section of the PMP describes how far out the project has been detail planned, how the future rolling waves will be managed, how many waves are anticipated, etc. It also describes how the high-level planning packages have been defined/structured and how they will be reviewed on a regular basis.

18. **Time-Phased PMB.** This section confirms that the project budget has been planned out over the duration of the project life. The information helps the organization develop out-year budgets. Customers, especially government customers, may also have fiscal budget constraints for multiyear projects. This section confirms the team has planned the project to accommodate those annual spending constraints.

19. **Billing Milestones.** This section contains a list of key billing milestones, the events that will

trigger significant customer funding payments. Highlighting and monitoring these events can focus the team on assuring the events are accomplished so that the money flows in when planned. This item only applies to externally funded projects.

20. **Working Capital Plan**. This section is a further refinement of the cash-management effort. It documents what the teams will do to focus on assuring customer payments are made on time, reducing the amount work in process (labor and material that the firm has paid for but that the customer has not yet paid the firm for), and so forth. Some organizations may elect to ignore this section because their finance group is not staffed to effectively support the project teams in such initiatives.

21. **Communications Plan**. This is where teams describe how they will interface with the customer, senior management, subcontractors, functional departments, and team members. The narrative describe such things as key interfaces, frequency of interfaces, how information will be disseminated, how the health of the interfaces will be monitored, and the role the project team wants senior leaders to play. Communications plans are more important when teams include personnel and organizations around the world working collaboratively. Teams may elect to document the communications plan in a separate document, describing in the PMP only the key points of the plan.

22. **Subcontract Management Plan**. This section describes how the team intends to identify and manage its subcontractors. It should be tailored specifically to each program. It should describe

how selections will be made, how progress will be monitored, and what communications will occur. Teams may elect to document the sub-contract management plan separately, describing in the PMP only its key points.

23. **Risk/Opportunity (R/O) Management Plan.** This section describes the project team's current assessment of project R/Os along with a summary description of the team's action plans for managing those R/Os. It also includes a description of the team's plan for modifying their R/O assessment as the project proceeds. Senior leaders should refer to this section to find out what challenges the team foresees and to learn what the organization can do to help the team address these uncertainties most effectively.

24. **Capital Equipment Acquisition Plan.** This section describes the capital equipment commitments that is essential to support the project execution plan. It should state the item, the rationale for its use, and date it is needed. It is a chance to reinforce the organizational commitment to provide that equipment.

25. **Quality Assurance Plan.** This section may refer to a separate quality plan. But the PMP must contain a description of any deviations from normal practices and policies and special areas of focus or concern, and it must describe how the team intends to meet the program quality goals.

26. **Configuration Management Plan.** This section describes how the team intends to manage the product, test equipment, and other platform design configurations. It should document any requested exceptions to standard practice.

27. **Material Acquisition Plan (MAP).** This section describes how the team intends to manage

acquisition and distribution of material required for the project. Will it share inventory among projects? How will it maintain control of customer owned material? Are there any unique material-acquisition challenges? If so how will they be addressed? The MAP confirms to senior leadership that the team understands and has a plan to address the material challenges.

28. **Manufacturing Plan**. This section describes how the team will accomplish design-for-producibility and design-to-production-transition requirements.

29. **Make-or-Buy**. This section addresses how any make or buy decisions will be determined and approved.

30. **Data Management Plan**. This section describes how the project team will assure that data items are developed, verified/tested, delivered, and accepted on time.

31. **Design-to-Target Cost (DTC)**. This section documents the established recurring target cost goals, the approach for achieving them, and how progress will be reported.

32. **Technical Data Plan (TDP)**. This section describes how the team will develop and manage configuration control of technical data.

33. **Design Requirements Checklist (DRCL)**. This section describes the key design technical requirements and how each of them will be verified, whether through analysis or formal test.

34. **Systems Engineering Management Plan (SEMP)**. This section typically refers to a separate document that is developed by the engineering team to address specifically how they will accomplish the technical challenges of the project including the test equipment approach,

quality requirements, parts selection, and a host of other topics. The SEMP is typically only developed for technically challenging projects. The PMP should include a summary of the unique challenges or unusual approaches documented in the SEMP.

35. **PMP Revision Plan.** This section documents the project team's expectations for PMP revisions. Integrated project plans and PMPs are not static. They cannot be because the project environment is rife with assumptions, unknowns, discoveries, risks, and opportunities, all of which make the future unpredictable. The project environment is in constant flux and so the integrated project plan and PMP must constantly adapt. Therefore teams typically indicate an intention to review and revise the PMP after any major project-scope change (perhaps 20 percent of the estimate-to-complete project value), after key project milestones (e.g., critical design review, product qualification testing, design release to production) or annually, whichever comes first.

A particular project's PMP may not need some of these 35 items, but it will likely need to have a few sections that are not included on this list. Examples of project-specific additional items include a test plan for a particularly complex system and each of its subsystems, a technology-alternatives plan for a specific and risky technical approach, or a plan for assuring coordination between two critical subcontractors that must work closely together. On the other hand, large and complex product development projects may need to address all 35 topics on the list and them some. Each project team should determine the PMP content that best fits the particular project, and then share the rationale for their decisions with senior leadership. Leaders should encourage project-specific tailoring but also insist that all relevant sections are included and addressed appropriately.

As noted earlier, PMPs have a tendency to become bureaucratic tools, rather than what they are meant to be—a useful tool that helps facilitate project success. For example, an organization may mandate a specific table of contents for all projects, thereby levying on the project team a requirement to address topics that are irrelevant to the particular project, and failing to levy a requirement to address unique topics that are critical to the project success. Teams may elect to populate the PMP with generic material or with slightly modified material from earlier projects, hoping that the volume of the submittal will intimidate those assigned to review and approve the PMP into doing only a cursory review. The root cause for such bureaucratic responses to the PMP often lies with senior leadership. Leaders who do not understand or appreciate the value of integrated planning, or of a PMP, will inevitably send clear signals that planning discipline is not valued, no matter what official policies may be in place. When that happens only the most dedicated and experienced project managers will persist with robust and effective planning. Senior leaders who appreciate the value of project planning insist that the planning be done, monitor to assure it is done, engage personally to review project plans, publically acknowledge examples of good planning, and coach project managers in the development of stronger project plans. That intelligent attention is the antidote for bureaucratic PMPs.

SUMMARY

Integrated project planning and the project vision development are perhaps the two most important of the eight habits of successful project teams. The plan is the roadmap for turning the vision into reality. Plan development contributes to project team building. A shared plan is a catalyst for continued team commitment. The plan is the yardstick against which progress is measured. Planning matters. Plans matter. Teams that do integrated planning well are much more apt to succeed than those that do not.

CHAPTER 5

HABIT # 4—
CONTINUALLY MONITOR
PERFORMANCE
AGAINST THE PLAN

"The last ten percent of performance generates one-third of the cost and two-thirds of the problems."
—*Augustine's Laws* (no. XV), Norm Augustine,
CEO Lockheed Martin[1]

S uccessful project teams understand their progress or lack of it from the start because they have installed both a plan and a monitoring system that measures their progress against the plan. They are able to avoid guessing about their rate of progress. Guessing optimistically is always less embarrassing and less painful— until about the 90-percent point when all that optimism is finally exposed as unfounded. Tracking progress from the start is less painful. Norm Augustine's words also ring true because many projects begin with huge challenges about which the project team and organization are in denial.

Peter Drucker distinguished between "control" and "controls," arguing that "control" is proactive and concerned with what ought to be; whereas "controls" are reactive in that they provide feedback about past activity. According to Drucker, the manager exerts control by providing direction and the appropriate guidance, incentives, and resources to enable the direction to be carried out. The manager also establishes a system of controls to determine whether progress is being made in the desired direction and whether the guidance, incentives, and resources are having the desired effect. The effective manager both sets direction (exerts control) and monitors the performance of (controls) the organization.[2]

Many textbooks also address the command and control concept, or to use Drucker's terminology, the "control and controls concept", asserting that the four management functions are to plan, organize, lead, and control (POLC). The reader who is not familiar with the POLC model should refer to one of the many excellent management books that discuss it. Peter Drucker's *Management: Tasks, Responsibilities, Practices* (1973) is a fine choice, although it predates the use of the specific POLC vernacular. *Management* by Robbins and Coulter specifically addresses the POLC model.[3] Both planning and leading are acts of setting direction, although for Robbins and Coulter, control is the monitoring and course-correction activity, the opposite of how Drucker uses the term. In the military vernacular, leading is the counterpart to command; however, control has the same meaning in both the traditional management vernacular and the military vernacular. No matter what terminology is used, it is generally agreed that both commanding and controlling are essential management activities, including project management.

This chapter focuses on the feedback and monitoring system that informs the manager about progress, a system that is especially important for effective project management. The material in this chapter focuses on the unique aspects of project management control, aspects that require adaptation of the traditional lore.

Project management monitoring is different than process or task work monitoring and those differences should influence how the work is monitored and controlled. The differences are rooted in the fundamental characteristics that distinguish project work from other work.

First, the project manager must build from scratch an ad hoc monitoring system for each project then deploy that newly created system across a still-forming project team because a project is a one-time activity (a temporary work group that forms rapidly, works together for an extended time, then disbands once the work is completed). Some of the more competent project-based organizations have a generally accepted monitoring philosophy and techniques that can be adapted for each new project but many organizations leave it to the manager to build the project monitoring system from scratch. So, project managers must be more adept than most managers at designing and deploying such systems.

Second, the project manager must craft a unique monitoring system tailored to the current need because every project is unique. No two projects face the same project vision, the same stakeholders, the same technical challenges, the same staff and skills, and the same resources, at the same point in time. Even if an organization has a generally accepted project monitoring system it must be adapted to each unique project situation. So, project managers must be more adept at creating and installing a unique system or at adapting a generally preferred system for each project.

Third, project managers must establish a means of monitoring learning and knowledge sharing as well as monitoring the pace and quality of that learning and sharing because project efficiency is much less about economical use of resources than it is about rapid learning. Teams that learn early what they do not know and then adapt quickly to that new learning are much more efficient than teams that manage to do work with fewer staff or finish work a few weeks earlier than planned. Of course, they must also monitor the traditional concerns about resources and their efficient use. So, the project manager must monitor some unique aspects of the project work activity.

These three work activity differences create unique demands for project monitoring systems and for the managers who craft, deploy, and rely on them. Those who understand the challenge and do the work will improve the chances their project will find success.

WHAT MUST THE PROJECT MANAGER MONITOR?

Managers and teams must monitor many project dimensions. Projects exist in complex dynamic environments and are susceptible to failure from any number of factors. The project manager must build a feedback array that will keep him and the entire team informed about all the critical factors. Some would say every factor, no matter how seemingly trivial, is in fact critical and must be monitored. Are the stakeholders still committed to the vision? Is the team on schedule? Are the expenditures resulting in the planned work accomplishment? Are the technical requirements being met? How has the current plan changed from the baseline plan and does the current plan reflect the work actually being done? Are the team's current skills appropriate for the current challenge? Are the risks increasing or decreasing as we learn? The list of on-going questions seems endless. Of course each project presents a unique set of challenges, challenges that may introduce their own unique and truly critical monitoring system requirements. Further, team members must know how the project leaders will measure their performance and project leaders must know how senior leaders and customers will measure the overall project performance, needs that exert some additional influence on the content of the project monitoring system. The list of potential monitoring requirements does seem endless.

The project manager must distinguish what is critical from what is important and what is important from what is merely interesting then have the savvy to build, deploy, and use the appropriate monitoring system for each project. The following paragraphs describe a few dimensions of project work activity that must be addressed. Remember, this is not a comprehensive list. Nor do the observations made about the topics below fit every project. Building a useful project monitoring system demands both craftsmanship and artistry.

The project vision and the stakeholder commitments to that vision must be monitored. Customers and other stakeholders may drift from their original interpretation of the project's purpose, a hazard that puts the project in grave peril. Team members may be tempted to reinterpret their original understanding of the vision as they feel the pressure to perform in the face of unexpected challenges. Changing environmental factors may force modification of the original vision, modifications that must be recognized, negotiated, and communicated. All these factors and more make it vital for the project manager to establish feedback channels that allow him to continually assess the various stakeholders' current interpretation and acceptance of the project vision.

Recall from chapter two that one project manager made it a habit to begin every presentation with a project vision chart. This practice certainly reinforces the vision—it serves a command function. It also facilitates a monitoring function because it prompts on-going dialogue about the interpretation of the vision. As a result, the project manager may be able to determine that a particular stakeholder's commitment to the vision is wavering, or that some team member has misinterpreted the implications of the vision, or that a new stakeholder does not fully understand the vision. The mere practice of starting every presentation with a vision chart is both a command device and a piece of a monitoring device.

Another vision command and monitoring technique is the "elevator speech." Every member of the project leadership team should know verbatim a brief summary of what their project is working to accomplish, a summary that can be communicated in the length of time it takes to travel a few floors on the elevator. The project manager exercises command by repeating that brief speech frequently to many people, thus communicating what the stakeholders and team members should be rallying around. However, this also serves a monitoring function. A savvy manager my occasionally misstate the vision, testing to see if someone corrects her. The response indicates whether or not people understand the vision, whether they have accurately internalized the vision, and whether or not they are committed to it.

Effective project team leaders sometimes build qualitative metrics for monitoring project vision health. They use a color-coded matrix to indicate the current status and trend of vision commitment for each stakeholder. They review the matrix quarterly with project leaders, with organizational leaders, and with key customer leaders to encourage everyone to be sensitive to stakeholder and team member vision commitment, to encourage them to recognize and seize opportunities to validate that commitment, and to learn if the visioning communications are effective.

The product, system, or service requirements must be monitored. Are the originally agreed requirements still agreed?

Are they valid and appropriate in light of current knowledge? Have all requirements been identified, specified, and negotiated? If not, is the rate of closure satisfactory? Have any new or reinterpreted requirements arisen? Is progress being made toward meeting the requirements? Do we still have appropriate margin given the uncertainty of meeting the requirements? Is the requirements test and demonstration approach still valid? Every day the project team learns more about factors that may influence the product, system, or service the project is working to provide. Every day the outlook changes. The project team must have in place an effective and timely means of monitoring the impact of new learning on the project requirements.

Requirements, unlike visioning, lend themselves to quantitative monitoring. Systems engineers spend a great deal of time establishing, allocating, and tracking requirements. One can find an array of requirements management software tools; the DOORS software by IBM is a popular example. The engineering design and product development literature offers many examples of requirements metrics. Yet, teams that make use of these tools and metrics often fail to effectively control and monitor project requirements. Just as EVMS may be necessary but insufficient, so too these tools may be necessary for some large complex projects but they are insufficient because project teams must understand what they are trying to accomplish then adapt the tools to meet the project need.

Project teams must also deal with the political and social dimensions of requirements development, qualitative rather than quantitative dimensions. Customers do not always know just what they want. Customers cannot always articulate what they want in terms the team can grasp. Design teams may have to distill requirements from marketing data and technology trends. Customers and stakeholders may disagree about requirements and be unable to resolve the disputes. Yet, the project team has been directed to begin work toward meeting those contradictory requirements. New information or changed priorities may cause stakeholders to revise their interpretation of requirements but not admit their interpretation has changed because they do not want to admit responsibility for the consequences of the revised interpretation. Systems engineering techniques and tools like DOORS cannot by themselves deal with these political and social challenges. Nonetheless the project team must continually monitor and control these dynamics.

Project teams must establish and use requirements monitoring techniques to manage the identification of requirements, the negotiation of requirements, the communication of requirements, the changing of requirements, and the demonstration of requirements compliance.

Quantitative monitoring can help; it can even be essential. Teams should know how many requirements remain open and whether they are moving toward closure. They should know how much design margin exists for each critical requirement and whether they are adding or losing margin as the design matures. They should understand which requirements are critical and which can be compromised if necessary. The project team may refer to a family of quantitative metrics to monitor requirements. The literature on product development methodology is filled with examples of such metrics. Teams can refer to similar previous project monitoring systems to identify both useful and misleading or ineffective metrics. The project manager must assure that an appropriate family of metrics are established, understood, and then monitored.

But, qualitative monitoring is equally important. Teams must continually monitor how the customers interpret the requirements and how that interpretation changes over time. Teams must monitor their internal engineering activity to assure requirements do not creep into the design because engineers think they can improve the product.

The qualitative dimensions of requirements monitoring rely on three project team dynamics. First, teams must practice requirements management discipline, discipline within the team and discipline with the customer. Every member of the team must insist that requirements be articulated, understood, documented, and communicated. That effort forms the baseline against which change can be detected. Here the systems engineering disciplines and tools can provide feedback to monitor progress. Second, teams must practice sensitivity to potential change. They must persistently monitor the internal and external environment looking for hints that requirements must change to accommodate new budget realities, new market dynamics, new technologies, etc. Here the project manager's focus, engagement, and enforcement can foster the appropriate sensitivity and thus generate the informal feedback about potential change and whether it is being dealt with. Third, teams must practice rigorous control of requirements change. They must engage potential change, identify it, understand it, resolve it, and formally control whether or not the change is accepted. Here project teams must blend the quantitative and qualitative feedback to monitor how effectively the team is controlling change.

The project manager determines whether these three dynamics are healthy and active or stagnant. He must display interest in these dynamics. He must role-model the desired attitudes and responses. He must reinforce the desired behaviors.

The underlying technology or technologies must be monitored. Is the selected technical approach still viable? Is it the most viable option? How is the technology trend evolving? Is the team equipped to deal with the technology? The team must have a means of monitoring and assessing new insights and perspectives about the technology. A three-week long local IT network upgrade project may have no need to monitor technology trends once the project begins, but a three-year project to develop a new flat-panel display for a Coast Guard search and rescue helicopter has reason to be concerned about evolving technologies. Hugh investments from the lap top computer, cell phone, personal digital assistant, and e-reader industries are driving rapid change in glass, coatings, display electronics, and display software. A technical solution that makes good sense when the helicopter display project starts may turn out to be obsolete less than a year later. Project teams must understand how technology trends may affect their project and then build appropriate feedback channels into their project monitoring approach. Here again the monitoring approach is both qualitative than quantitative.

Project teams must assign responsibility for and fund on-going effort to monitor the relevant technology trends. They must establish periodic technology status reviews and project leadership must engage in those reviews. Thus, the technology monitoring system relies on smart focused individuals working in a reinforcing project management discipline.

The technology monitoring system may also rely on quantitative assessments. The project team may establish a set of metrics comparing the original project technology performance assumptions, to the current technology capabilities, to the technology rate of change. It can also establish thresholds to trigger reassessments when technology changes may prompt project changes.

These qualitative and quantitative dimensions combine to form an integrated project technology monitoring system, a system the team can use to effectively control project technology.

The team members and the team dynamics must be monitored. What is the current state and direction of team morale? Does the team have a proactive or a fatalistic outlook? Is the social environment conducive to rapid learning and sharing? Are morale shaping initiatives having the desired effect? The project manager must understand how team performance is improving or declining and why it is changing.

Here the primary feedback sensor is often the project manager him or herself. Daniel Goleman[4] introduced the notion of emotional intelligence arguing that it may be more important than IQ. Goleman described emotional intelligence as the ability to identify, assess, and control one's emotions, and to identify, assess, empathize with, and influence the emotions of other individuals and groups, a useful ability for any manager. Some project managers may have powerful intellects but be emotionally insensitive while others may be charismatic and empathetic yet be less powerful intellectually. So, one project manager may innately know through day-to-day interaction how emotionally and socially healthy the individuals and the team as a whole are, while another manager may have no clue.

An organization and a project manager can employ several monitoring techniques to supplement their intuition, be it strong or weak. Some organizations insist on periodic project management health surveys as a way to gather insights to team member attitudes. Other organizations conduct periodic sensing sessions with selected team members. Both can be useful if the organizational culture fosters truth-telling and problem solving rather than power politics. Some project managers, recognizing their own insensitivity to the emotions of others, rely on trusted associates to read the emotional and social health of their team. The point is that the project leadership team must monitor the team members and team dynamics to assure the team is capable of accomplishing its work and motivated to do so.

Processes must be monitored. Recall we said in chapter one that project work may contain within it process work and may be influenced by processes outside the project itself. Teams must know whether those processes are effective and efficient. Are those processes, procedures, and disciplines, whether inside or outside the project, accomplishing their objectives? Are the critical reviews occurring when intended? Are they accomplishing the intended result? Are the interfaces between activities and subsystems being managed tightly? Are handoffs effective and timely? The project manager must continually verify that the management processes are accomplishing their intended purpose.

Again, the monitoring system for processes must contain a balance of quantitative and qualitative feedback. Teams may elect to use quantitative metrics to regularly examine process consistency, cycle-time, and efficiency. They may elect to quantitatively examine the quality of the process outputs. They also need to regularly assess whether the processes are still necessary, need to be revised, or must be reinforced. Project managers and their teams should identify the processes critical to project success then install the metrics to monitor those processes. They should also conduct periodic process reviews to interpret the metrics, to subjectively assess the processes value and health, and to direct appropriate actions.

Resources must be monitored. Are equipment, and other resources arriving and departing the project when planned? Are the resources as capable as planned? Are there any necessary changes to forecasted resource needs and are those changes being communicated appropriately? Project managers are responsible for assuring the appropriate resources are available when planned and that they are used effectively. That responsibility can only be accomplished if the appropriate monitoring channels are in place.

Yet again, the monitoring must be both quantitative and qualitative. One can tally the number of people needed versus the number available. One can count the number of test fixtures completed and the number of days until the last units will be available. But, it is not so easy to assign a number to the relative skill level or relevant experience of the key staff members. Some project managers make it a habit to establish trend charts depicting the month-by-month staffing plan versus the staffing actually provided as a way to identify growing problems and prompt corrective action. Some managers also identify critical skill positions well ahead of time and independently track efforts to fill those specific positions.

Effective project managers expand their monitoring system to embrace all resource needs, not just staffing needs. The project resource monitoring system should keep track of test equipment and fixturing, facilities, materials, and tools to name only a few critical resources.

Schedule and cost performance must be monitored. Are the schedules current and reflective of the work being done? Are the cost plans current and do they reflect work being done and planned? Are there any signs of cost being incurred without appropriate progress? Are changes to cost and schedule plans being incorporated as quickly as necessary? Is the team working from a single integrated schedule? Is the number of schedule interdependencies growing or shrinking? Is the project gaining or losing slack on the critical path? Are the number of early or late task starts and task completions increasing or decreasing? Project teams must use such an array of metrics and qualitative feedback to understand how they are progressing along the integrated project cost and schedule plan.

Here the project manager can be overwhelmed with tools and metrics. Sophisticated earned value measurement system (EVMS) tools can parse mountains of data into as many metrics and trend lines as a manager is willing to tolerate. Books have been written about cost and schedule monitoring. Formal weeks-long courses are available. Various agencies and councils offer formal certification for individuals and organizations. The challenge here is not merely to identify metrics to monitor but instead to sort from all the candidate metrics what ones are relevant to, and most appropriate for, each project and each project phase.

Project management literature often refers to a project management information system (PMIS). The PMIS is typically described as being made up of three tools; the WBS/SOW, an integrated schedule, and aggregated cost account budgets all combined with an EVMS. Some organizations and some project managers have concluded that the PMIS satisfies the need for a project monitoring system but such is not the case. The abundance of cost and schedule monitoring tools and the advocacy of an EVMS-based PMIS as the prescriptive solution for a project management monitoring system is dangerous because project teams or organizational leaders may fall into the trap of relying on these tools as the primary, or even the only, indicator of project progress or effectiveness.

The three tools within the PMIS are not by themselves information systems. The first tool, a WBS/SOW and its associated cost accounts, describes an integrated set of work activities with individual accountability and specific activities. These work activity packages, or cost accounts, are the level where most work is monitored. The WBS/SOW is what Drucker would call a command tool because it communicates to the team what work is to be done and who is supposed to do it. It is not by itself a controls tool because it lacks a feedback mechanism. The second tool, an integrated schedule, with its interdependencies and critical path, is the benchmark against which schedule progress is assessed for each work activity and for the overall project. The schedule is an essential part of the integrated project plan. It, too, is a command tool used to tell the team when work must be done and how the various work pieces depend on one another. It is not by itself a controls tool because it, too, lacks a feedback monitoring mechanism. The third tool, aggregated cost account budgets along with any reserves, forms the overall budget baseline against which project expenditures are monitored. It communicates to the team what funds are allocated to each work activity. It, too, is a command tool but not a controls tool. These three PMIS tools are not by themselves a monitoring system although they do underpin such a system because they function as yardsticks against which the data from the project management controls are compared.

The EVMS is the controls part of the PMIS because it monitors progress against the baselines established by the three tools described above. It is what makes the PMIS a cost and schedule progress monitoring system. However, a fully and effectively deployed EVMS is only a modest part of an overall project monitoring system because it completely fails to address many of the areas that must be monitored. It offers little insight into technical accomplishments. For example, a team may be underspending and ahead of schedule but the work being accomplished will not yield a design that meets the specifications. This sort of PMIS also fails to monitor technology, requirements, vision stability, team morale, and so on.

THE EARNED VALUE MEASUREMENT SYSTEM

Let's discuss EVMS a bit further. The EVMS is the most commonly mentioned, and certainly the most widely supported, method for monitoring project performance. EVMS is often mandated, especially for government contracts. Millions of dollars and tens of thousands of hours are spent advocating, deploying, and using EVMS each year; a discouraging situation considering how badly it is misapplied and how poorly it is used.

The EVMS can be an effective, even an essential, tool, for spotting some types of project problems. EVMS data

can provide early indications of schedule or cost deterioration. Accurate data can provide the insight that leads
project managers to ask more pointed questions about
specific activities. The data can uncover the truth about
the productive use of resources. It can provide data that
when interpreted properly and acted on promptly will
enable teams to use resources more effectively, make better decisions, and exercise more control over the project.
When used properly, EVMS can help prevent the dreaded
"90 percent spent but only 50 percent complete" scenario
so familiar to project managers. An effective EVMS can
facilitate better project performance.

You need to be aware that an EVMS cannot do everything. First, the three PMIS tools that underpin an EVMS
are not always fully deployed or used correctly. For example, teams may have adopted a standard WBS not suited
for their unique project. The EVMS is in those situations
providing data that is either misleading or of no value to
the project team. Second, source data may be unavailable.
EVMS has been deployed on projects and across organizations even thought there was no project-level cost data
available. The organizational cost accounting system did
not collect cost data at the project task level, a core requirement for EVMS. So, the tools were deployed and the EVMS
was deployed but the teams could not effectively monitor
project activity. Third, the three tools are often not integrated. It is common practice to develop a project WBS/
SOW, a project schedule, and a cost budget that are independent of one another (refer to Chapter 4). When that
happens the EVMS data inaccurately monitors progress
against a broken project plan. Fourth, EVMS tracks work
activity progress versus a plan. It does not track the quality,
effectiveness, or the appropriateness of that work activity.
Fifth, project teams must use milestone progress standards
rather than percentage complete judgment standards to
assess cost and schedule progress. EVMS is of little benefit

when it is founded on percentage complete estimates. The EVMS is perfectly capable of reporting great progress toward doing the wrong work badly. So, teams that rely solely, or even primarily, on EVMS often go astray. Even so, EVMS can be a useful segment of an overall project monitoring and control system.

Steve Crowther, of British Aerospace said, "Whilst you can practice good project management without EVM (referring to EVMS), you cannot practice EVM effectively without good project management."[5] EVMS can help a team understand its progress against the cost and schedule dimensions of a project plan but; the team must first have a viable integrated plan, it must be actually working to the plan rather than doing work outside the plan, it must practice disciplined plan change control, and it must accurately measure real progress rather than use optimistic guesses about percentage completion. EVMS is a powerful tool for competent project teams, not a substitute for that competence, and certainly not a creator of that competence.

Going beyond Crowther's comment, EVMS also requires organizational level project management competencies. For example, one organization spent over $1 million trying to deploy a certified EVMS system. However, their accounting systems and cost collection systems lacked the ability to accurately capture the actual costs incurred for specific project tasks. They simply could not gather the basic information necessary to feed the EVMS they had been working so hard to deploy. The organization also lacked the finance department staff and bureaucracy to gather, sort, process, and analyze the task-level cost data even if it had been available. The organizational leaders had been told that EVMS could help them better manage projects; that it could help them avoid the serious cost overruns and delays they so frequently encountered. So, they had invested to deploy an EVMS not understanding the infrastructure and discipline prerequisites for effective use of that EVMS. Effective EVMS must be built on a sound organizational and project team competency foundation. EVMS is a tool that supplements existing good practice. It does not create that good practice.

Some organizations avoid EVMS because they have heard about or had their own frustrating experiences like the one described above. Others do so because they mistakenly believe it is an overly formal tool that is expensive to operate. Indeed, it often is overly formal and expensive although it need not be so. The fundamental intent of EVMS can be accomplished using simple tools. First, the project must have a documented integrated plan including frequent and verifiable progress milestones against which to measure earned value performance. Second, the project must be able to gather periodic, at least monthly, schedule progress data at the work package level. Third, the project must be able to gather periodic, at least monthly, actual cost data at the work package level. The project team can then use pencil and paper to perform simple four-function mathematic calculations to derive the EVMS metrics. Even very large projects can employ EVMS if these requirements are met, although they usually make use of commonly available software. Complexity arises when organizations and project teams introduce sophisticated software and burdensome bureaucracy without first establishing the required discipline of integrated planning and without installing accurate cost and schedule data collection methods. These simple but not easy requirements get entangled in a bureaucracy that makes the simple-but-not-easy into the complex-and-not-easy. The failure is not with EVMS but instead with organizational weakness and misunderstandings about the fundamental tenets of effective project management.

Project teams sometimes deploy EVMS as a part of their project controls because they are forced to do so.

Such coercion often comes from one of two sources. First, organizations may mandate EVMS for projects. The organization may have become frustrated with poor project performance and so adopt EVMS in an attempt to improve outcomes. These organizations do not always understand the underlying project management disciplines but they have heard that EVMS is an essential tool. Second, external customers may mandate that the supplier use EVMS for their projects perhaps because their higher-level customer has imposed the requirement or perhaps because they believe EVMS to be an effective tool. No matter the source of the coercion, mandated deployments rarely benefit the project absorbing the mandate. It is worth repeating that organizations and teams must first embrace the fundamental project disciplines. Then they can take advantage of tools like EVMS. Deploying EVMS ahead of that understanding is disruptive and futile.

EVMS, like all tools, is not without its flaws. It can lead a team astray even when it is deployed in an organization and a project with good foundational skills and resources. Those who use EVMS as their primary project-monitoring tool are essentially trying to drive while relying on what they can see in the rear-view mirror. The system, when it is deployed and used properly, provides a somewhat accurate picture of what has been accomplished so far. Algorithms are used to project that same performance forward as an estimate of future project performance. The assumption is that if a project has performed well to date then it is going to perform equally well in the future and if a project has performed poorly to date then it is going to continue to perform as poorly in the future. EVMS theory asserts that future project performance is accurately predicted by past performance.

Certainly many projects start poorly and end poorly while others start well and end well but many projects appear to start well then end poorly (Rarely do they start poorly and end well.). Their past performance was not, and could not have been, predictive of their future performance.

Consider a project that begins well. The project vision is clear and shared by the stakeholders. The effort is planned in detail. Appropriate resources are made available. The work starts well and proceeds smoothly. The EVMS data indicates excellent progress for the first 70 percent of the project. However, the project is attempting to build a custom mechanical device for use with a scientific payload on board a NASA deep space probe satellite. The device specifications are extremely challenging and the testing will be rigorous because the device must work precisely as intended and obviously there will be no opportunity to repair any problems after the satellite has been launched into space. A failure after launch could mean the entire $500 million experiment would be wasted. The mechanical device project team has made an array of complex technical decisions about materials, processes, and assembly techniques they and the NASA believe will yield a satisfactory rotating device that will enable the experiment to survive the launch stresses then operate for years as the satellite travels to the fringe of our solar system.

This team faces a major hurdle late in the project. This mechanical device will not operate on earth in the same way it will operate on orbit. The mechanism will feel the effects of earth's atmosphere and gravitational pull while being tested, effects that will not be present in space. Further, the mechanism will operate through dramatic temperature extremes while in space because part of the device will at times be exposed to direct sunlight while simultaneously another part will be exposed to dark space, a difficult thermal environment to simulate in the laboratory. The team and their customer, NASA, have agreed on an elaborate and exhaustive test and analysis plan they believe will verify the mechanism will work properly but the test and analyses methods and results will be subject to wide interpretation. The NASA engineers will insist on checking, verifying, reanalyzing, and second-guessing every aspect of the test data then perfecting every aspect of the design. So, this team may make steady progress through 80 percent or 90 percent of the project but end up with massive delays, redesign, or perhaps complete project failure during the last 10 percent of the project when final testing and analysis occurs. This project's past success as reported by the EVMS system may well not be a harbinger of what is to come. The project team and the NASA customer would be foolish to assume otherwise.

Consider the opposite situation. A project team has been assigned to refurbish an existing office building; installing a new roof, reworking the heating and air conditioning, reconfiguring several walls, and upgrading the interior. Within the first month it discovers asbestos in a section of the ceiling. Neither the owner nor the project team knew about the asbestos, and so the project plan did not anticipate having to deal with it. After only 30 days the project has realized it will face a schedule delay, additional unplanned costs, and the need for an additional subcontractor specializing in asbestos removal. About three months later the asbestos has been removed and the OSHA inspector has given the project team approval to proceed. Everything goes smoothly from that point. The project team's early difficulties were not a predictor of its future performance. The poor initial cost and schedule performance, as reported and projected into the future by the EVMS, was not a harbinger of the future.

Certainly, every project team should be challenged to explain its past performance successes or failures. Just as certainly every project team should be tasked to explain why it believes its past is or is not a prologue of its future. That dialogue brings to light the relevant facts and understandings, interpretations of those facts and understandings, and the implications for the project work ahead. The EVMS data may offer insight into past project performance, but its more important function is to be a catalyst for a rich dialogue between the project manager and the organizational leaders about current and future project performance, a dialogue that sheds light on just how well the project manager and the project team understand the challenges and their path forward.

EVMS often suffers from another problem. It tends to become entangled in cumbersome bureaucracy, entanglement that adds cost while also diminishing the monitoring value of the system. EVMS has been around long enough to develop a specialist cult. The federal government has fostered that cult within its own ranks and it has spread to many contractors. Functional groups within organizations too often become enamored with the rule making, policy development, compliance enforcement, and ritual that is often wrapped around the EVMS tool. There are many instances where an organization has unduly burdened itself, so much so that project teams find themselves serving the tool and its entrenched bureaucracy rather than using the tool to manage the project effectively. Senior leadership and project managers must understand EVMS principles well enough to detect and limit this sort of organizational behavior.

Notwithstanding its shortcomings, EVMS is an essential part of a project management monitoring system. Some dimensions of project performance can be very effectively monitored using an EVMS and the three tools on which it is founded. The EVMS provides actual cost of work performed versus the planned cost of work performed and the actual time taken to perform that work versus the planned time to perform that work. We strongly advocate using EVMS as one element in a much more comprehensive project monitoring system, although it must be surrounded by an array of formal and informal feedback channels that keep the project leadership team informed on all the important project dimensions.

ANOTHER ELEMENT OF THE MONITORING SYSTEM: PROJECT REVIEWS

Let's step away from the quantitative and metrics portion of the project monitoring system long enough to describe another vital element—frequent periodic project reviews. Effective project teams, especially those working on large and complex projects, are in a perpetual state of review. Perhaps a six-week long project to upgrade the local area network in a building needs very little review after it gets under way but a challenging and long-running project must include an ongoing review scheme as part of its monitoring and control network.

Below is a description of some of the reviews found useful for many projects. This is not an all-inclusive list, nor do all of these reviews fit every project. Each industry and each technical discipline tends to have its own customs and vernacular regarding reviews. The project manager should work with the organizational leadership and with the project team to construct a suite of reviews and a review schedule best suited for the project.

Initial project plan review—Chapter 4 described the importance of integrated project planning and capturing the overall project plan in a formal Project Management Plan (PMP) document. Organizations that consistently conduct formal and rigorous PMP reviews more often find project success. The leadership at one business unit, striving to improve overall project performance, instituted a practice of requiring that every new-start project conduct a PMP review with the senior leadership team. The reviews, lasting for several hours, involved an in-depth critique of the vision, requirements, integrated plan, monitoring system, risks and opportunities, and several other topics. The benefits were real for both the leaders and the project teams. Leaders came to better understand the unique challenges faced by the team, whether the team was up to those challenges, and what the organization must do to facilitate project success. The project team benefited in that it was able to articulate what it needed from the functional departments and then it was able to receive commitments to meet those needs. The team learned early on whether or not it would be allowed to deviate from policy or procedural constraints that could handicap its chance for success. It was able to gain the confidence of the organizational leadership team. These reviews also fostered the application of best practices through the real-time training of project managers and project teams. Finally, these reviews fostered a cross-organizational appreciation for the importance of the project, an appreciation that translated into organizational assistance rather than resistance.

Recurring project plan reviews—Projects that run for a year, or for several years, will go through changes that dramatically impact their plan and their likelihood of success. Effective organizations insist on a formal revision and review of project plans when such change occurs. Best practice organizations mandate at least annual PMP updates and formal reviews, with more frequent revision if appropriate. For example, a team should be required to revisit its PMP when it encounters scope change greater than some threshold, perhaps 25 percent of the overall effort. Teams should also revisit their PMP after critical events like a major product design review, a major test activity, or the completion of a key subsystem installation. The point is to insist that the team and the organization be sensitive to significant change events and adapt to them in a disciplined way. The recurring project plan reviews foster that discipline.

Periodic project reviews—Projects need to be reviewed frequently, at least quarterly, and more often if they are large, complex, dynamic, or being conducted by an immature team. Periodic senior leadership review from outside the project team serves both a command and a controls function. As a command function it communicates what matters. As a controls function it provides a venue for assessing project performance. There is no substitute for real time dialogue about the project's recent past performance, its current state, and the outlook. Metrics alone communicate facts and data about project performance but real-time interaction provides a venue for understanding the unmeasurable dimensions of a project's condition. An astute leader can often tell more about a project from the mannerism, tone, and competence communicated during a well-run periodic review than could possibly be communicated with metrics alone. Quite often, hesitancy in answering, a casual aside, a vague response, or even the sudden tensing of the project manager's brow when a question is asked can lead to further questioning and insights that can be gained in no other way. These periodic reviews serve other functions as well. They offer a venue in which the project team can remind the organization as a whole or the functional departments about their commitments to the project plan. They also offer a venue for coaching project managers and their teams, for sharing organizational best practices, and for quickly adjusting priorities to adapt to new learning. Periodic project reviews help both the project team and the organization find success.

Project management review formats are often a point of contention and confusion that unnecessarily distract people and sometimes lead to less-than-optimal reviews. Organizational leaders often become enamored with standard templates for all project reviews. Leaders sometimes complain that the different project review formats and content may cause them to miss, or to misunderstand, key points. They also dislike having to interpret a variety of formats, preferring to be able to skim quickly across standard formats to get the information they seek. Some project managers complain about having to fill out standard formats that contain irrelevant information or inhibit clear communication about their particular project. Other project managers ask for a standard and consistent format so they can simplify the chore of putting together the review package each time.

Most of these arguments, whether pro or con, miss the point. The project reviews are most beneficial when they foster clear communication between the project team and organizational leadership about project status, progress, change, and issues. Teams may need to adapt, tailor, or supplement standard formats in order to accomplish that communication. Leaders should encourage useful modifications, even if it means they must concentrate a bit harder to understand the differences.

Best practice organizations and project teams use standard templates and formats as a starting point but adapt quickly to unique project needs. These organizations begin by asking the project team to address in their PMP how it will structure the project review activity. The team typically reviews a standard list of review topics, adding or deleting topics as it thinks appropriate. The team then reviews the standard formats for the selected topics and adapts them as appropriate. The team presents its recommendation to the organizational leaders during the formal PMP review, seeking concurrence for its decisions. The leaders and the project team can then reach a mutual understanding about what should be reviewed and how it will be reviewed. Finally, the team may continue to modify the agreed format as the project needs change but each time it returns to the senior leaders to get concurrence for the modification. This approach allows the organization to have a controlled yet flexible process, a hallmark of successful project management based organizations.

Appendix II contains a sample project review template. Project managers may find it a useful place to begin the work of building a template that meets their project needs and satisfies their organizational needs.

Focus reviews—Projects may involve many disciplines and many interrelated but somewhat unique activities. Production depends on Procurement to make the correct materials available when needed. Test depends on Design and Systems to provide a clear understanding of what is to be tested and how. The hardware and software engineering teams depend on Systems to establish the boundaries and interfaces between them. Project risks and opportunities must be assessed and reassessed periodically. Technologies must be monitored. These challenges and many others must be monitored throughout the project. Effective organizations do not try to address all these topics during the periodic project reviews. Instead, they may identify special focus topics needing additional attention or understanding. Ad hoc focus reviews provide a venue for the in-depth probing of those areas while also allowing the periodic reviews to accomplish their intended purpose rather than be consumed by every critical issue that comes along. Project teams should be conditioned to expect such reviews from time to time.

So far we have described several project review formats to foster interchange between the organization and the project team. Now we shift to a description of internal-to-the-project reviews that enable project execution, monitoring, and control.

Monthly work activity reviews—Effective project managers conduct monthly reviews with each work activity (control account) leader. These reviews serve a command function in that they provide a recurring opportunity for the project manager to issue guidance. But, when done well, these reviews serve an even more vital function of allowing the project manager to monitor work activity progress. Find below a few specific recommendations for making these reviews as powerful and effective as they need to be.

- Be religious about holding them—Best practice organizations consider these reviews to be vitally important and cancel them for only the most critical reasons. This discipline reinforces accountability for progress. It also provides the project manager an opportunity to get that visceral feel for how the work activity is progressing.
- Include the appropriate participants—Attendees should include the work activity leader and the project manager. The project technical leader and the project planning leader should also attend because both of them can spot implications that may impact other work activity areas.
- Spend some time on every work activity (control account)—Best practice project teams make it a standing practice to review every work activity every month. Major problems can arise in any work activity no matter what its size. Events or learning in one work activity may have only a minor impact for that activity but have a major impact for other work activities. Work that deserves to be segmented as a separate work activity (control account) deserves to be reviewed monthly. These need not all be long reviews. Some work activity can be reviewed in ten or fifteen minutes if the work scope is modest, if there has been little activity during the past month, or if the activity remains under control. Nonetheless, each work activity deserves its time in the spotlight.

- Have Planners prepare beforehand—The project planning staff should review all the work activity EVMS data, analyze it, and prepare summary observations for the project manager. This pre-work helps assure the important topics are addressed during the session.
- Learn and help rather than chastise—These reviews are intended primarily to give the project manager feedback about the work activity. The environment must be one in which that feedback is encouraged and appreciated. Work activity leaders who are heard and helped as appropriate will continue to provide useful feedback. Those who are chastised will not. Project managers must find a different arena for delivering criticism.
- Discuss risks and opportunities—These reviews should have three distinct segments. First, discuss progress versus plan for the preceding month. Second, discuss leanings and implications. Third, discuss the current understanding of work activity risks and opportunities, the implications of any changed understandings, and what actions are planned to influence the likelihood or impact of those risks and opportunities.
- Agree on short-term goals—Each review should end with a recap of the goals and objectives for the coming month.

Focus reviews—Project managers should establish appropriate internal focus reviews on topics important to project success. Most projects longer than a few months benefit from periodic risk and opportunity reviews (a topic to be addressed in more detail later). Engineering design projects benefit from iterative design progress reviews (preliminary design review, critical design review, etc.). Some projects benefit from design-to-production transition reviews where the team addresses progress toward a design that will meet target cost goals, or assess the ease with which the product can be manufactured. It is up to the project manager to determine what focus reviews are appropriate. It is up to senior leadership to assure the determination is made and is sound.

Reviews are only beneficial when done with informed engagement, noble intent, and a constructive attitude. Ritual alone does not add value. As has been stated often, these reviews often perform both a control and a controls function. They provide a venue for sending guidance to the project team. They also provide a venue for monitoring project progress. Project managers must establish the tone and the culture that facilitates both.

THE CHALLENGES OF DEVELOPING AND USING MONITORING SYSTEMS

Developing a project monitoring system is no easy task. Project teams must be cautious as they determine what must be monitored, build the metrics within the monitoring system, and interpret the feedback from the system and metrics. Drucker described three considerations of business controls, considerations that also apply to project controls.

First, Drucker said, "Controls can be neither objective nor neutral."[6] He argued that the act of monitoring an activity or outcome highlights its importance to the detriment of other activities not being so closely monitored. People may begin to manipulate the environment to make the measurement appear better, whether or not the desired outcome actually gets better.

Several years ago the leadership at an aerospace business unit decided to measure their on-time delivery performance. They had seen an industry study asserting top tier competitors were meeting their contractual delivery obligations about 95 percent of the time. The business unit was only meeting contract delivery obligations about 65 percent of the time. The old saw that what gets measured improves held true again. Project teams began reporting on-time delivery improvements within a few months after the new metric was announced. The problem was that the metrics improved but customers were not happier because they were not seeing the improvement. Some project teams felt they could claim on-time delivery if they made the delivery during the month stated in the contract but not necessarily on the specific date promised. One project manager said, "After all these projects are challenging and within a month is close enough." Other project managers asserting on-time performance improvement had called their customers asking for a contract revision so they would not miss the delivery. Still others asserted that the team should not be accountable for supplier delays. The business unit leadership team learned again that people instinctively look for the easy way to appear successful. Manipulating the score keeping was certainly easier than actually improving the performance.

The business unit leaders had to patiently but persistently remind everyone that the objective was not to make the data look better. Instead, the objective was to learn what was preventing better on-time delivery performance so that those obstacles could be removed. Change came slowly. Several project teams continued to interpret the rules and the data in the most favorable light but after several more months a few teams began to point out problems with too little test equipment, some overly bureaucratic procurement processes, chronically late test equipment, and several other issues that were too-often impeding on-time delivery. The organization began making structural changes that fostered better project schedule performance, and within a couple of years on-time delivery had improved (in fact, not just in metric manipulation). During the third year after the new on-time performance metrics were put in place the business unit reported an average of 97 percent on-time delivery, the first of five consecutive years achieving better than 96 percent on-time delivery to original contract promise dates.

Drucker's second consideration was, "Controls need to focus on results." He argued that measuring efficiency is equivalent to measuring effort, but it is effects that matter rather than efforts. A project team may use EVMS to track its progress against a schedule and budget (efficiency) but a team may finish work activity under budget and ahead of schedule while delivering a result that does not meet the intended needs (no effectiveness). Teams need to monitor both efficiency and effectiveness (tangible results).[7]

This topic presents an opportunity to revisit the dreaded "80 percent complete" syndrome. Every experienced project manager can tell a story about work activity that seemed to be more or less on track through about 80 percent of the effort and then dramatically stalled, taking nearly as long and as much money to complete the last 20 percent of the effort as it took to accomplish the first 80 percent. The phenomenon is so common that some project professionals and organizations assume it is unavoidable. When this occurs it is almost always due to a mistake that occurred when the work was first planned, a mistake that disabled the PMIS part of the project monitoring system, a mistake that made the 80 percent complete syndrome inevitable. The following paragraphs describe why this occurs and how to prevent it.

Recall from chapter four that projects must be based on an integrated project plan, one that integrates the work scope with a compatible schedule and budget. The work scope is divided into work activity packages (control accounts or cost accounts). Each work activity package has its own schedule and budget forming an integrated plan for that sub element of the overall project. The sub elements are interconnected and coordinated to form the overall integrated project plan.

Not all the work activities are equal. Those that will take more than a few weeks to complete must be monitored differently than longer tasks. Some of the work activities are brief. Examples include; a six-week task to design an interface cable between two electronic boxes, a two-week task to review an existing test plan and adapt it for the current project, a 21-day task to support installation of equipment at the customer's site, or a series of brief trips to a subcontractor facility to review their progress. Other work activities are not so brief. Examples include; a six-month long effort to jointly development with the customer a set of top-level requirements for a new hydroelectric dam, installation and test of twelve generators, installation of a security system and control center, or construction of a spillway. The progress in accomplishing the former kinds of work activities should be monitored differently than the later. The key notion is, as Drucker said, to determine progress on the basis of tangible outcomes rather than judgment. Longer tasks need intermediate milestones against which to assess progress.

For example, a team assigned to upgrade the local area network within an office building plans to complete the work in three weeks. The tangible project completion will be self-evident; the users will all be connected and the network speed will be faster than before. The project manager has identified several work activities within the overall project including; 1) all equipment delivered and ready for installation, 2) old equipment removed and new equipment installed during shut-down weekend, 3) new software installed on new equipment during second shutdown weekend, 4) new system is stable and operating at expected speeds, 5) all changes documented and IT team trained, 6) project completed. The project manager knows how much time and how much budget is planned to accomplish each of the six work activities. She can compare the actual time and cost incurred to the planned time and cost incurred for each, maintaining almost real-time awareness of progress versus plan. The project manager may have elected to not identify interim milestones and then build a detailed budget and schedule for each of them. After all, the entire project is only three weeks long, some of the identified work activities are only a few days long, there are only 4 people working on the project, and she is directly engaged with each of them daily. She can simply rely on her judgment about progress. She may decide that the cost and time required to build the detailed plans and track them is not worth the effort. For that matter, the organization's cost control system may only be able to provide monthly cost information, making the work activity data of no use for a three-week long project.

On the other hand, a hydroelectric dam project is scheduled to take five years to complete. The integrated project plan includes work activities that will each take several months to complete. Each work activity has a schedule and budget plan. The project manager may elect to rely on her personal judgment, or the judgment of work activity leaders, to determine whether work is proceeding according to plan. But, judgments are not always sound, and they are certainly not always accurate, especially for such large and long-term tasks. Individuals will be hopeful or optimistic about the work actually accomplished and about how much can be accomplished in the future. Individuals will be prone to give positive progress reports because delivering negative progress reports will lead to criticism, or additional probing, or undesired help. In short, the project managers' decision to rely on judgment to determine progress leads to a high likelihood of the project stumbling into the 80 percent spent but 50 percent complete syndrome.

What should the project manager do? The solution is found in the specifics of how the EVMS is configured to monitor progress. There are essentially three approaches to monitoring work activity progress (see Table 5.1). Successful project teams have a strong bias for specific milestones rather than percent complete or level of effort monitoring. Project managers enable the dreaded "80 percent spent but 50 percent complete" syndrome when they rely on percent complete monitoring. Having made clear

Table 5.1   EVMS Progress Metrics

Examples	Weaknesses	Strengths
Milestones		
Requirements documented and approved	Requires time and energy early in the project to identify and negotiate milestones	Prevents 90/50 syndrome
System design completed and approved		Reduces debate about what has been accomplished
First-pass software released	Team members may resist specific milestone measurement	More accurate reading of project progress
Test completed successfully		
Percent Complete		
Work activity leader uses judgment to report progress toward completion	Requested when plan is flimsy	None
	Requested when work scope not well understood	Should rarely be used
Applied to any work activity	Judgment is subjective	
Level-of-Effort		
Support tasks (e.g., planning, project manager)	None when used for true level of effort work activity	Streamlines monitoring of level-of-effort work activity without hurting accuracy
Field/customer liaison	Useless when applied to other work activity	
Quality or production engineering support to build/test		

the preference for the milestones approach, each technique is described further below.

Let's begin with the "percent complete" approach. The project team establishes a scope, schedule, and cost plan. A start and complete date is established for each major work activity, whether short duration or long duration. Once work begins, the work activity leader is asked periodically to provide an assessment—an opinion—of the percent of work accomplished so far. That assessment is matched against the amount of money spent and the time remaining until the planned completion date to estimate if the work is being accomplished as planned.

The "percent complete" metric is strongly discouraged by nearly every piece of EVMS literature and most, if not all, EVMS instructors. First, real-time personal judgment of accomplishment is subjective. One individual may sincerely believe half of the work has been accomplished while another individual may believe only one-quarter of the work has been accomplished. Whose judgment is to be believed? Second, an individual's reluctance to deliver a disappointing progress report may cause him to be overly optimistic about what has been accomplished, a false estimate that will not be exposed until much later. Third, individuals who are feeling the pressure of being behind may become overly optimistic about how little work remains and how easy it will be, using that as a rationale for claiming more than appropriate progress to date. Fourth, for whatever reason, whether one of the three listed above or some other, the 80 percent syndrome nearly always arises on projects where "percent complete" is used as the EVMS progress metric. The correlation is too high to ignore.

Yet, the "percent complete" measure is frequently used. Why? One reason is that some project managers do not understand the consequences. Another reason is that it is simple, requiring no organizational or project infrastructure, no software tools, and very little data collection process. Yet another reason is that project teams feel pressured to begin work as quickly as possible, forgoing disciplined up-front planning—they believe they do not have time to work on progress milestone development. That sense of urgency can lead teams to charge ahead with only sketchy plans, telling themselves they will catch up later. Another reason is that teams with a sketchy project vision, poor requirements, and a vague plan do not have sufficient detailed baseline information to establish more rigorous metrics. Yet another reason is that senior leaders do not appreciate the need for more rigorous up-front metrics development, and so they do not insist on them and may even discourage teams from developing them. So, the use of "percent complete" is often a symptom of much deeper problems. Successful project teams distrust "percent complete" and avoid it whenever possible.

"Milestone" metrics are a much more effective means of assessing work activity progress. Each major work activity is broken down into smaller specific and clearly definable segments with tangible outcomes. The work activity is segmented into increments no more than two months long, preferably one month or shorter. For example, a team has allocated six months time and a budget of $150,000 to design a power supply for a new security system. The work activity will begin when the systems engineer finalizes and releases the power supply requirements document and will end when the power supply design team gets systems engineering approval for their design.

The project manager has asked the power supply design team to identify five to eight intermediate progress milestones that will be used to track progress. The team submits the following;

1. Systems engineering approval of top-level power supply architecture, showing major functional blocks, interfaces between blocks, all power

supply inputs and outputs, approximate weight and dimensions, and a summary of design margins for all key requirements. The team believes this work will take six weeks and will consume 15 percent of the total budget.

2. All initial detailed drawings submitted to configuration control and systems engineering review. The team believes this work will take six weeks and consume 20 percent of the total budget.

3. Complete electrical and mechanical design analysis and conduct preliminary design review. The team believes this work will take ten weeks, running in parallel with some of the other tasks and will consume 20 percent of the budget.

4. Revise all drawings and documents to reflect any changes from the preliminary design review. The team believes this work will take two weeks and will consume 5 percent of the budget.

5. Develop preliminary parts list and purchase information. Get procurement department approval of preliminary list. The team believes this work will take eight weeks and consume 10 percent of the budget.

6. Prepare for and conduct final design review. The team believes this work will take two weeks and consume 10 percent of the budget.

7. Revise all drawings and documents to reflect any changes from the final design review. The team believes this work will take two weeks and will consume 10 percent of the budget.

8. Submit all final drawings and documents to configuration control. Submit final parts list and procurement information. The team believes this work will take two weeks and will consume 10 percent of the budget.

The project manager and the work activity leader agree on these eight performance milestones, their time durations, and their dollar values. As the work progresses the work team will received performance credit for each milestone after it has been accomplished. There is no need for judgment about progress. There is little likelihood of undue optimism creeping into the EVMS data. There is little chance of the 80 percent syndrome emerging.

The third approach to EVMS progress metrics is "level-of-effort." This approach to assessing progress can be useful for some work activity. The level-of-effort approach essentially acknowledges that schedule performance is irrelevant for the activity being measured. Some project work activity is indeed not subject to intermediate schedule progress milestones. For example, the project plan may call for a full-time planner from the start to the end of the project. The planner will help establish the initial project baseline plan, manage changes as they occur, prepare monthly status reports, and assist the project manager in analyzing the progress data. The planner's administrative and analytical work is on-going. There is no clear milestone event to designate that a specific amount of the planners work activity has been accomplished. As another example, a project team may plan to send a small engineering team to the customer facility to advise and assist in integration testing. The engineering team will be there for six months. It has no interim milestones to accomplish because its role is simply to be of assistance. The project does not benefit from imposing artificial milestones to monitor the work scope in progress for such activities.

Effective project managers take the time to develop frequent, tangible, accomplishment-based milestones against which to assess work activity progress. They use "level-of-effort" when appropriate. They do not allow the team members to use "percent complete" estimates as their measure of work activity progress. Therefore, they rarely fall victim to the 80 percent syndrome.

Recall that Drucker identified three considerations of business controls. The first two considerations were "controls can be neither objective nor neutral" and "controls need to focus on results." Drucker also argued that, "controls are needed for measurable and nonmeasurable events"[8] echoing Albert Einstein's reputed assertion that, "Not everything that counts can be counted, and not everything that can be counted counts." Consider the strength of our relationship with our significant others. It counts very much, but one would be hard pressed to find a useful way to quantify it—try telling your mate that your relationship is a 7.4 on a scale of 10 and see what reaction you get. Similarly, a stakeholder's commitment to the project vision counts but cannot be quantified. Leadership confidence in the skills and commitment of the project team members counts but that too cannot be quantified in any useful way. Conversely, one can easily count the number of hours that were spent preparing a test plan, but what really matters is the quality of that plan, something that is not so easily quantified. Project monitoring systems must successfully monitor both measurable and nonmeasurable events. Successful project managers employ stoplight charts, Likert scales, better/worse directional arrows, and especially group assessment discussions as a way to keep tabs on those areas that matter but do not lend themselves to quantification.

ADDITIONAL CONSIDERATIONS OF PROJECT MONITORING SYSTEMS

Drucker pointed out three major considerations of business controls, or in our case, project monitoring systems. Here are a few additional considerations.

It is better to measure poorly the important than to measure well the unimportant. Do not trust substitute metrics. Two decades ago Steven Kerr,[9] who at the time held the position of Chief Learning Officer at General Electric, wrote a brief but powerful article titled "On the Folly of Rewarding A, While Hoping for B." Kerr reminded everyone that we should expect every person to do, or at least pretend to do, the things they are rewarded for doing rather than the things we ask them to do. Yet, time and again we fail to heed Kerr's reminder.

One glaring example is occurring now in many, perhaps most, organizations around the globe. GE, Honeywell, and many other organizations value employee learning. They understand the benefits of having a workforce that continually becomes more knowledgeable and so they spend millions of dollars each year on employee education and training. These firms have developed expensive and time-consuming internal training programs to develop key managers and executives. So, how do these firms measure progress toward achieving this more educated workforce? What does their monitoring and controls system actually measure? Butts in seats. That's right, most organizations have elected to track the number of hours employees spend in training, rather than the actual advancement in employee education. Most organizations commit the folly of measuring the number of hours employees spend sitting in class but hoping for a better-educated workforce.

Why do they commit this folly? Because they can easily figure out how to measure attendance at training but they cannot so easily figure out how to measure advancement in learning. They have all elected to measure well the unimportant because it is so difficult to measure, even to measure poorly, the important. They are measuring A while hoping for B.

What are the consequences of this folly? One consequence is that the individuals and managers set about making the metrics look favorable—recall Drucker's observation that controls can be neither objective nor neutral. If Tom's performance appraisal is influenced by the number of hours of training he completes then Tom will make time to attend training. Tom has been assigned to a challenging project that has been struggling with a major requirements change. He has not so far had time to attend training but it is now late in the year and Tom has to do something quickly. So, he signs up for the only training event with an available seat. The training has little to do with Tom's work, and he has no interest in the topic, but at least he will be able to complete enough training hours to satisfy his boss and not hurt his performance appraisal.

Another consequence is that Tom's engineering department manager, Jane, will set about trying to make her department, and herself look good. It turns out that the organization's monitoring system measures the number of hours of individual training as well as the average number of hours of training per employee for each department. Jane's department has just installed a new set of design analysis and simulation tools that should dramatically improve the speed and quality of new product designs. Ten of the 65 employees in Jane's department should receive extensive training on the new tools, about 320 hours each. The department training budget was built on an assumption that the 65 employees would receive an average of 80 hours of training during the year (a total of 5200 hours). But, the ten employees learning to use the new tools will consume more than half (3200 hours) of the department training budget.

Jane has a serious dilemma. She can see no good choice. She can elect to authorize training for the ten employees on the new system and the 80 hours of training for the other 55 employees. This decision will enable the department to improve its productivity and work quality. Several product development projects planned for next year will benefit greatly from the change but there will be little benefit to this year's projects. The decision will also enable all her employees to meet their annual training goal. But this decision may cause Jane to overrun her department training budget by as much as 40 percent and her boss has already warned everyone that budget overruns will reflect badly on their appraisal. Jane is a candidate for a promotion and she does not want to hurt her chances for the job.

Jane's second alternative is to stay within the department training budget by funding every employee's 80 hours of training and deferring most of the new tools training until next year. Her employees can meet their training goals. She can meet her department training and budget goals. But, the benefits of the new tools will be deferred for several months, thus adding otherwise avoidable cost and risk to some upcoming projects.

Jane's third alternative is to stay within the department budget by funding the tools training while restricting any other training for the rest of the year. She can meet her department training and budget goals. She can also support the upcoming projects. But, many of her department employees, including Tom, will be unable to attend training and so will miss their personal training goals.

In this situation the training monitoring system (and the budget monitoring system) is using metrics that drive Jane to consider a short sighted, perhaps even harmful, decision. Why? This dilemma arose because those building the monitoring system wanted to monitor improvements in employee education. They could not come up with easy-to-collect data about actual learning improvement but they could come up with easy-to-collect data about training hours (butts in seats). They chose to use a substitute metric that could be measured well. In doing so, they committed the folly of rewarding A (and getting A) while hoping for B.

Why does this happen so often? What drives groups and individuals, including project teams and project managers, to ignore Kerr's reminder? Again, the reason is simple, but the solution is not easy. Many of the things that matter greatly cannot be easily measured yet we desperately want to measure them. Now comes the flaw. Rather than accept the awkward assessment of what matters managers succumb to the temptation to use the easier substitute metric, telling themselves that they understand the distinction and will not be led astray. What happens of course is that all the others on the project team, in the functional departments, at the suppliers, and in the customer community do not appreciate that compromise. They only know that for some strange reason the project manager wants to measure the number of hours that butts are in seats attending training, or the cost variance on every piece of work in progress, or the average number of field service complaints from customers. Others cannot easily determine what their leaders are hoping for. They can only determine what is being measured and rewarded.

The managers who make these compromise decisions also tend to fall victim to them. A manager may acknowledge that hours-of-training is a poor substitute for measuring the improvement in learning but as time marches on the metric takes on a life of its own. It gets embedded in department and individual goals. A bureaucracy develops to articulate ground rules and procedures for collecting and interpreting the data. Other metrics are derived from the training metric. Before long, all the attention has shifted from achieving the original desire of a more learned workforce to a new desire of more training hours delivered. The substitute metric redirected effort away from what matters to what can be easily measured.

Project managers must accept responsibility for establishing an effective monitoring system, including the metrics that system uses. They must understand that Kerr's advice is still relevant and they must heed it. They must be

willing to measure poorly the important rather than measuring well the unimportant. They must beware of substitute metrics. Finally, they must guide the project team and
the entire stakeholder community to understand the haz-
ards of deploying inappropriate metrics and then being
duped by the metrics they created.

*It is much more important to be about right than to be precisely
wrong.* Norm Augustine's Law of Definitive Imprecision
(Law Number XXXV) states facetiously, "The weaker the
data available upon which to base one's conclusions, the
greater the precision which should be quoted in order to
give the data authenticity."[10] Project monitoring systems
must be built and managed to avoid giving the data undue
authenticity. In other words avoid great precision where no
accuracy exists. Augustine offered the following example
of undue precision. "Consider the following evidence: As
reported to Congress at the time development was to be
initiated, the total program cost for the Navy's Harpoon
missile program was stated to be $1031.8 million. For the
Air Force A-10 aircraft program, the corresponding cost
was defined as $2489.7 million. Not $2400 million; not even
$2489 million. Rather, the cost would be two thousand four
hundred eighty-nine *point seven* million dollars. In the case
of the Navy's F-18 aircraft program it was originally stated
to the Congress that the cost would be twelve billion eight
hundred seventy-five point three million dollars. A few
years later an updated version of the same report listed the
probable cost as twenty-four billion twenty-three million—
and (still!) point three million dollars."[11] Augustine went
on to comment, "history shows the first digit of past program cost estimates to have been in error, on the average,
by about 100 percent." He went on to note that at least the
last digit is correct 10 percent of the time.

Allowing the project monitoring system to use undue
precision encourages destructive misbehavior in three
important ways. First, it is a waste of time, energy, and

resources. People find themselves tracking down, analyzing, cross-checking, and auditing figures in an effort
to make the math tie out to the fourth, or even the four-
teenth, significant digit when, as Norm Augustine pointed
out, even the first significant digit is likely wrong. All of
that effort should be put to some potentially good use.
Second, it lends an aura of accuracy that deceives and
misleads. It is human nature to infer some level of rigor,
analysis, and thus accuracy when one sees the number
$1,974,635, much more accuracy than one infers from the
number $2 million. This false sense of accuracy, bestowed
by the undue precision, creates a corresponding false
sense of confidence in the number. Third, such precision
misdirects one's attention away from the critical assumptions and uncertainties underpinning the number and
toward the relatively trivial mechanics and details of the
calculation.

The following example illustrates this third destructive misbehavior. Francis, a test engineer on a new project, has been asked to estimate the cost of developing a
test-plan document that will be delivered to the customer,
who must then approve it before testing can begin. Francis
makes some assumptions about the kind of hardware and
software that must be tested. He makes some assumptions
about what testing will be required. He thinks about the
last test plan he wrote and how difficult it was to get the
customer to approve the document. He also thinks about
the four other projects to which he is assigned and how
little time he has to put this estimate together. He does
not bother to find out that the customer has asked that
the test plan be prepared in accordance with a new test
policy their firm has just released; instead, he assumes the
format will be one he is familiar with. Francis assembles
his estimate, concluding the document will be 120 pages
long including tables and charts. He assumes, based on
historical data, that it will take an average of eight hours

per page to complete the document. He also assumes that the customer review will result in changes to 20 percent of the document (24 pages) and that the changes will require another four hours per page to make. Francis submits an estimate of $104,530 to prepare the test plan.

The project manager receives the estimate and immediately dives into the pages of rationale. He notices that Francis has assumed a senior engineering labor rate rather than a mid-range labor rate. He remembers that the test plan on the last project was less than 100 pages long and wonders if this plan will have to be 120 pages long. Francis and the project manager discuss these and a few other details before agreeing on an estimate of $98,071. Each moves on to his next task.

Notice that Francis and the project manager never discussed the key assumptions critical to the estimate, assumptions that may have doubled or halved that estimate. Why, because they let themselves be seduced by the precision. If Francis had instead said my estimate is between $70,000 and $120,000 depending on three key assumptions then the project manager would have said, "Let's discuss those assumptions." If the project manager had not been seduced by all the detailed rationale and the precision of Francis's estimate he would have asked, "Francis what key assumptions and uncertainties most influenced your estimate?" Undue precision draws one away from such discussions, diverting us into the less important mechanics.

Project managers are responsible for deploying an effective and helpful project monitoring system. Therefore, they must assure that the monitoring system does not abide inappropriate precision that will infer accuracy where it does not exist.

What do you mean by that? We often misunderstand one another. A project team is a perpetual learning organism. The team members are in perpetual contact with stakeholders and with one another, sharing information and gaining new insights as they work to accomplish their unique one-time activity. Sadly, it is the human condition to be frequently misunderstood, as Table 5.2 shows.

It is not just soft phrases like "improbable" that are interpreted differently. Recall the example about the on-time delivery performance metrics. What could be simpler than counting whether or not a project team actually made a contractually required delivery on or before the due date. After all, the contract contains the mutually agreed date and the shipping documents contain the date the item was delivered. What could be simpler than comparing the two dates? Yet, the business unit had several interpretations of "on-time delivery" in play for nearly two years. Some people asserted that delivery within the promised month was close enough to count as being delivered on time. Other people asserted that missed deliveries due to supplier problems should not count. Some people would count a missed delivery as a miss but then

Table 5.2   Same Words but Different Meanings

Statement	Range of interpretations
Almost certain	60% to 100%
Highly likely	60% to 100%
Very good chance	60% to 100%
Likely	60% to 90%
Probable	60% to 90%
We believe	60% to 100%
Better than even	60% to 70%
We doubt	20% to 40%
Improbable	20% to 40%
Unlikely	20% to 40%
Probably not	20% to 40%
Little chance	20% to 30%
Almost no chance	5% to 10%
Highly unlikely	5% to 10%
Chances are slight	5% to 10%

Source: Data derived from results of a 1989 study by Reagan et al. cited in Vick (2002), as well as a study by Chew (2006).

give themselves credit for that delivery when it was subsequently made—eventually they got back to 100 percent on time. They were just a little tardy in doing so. Some argued that a miss counted against the team every month until it was delivered—thus a single delivery made four months late counted as the equivalent of four missed deliveries. Some wanted to count early deliveries as an offset to any late deliveries. Many of these interpretations were informal, even hidden, interpretations that had to be searched out and challenged. Metrics seldom mean to others what they mean to us.

Project managers and team members must continually test and challenge understandings. One project manager used to end every discussion by insisting that the other party restate what had been discussed and their understanding of the discussion. It was often a frustrating exercise but the manager insisted that it was the only way to verify the parties had communicated effectively. Whatever the technique, project leaders must build a project culture that appreciates the likelihood of misunderstanding one another and the need for diligence to deter those misunderstandings.

SUMMARY

The path to a helpful project monitoring system is simple but not easy. First, project teams must have an integrated plan against which to monitor performance. It is wasteful and futile to monitor performance against a bad plan. Second, the team must work to the plan. The monitoring system will report progress versus the plan. It will not provide feedback about work done outside the plan. Third, the project manager must craft a monitoring system tailored to the unique project challenges, and not rely on the generic or bureaucratically provided monitoring system. Fourth, the team must use multiple feedback paths for critical areas, not trusting one source when it really matters. Fifth, the team must remember that numbers aren't everything. Some critical dimensions must be monitored subjectively. Sixth, teams must diligently search out the gaps and weaknesses in their project monitoring system, for those weaknesses are surely there. Finally, project managers must be guardians of the big picture (monitoring system and usage) as well as the details (metrics use and abuse). No one else is better equipped to do so, and no one else will do so.

The list of considerations for project monitoring systems is long, too long to address every consideration here. Nonetheless, project teams must establish, manage, control, and use a monitoring system to track their performance against the integrated baseline plan, the requirements and specifications, and the vision. The effective project teams meet that difficult challenge. The ineffective ones do not.

CHAPTER 6

HABIT # 5— ACKNOWLEDGE AND ACCOMMODATE BOTH UNCERTAINTY AND IGNORANCE

"No plan of operations extends with certainty beyond the first encounter with the enemy's main strength."
—Helmuth von Multke,
WWI German Field Marshal

The uninitiated may conclude after reading this chapter that project success may be unachievable. Indeed, no one can deny that projects are often difficult and challenging. Some are destined to fail from the start. This chapter embraces the notion that the project environment is awash in ignorance and uncertainty. But it also embraces the notion that project managers, their teams, and their organizations can act to constrain and manage that ignorance and uncertainty. They can improve the likelihood of project success through their own actions.

Uncertainty is best thought of as variability in assumptions or estimates. We continually estimate how long tasks will take, how many miles it is to a destination, how difficult a task may be, how well our recommendation will be received, how sure we are about an outcome, and many other things. Project uncertainty is best thought of as variability in the estimate of project scope (effort, cost, features).

Teams are also beset by the consequences of their ignorance about many aspects of the project and its environment, including technologies that do not perform as advertised, at-risk customer funding, erroneous documentation, oversold resource skills, fatal errors in preexisting software, team ignorance of technology that could dramatically simplify a design, and many other factors. Teams must deal with the uncertainty of cost estimates, schedule estimates, technology capability, staff performance, resources availability, supplier performance, stakeholder support, and a long list of other factors. As stated earlier, project efficiency is best measured in terms of how rapidly the team learns what it does not know and then adapts to that new learning. Project teams are efficient when they accept the fact that theirs is a world filled with ignorance and uncertainty, when they drive to uncover and resolve those variables, and when they adapt to them quickly.

Human behavior and thought patterns contribute mightily to our personal ignorance and uncertainty and in turn to project ignorance and uncertainty. For example, our brains are not logical. Jonah Lehrer, a renowned science writer, put it well, stating that, "we weren't designed to be rational creatures. Instead, the mind is composed of a messy network of different areas, many of which are involved with the production of emotion. Whenever someone makes a decision, the brain is awash in feeling, driven by its inexplicable passions. Even when a person tries to be reasonable and restrained, these emotions secretly influence judgment."[1]

We, too, often make up facts in our search for insight. We humans, either as individuals or as groups, seek to explain everything. We are willing to draw inferences and extrapolate from snippets of information in order to make sense of what happens around us. We see a few pieces of a mosaic and our imagination begins to fill in the rest. As the work proceeds some of the additional tiles we see reinforce our imagined image but others do not. We try to reinterpret the odd pieces of tile, clinging to our original, ill-founded image until we have no choice but to admit we are wrong. Our original assumptions cause us to reject new learning.

We continually revise our memories. In just the last ten years or so researchers have learned that the conventional wisdom about long-term memory has been completely wrong. It has always been thought that those memories were permanently wired into our brain. Everything that happened to us was there waiting to be recalled. Now it has become clear that our memories actually change over time to align with our current biases and perspectives or to better fit with our self-image. Karim Nader, a memory researcher, says, "For a hundred years, people thought memory was wired into the brain. [...] Instead, we find it can be rewired—you can add false information to it, make it stronger, make it weaker, and possibly even make it disappear."[2]

We often don't know what we think we know. For example, we all know from junior high school science class that water freezes at 32°F (0°C) and boils at 212°F (100°C). But, this is not always true. Water boils at 100°C at sea level, but it boils at 72°C on Mount Everest because the atmospheric pressure is lower at higher altitudes, something many of us have forgotten. On the other hand, atmospheric pressure has very little effect on the freezing point of water because the melting process does not involve gas-phase molecules. But it turns out that water does not actually freeze at 0°C because the removal of the "heat of fusion" is necessary for water to change phase. Water must cool to slightly below 0°C and remain there until it has crystallized into ice. Once it is frozen, it will remain so at 0°C. That is, of course, unless the water contains salt or impurities because their presence lowers the freezing point of water. We don't always know as much as we think we know about something.

We humans, with our personal ignorance and uncertainty, find ourselves working in a project environment rife with its own ignorance and uncertainty. How can project teams cope? How do they handle the inevitable conflict when their project plans makes first contact with the realities of their world?

RESERVES ARE A WAY TO DEAL WITH PROJECT UNCERTAINTY AND IGNORANCE

Project reserves are needed to cope with the inevitable discoveries that arise as a project unfolds. Norm Augustine, past CEO of Lockheed Martin said, "There are also a large number of more subtle characteristics that seem to distinguish the effective program manager from his or her less successful counterpart. Somewhere near the top of that list is the ability to plan an undertaking so as to ensure some degree of reserves; reserves in dollars, time, product performance, or whatever."[3] Reserves give teams the capacity to adapt to change rather than experience every new piece of bad news as another trauma. One veteran project management executive said that he could tell within 15 seconds whether a project was in trouble. He believed that two figures gave a strong indication of project status. If a project had less than 10 percent dollar reserve versus the project cost estimate-to-completion (ETC) it was in trouble. If a project had less than 20 percent schedule reserve versus the project time ETC, it was in trouble. He asserted that any reasonably complex project will experience at least that much cost and schedule uncertainty and ignorance, and failure to plan the necessary reserves make the it impossible to deal appropriately with the coming surprises.

Project reserves foster success for several reasons. First, plans containing reserves are more representative of the project's likely outcome. Because initial plans are often optimistic, reserves, especially when they are based on a risk and opportunity analysis, add a degree of realism to the plans. Second, reserves empower teams to take the actions that influence their future. Someone who is barely able to pay the rent will likely forego repairing the oil leak in his car's engine, but later, when the car breaks down and he loses his job because he has no transportation, that "unaffordable" repair expense suddenly seems to have been very affordable. Project teams without reserves do not believe they can afford to make prudent decisions. Instead, they charge rashly ahead, hoping for the best, though they know the avoidable worst is around the corner. Third, reserves enhance accountability. Teams that have discretionary reserves are empowered to take actions that positively influence their project's future, and so they can be held accountable for making good use of those reserves, empowered and accountable for project success.

TYPES OF PROJECT RESERVES

There are four primary types of project reserves. *Financial reserves* are an integral part of the EVMS and are frequently discussed by organizational leaders and project managers, but often are not actually included in the project plans. *Schedule reserves* are the second most frequently mentioned form. They are not directly incorporated in EVMS, and they are seldom used in a disciplined way. *Requirements reserves* are found in some project baselines but are typically described as design margins and not generally appreciated as a part of overall project reserves. *Resource reserves*, including staff, critical skills of team members, facilities, and equipment, are rarely addressed but are equally important. Notice that the first three reserve types directly address the three sides of the project triple constraint; whereas, the fourth type addresses the resources needed to accomplish the three elements.

Financial Reserves

Financial reserves are often called management reserves (MRs), implying that they are the only form of project reserve. MR is the only reserve directly addressed within the EVMS dogma (see Figure 6.1). The contract budget baseline (CBB) is the formal agreed value of the project

Figure 6.1   Earned Value Measurement and Management
(Financial) Reserve

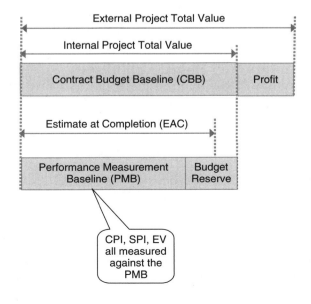

effort. An external project adds profit to the CBB, to become the "external project total value," representing the total cost of the project from the external customer's perspective and "total sales or revenue" (cost plus profit) from the project organization's point of view. (Note that this assumes that the project is a fixed-price agreement with an external customer. Cost-plus-fixed-fee and incentive-fee contract treatments of MR are a bit more complicated, but are the same in principle. The CBB is the negotiated cost plus the estimated cost of any authorized but not yet formally priced or negotiated work. It represents the cost that has been agreed between the customer and the project team. The performance management baseline (PMB) equals the CBB less the MR. The PMB is the baseline plan against which cost and schedule performance is measured. It is the EVMS yardstick for calculating the cost variance (CV), schedule variance (SV), CPI, schedule performance index (SPI), and several other EVMS metrics.

The size of the MR is often determined by industry rule-of-thumb. It may also be influenced or determined by the organizational culture and policy and customer preference, or even individual leadership preference. An often heard product development rule-of-thumb is that the management reserve should be about 10 percent of the CBB for low-risk projects and 15 percent to 20 percent for higher risk projects. That reserve should then decrease as work is accomplished, being adjusted to be between 10 percent and 20 percent of the ETC, the estimated cost of the work not yet accomplished.

Some organizations establish specific guidelines for determining and adjusting the size of MR. They may derive the MR from an estimate of the project risks and opportunities, essentially converting the reserve into an accounting measure of the most likely final project cost. They may derive it from so-called project-fee analyses, adjusting the reserves to fit their current desire for more or less conservatism.

As shown in Figure 6.1, the MR is drawn from the proposed cost for the scope of work. In practice, this means the proposed cost estimates are adjusted. The adjustment can take place in several ways. A project manager may declare a "tax" on all work activity estimates, reducing them by the desired percentage to create the reserve. In essence, each work activity manager is challenged to do the work for, let us say, 10 percent less. Some will succeed and some will fail. In theory, the reserve will cover the costs above the more aggressive goal and leave some additional amount to cover unplanned but necessary costs. A more thoughtful approach is to review selected work activities, searching out alternate and less expensive approaches to getting the work done. Thus dollars are freed up to fund the MR pool. The project manager may also elect to redefine or even eliminate some work activities that she deems optional, thus generating dollars for the MR pool.

Some organizations do not permit the establishment of an MR pool. Several reasons for this are given. Some organizations or some specific leaders assert that the MR is merely a slush fund that allows project teams to take the less challenging path. Sometimes projects are bid very aggressively out of desperation to win or naïveté about the scope of work, causing leaders to assert the project cannot afford to establish an MR pool. Yet projects seldom succeed without them and savvy project managers know they are at personal risk when their projects fail. In those instances the project manager may have to pad some of the initial or planning estimates in order to generate MR dollars. Those surplus dollars can remain hidden in the padded work activity plans until needed. Such deceit should be avoided unless the organizational culture leaves the project manager with no alternative. Our experience has been that in organizations where MR is denied, the project manager is in less peril if he creates and wisely uses hidden reserves than if he charges ahead without reserves.

One technique that avoids deceit and may help the organizational leaders come to appreciate MR is to frequently provide a project estimate-at-completion (EAC) accompanied by a probability of success. For example, the project manager may assert at some point that the $2 million project has spent one-quarter of its funding, is about two weeks behind schedule, and faces an additional $150,000 of net risks and opportunities. He further asserts that the project has a 15 percent probability of hitting that number, a 50 percent probability of hitting $2.4 million, and an 80 percent probability of hitting $2.6. This approach helps communicate the riskiness of hitting the more aggressive EAC, helps bound the range of that risk, and signals to leadership the potential for having to admit to problems in the future. The approach does not make the funds available to actually influence the project outcome, but it does set the stage for a dialogue that can lead to those MR decisions.

There is a great deal of debate about whether MR or any other project reserves are helpful, a debate that is often "religious" rather than reasoned. Naysayers argue that creating dollar reserves at the start of a project is merely an early admission of failure, or a team's attempt to make the challenge easier, or an admission that it is not up to the challenge. They also argue that giving a project team bold challenges—too little money, too little time, too few resources, and daunting technical goals—will compel it to do its very best, that it is at its most creative and efficient when striving to do the impossible. Reserves merely lighten the team's load and give it permission to be less creative and passionate. Advocates for the MR argue that it serves several purposes, some of which were identified above. First, they contend that it acknowledges that uncertainty is present rather than denying it. Such acknowledgment encourages action to resolve the uncertainties and uncover the ignorance. Second, they contend it provides a cushion to absorb or integrate the various ups and downs as the project outlook varies every time learning occurs. As a result teams and their organization are less prone to overreact to new information. Third, they argue that when managed appropriately dollar reserves empower teams and encourage savvy decision-making.

There is also great debate about how financial reserves should be created and managed. In fact, some customer communities may be conflicted about which philosophy they hold. The Air Force Space Command (AFSC) employs contractors to maintain, repair, and upgrade their satellite command tracking sites around the world. The contracts are worth several hundred million dollars a year and employ thousands of individuals. The AFSC officer in charge of each of these major contracts is typically a colonel, who holds the assignment for about two years before moving on to another assignment. Several years ago a new colonel was appointed, reviewed his contractor's project and declared that it had too little MR (dollar reserves). He directed the contractor to restructure some of the work to free up several million dollars to be held by the contractor's project manager and used at his discretion to deal with risks and surprises. Twenty months later that colonel was replaced by a colonel who immediately declared there should be no reserves. He quickly took control of the reserves that had just been created, removing them from the contractor's funding. He was replaced about two years later and—you guessed it—the new colonel declared that the project must have reserves, directed the contractor's project manager to find a way to create them. The point of this tale is that the MR philosophy is sometimes fickle, even within an organization. Nonetheless, project managers must take action to enhance their project's success, even when customers and other stakeholders make it more difficult. Reserves, especially financial reserves, improve the odds of success.

Schedule Reserves

Schedule reserves are less common than financial reserves, yet they are no less important. A team that has money but no time to deal with problems is still at risk. Figure 6.2 depicts the relationship between the baseline schedule and the reserve, a relationship similar to the financial reserves relationship to the baseline cost plan. Remember that the EVMS system does not formally acknowledge the existence of schedule reserves, only financial reserves. However, the following material describes the schedule reserve using the EVMS and financial reserve as a comparison. Notice that the schedule reserve is not part of the formal project agreement with the customer or stakeholders. Just as the cost EAC assumes the MR will be spent, so to the schedule EAC assumes the schedule reserve will be consumed whether for handling surprises, accomplishing contingency actions, or mitigating risks. The schedule reserve pool is established by techniques like those used

Figure 6.2   Baseline Schedule and Schedule Reserve

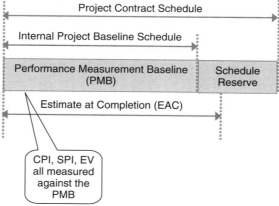

to create dollar reserves; the project manager may tax all schedules equally, may revisit and replan specific critical path work activities, or may redefine work scope to create the appropriate level of schedule reserve. Note that just as the financial EAC may be greater or less than the cost PMB plus reserves, so too the estimated completion date may be earlier than or later than the schedule PMB plus schedule reserves. Remember that EVMS does not directly account for schedule reserve in the same way it accounts for financial reserve. This description merely illustrates the concept of schedule reserves by comparing it to financial reserves.

Schedule reserves are different than financial reserves. One dollar is just like another in that any dollar can be spent to address any issue or opportunity. (This is a generalization with exceptions. In fact, "color of money" issues may make money from sources available for some uses but not others; for example, when capital improvement dollars cannot be spent on overtime costs). However, time at one point in the schedule may be more valuable than time at another point in the schedule. A project has a schedule critical path (see Figure 6.3), and time saved or lost along the critical path directly influences whether the project will end late. A two-week delay between point 5 and point 6 of the schedule flow chart in Figure 6.3a will result in a two-week delay in project completion. A two-week acceleration between point 5 and point 6 will result in the project being completed two weeks early. On the other hand, time saved or lost along one of the noncritical paths only affects the project end date if the change creates a different critical path. A two-week acceleration or delay in the activities between point 4 and point 5 may have no impact on the overall project completion date.

Schedule reserve is generally described as reserve along the project schedule critical path. The project contract schedule is depicted as 26 weeks long in Figure 6.3b, and there is no schedule reserve shown. The project team understands that even a 26-week project may well hold a few surprises, and so its savvy manager knows he must create a reserve because working to achieve a 26-week schedule with no reserve means a high likelihood of being late. The team decides it can accomplish the work

Figure 6.3a   Critical Path

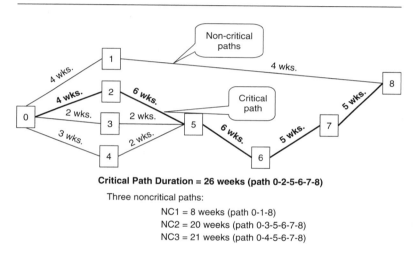

Critical Path Duration = 26 weeks (path 0-2-5-6-7-8)

Three noncritical paths:

NC1 = 8 weeks (path 0-1-8)
NC2 = 20 weeks (path 0-3-5-6-7-8)
NC3 = 21 weeks (path 0-4-5-6-7-8)

Figure 6.3b   Revised Critical Path to Create Schedule Reserve

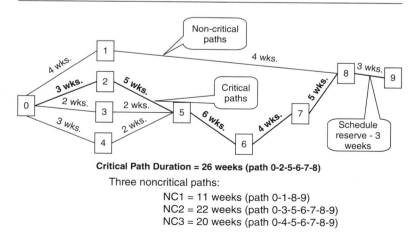

Critical Path Duration = 26 weeks (path 0-2-5-6-7-8)

Three noncritical paths:

NC1 = 11 weeks (path 0-1-8-9)
NC2 = 22 weeks (path 0-3-5-6-7-8-9)
NC3 = 20 weeks (path 0-4-5-6-7-8-9)

activity between points zero and 1 in three weeks rather than four weeks by putting in some overtime. It persuades the customer to make some requirements decisions two weeks early, which means it can accomplish the point 2 to point 5 activities in five weeks rather than six weeks. Finally, the team decides that it can complete the work between points 6 and 7 in four weeks by using a new software tool that simplifies one of the tasks. This plan revision takes three weeks out of the 26-week critical path schedule (see Figure 6.3b).

Note a few points about the exercise just described. First, the schedule now includes three weeks, just over 10 percent, of schedule reserve (point 8 to point 9) to deal with the surprises arising from the inevitable project uncertainty and ignorance. Second, the overall schedule critical path did not change. It was proposed and planned for 26 weeks and it is still planned for 26 weeks. Also note that the noncritical path lengths did change. Some got longer and some got shorter because of the revised assumptions and approaches for the work activities along those paths. Third, the critical path route did not change in this example although it may have changed. Suppose the team had identified a plan to shorten the schedule for the point-zero to point 2 work activity from four weeks to only two weeks and the point 2 to point 5 work activity from six weeks to only two weeks. Those activities would no longer be along the critical path, having been replaced by the five-week long point 0-4-5 path. Fourth, the reserve time is depicted at the end of the schedule. It may instead be placed anywhere along the critical path as appropriate. It may even be broken into a few pieces and placed at strategic points along the critical path. It should only be left within the tasks if the organizational culture does not appreciate the value of reserve and is apt to take it away, thereby giving the team an even more aggressive schedule. Fifth, the reserve was not created by merely challenging everyone to do 10 percent better, a scheme that seldom works. Instead the team identified different approaches, committed more resources, or negotiated new agreements that created a viable path to completing the work earlier— the team maintained the integrity of the triple constraint by keeping the scope of work approach, the schedule, and the cost in balance. Merely establishing a more aggressive goal knocks the triple constraint off balance. It does not actually create reserve. In fact, it does the opposite because it encourages higher risk shortcuts, discourages prudent risk mitigation activities, causes a loss of commitment to accomplishing what was promised, and induces other behaviors that add to overall project risk, thus making the project more risky than the amount of reserve created. It is a delusional approach.

Since EVMS does not provide accounting or metrics to address schedule reserves, organizations or project managers must develop their own systems for developing, monitoring, and reporting on them. Some scheduling tools do provide a way to monitor the presence or absence of a different interpretation of schedule reserve. Tools like Microsoft Project, ZOHO Projects, FastTrack Schedule, Primavera, and others offer the ability to track schedule performance metrics, including an accounting of the work activities started early or late and those completed early or late versus the baseline plan. They can also be used to track whether the work is progressing ahead of or behind schedule. The information can be used to calculate the amount of slack (also called "float") in a particular activity schedule. "Slack" is defined as how much more time can be spent on a task before it delays the project, which is before it becomes part of the critical path, and lengthens the overall project schedule. A project may have slack in several tasks that are off the critical path. Tasks on the critical path may or may not have slack. Thus, the overall slack across all tasks in a project schedule may give some indication of schedule pressure and the likelihood of project success, but it is not definitive. Some project managers use these tools to calculate the overall slack, or absence of slack, for every task along the critical path thus deriving some measure of how much critical path schedule reserve may be available if a problem arises. Monitoring slip and slack does not create schedule reserve but it is useful for tracking how much reserve is or is not being consumed as the project work proceeds. Managers can then decide whether or not they need additional schedule reserve.

Requirements Reserves

The notion of design requirements margin, or reserve, is certainly not new. Many engineering standards encourage or even mandate design margin. A piece of equipment required to operate reliably for 10,000 hours may be designed to operate for 15,000 or 20,000 hours to provide an extra margin in case some design assumptions or calculations prove incorrect. A software program may be estimated to occupy two gigabytes of memory, so the hardware team will be asked to design a three-gigabyte memory module, allowing some margin in case the software grows beyond the intended size. A structural engineer may add a safety factor to his calculations for the required tensile strength of the cables that will hold up a suspension bridge. Safety regulations and industry standards often impose such requirements margins. Project teams must embrace them.

Experienced project teams realize that the technical dimensions of the project are filled with uncertainty and ignorance, like every other aspect of the project. Even the most competent and diligent engineers make assumptions that turn out to be wrong. They misinterpret data and test results. They receive erroneous technical data from other sources. Simulations turn out to be imprecise or flawed and the errors are only recognized after the product is built. Teams know they need some degree of margin for each of the critical technical requirements that will give them more choices about how to address the inevitable unforeseeable events.

Certainly project teams should not, and cannot, establish margins for every single requirement, technical or otherwise. Teams should not impose margins where good technical practice deems them unnecessary. Nor should they impose additional margins on top of existing standard practice design margins unless warranted by special circumstances. What teams should do, what they must do if they hope to succeed, is identify the core set of requirements that the key stakeholders deem essential for a project to be considered a success. For example, a project team tasked to build an electronic assembly identified seven items (weight, peak power level, steady state power level, spare memory capacity, central processor unit nominal clock speed, central power unit high temperature clock speed, and the cost of each assembly) as parameters the stakeholders believed to be essential capabilities (see Table 6.1). Failure to achieve any of the seven requirements would make the assembly unusable, or cause significant technical interface problems for the greater system of which the assembly will be a part.

Table 6.1   Requirements Margin

Factor	Goal	Current Estimate	Margin
Weight	≤ 6 lb.	5.4 lb. ± 0.2	10%
Power			
Peak	≤ 12 W	13 ± 0.2 W	− 8%
Steady state	≤ 5 W	4 ± 0.2 W	20%
Spare memory %	≥ 30%	38% ± 2%	27%
CPU clock speed			
Nominal temp	≥ 2.5 ± 0.1 mhz	2.5 ± 0.3 mhz	0%
High temperature	≥ 1.8 mhz	2.0 ± 0.3 mhz	12.5%
Unit cost (2010 $)	≤ $10,000	$ 9,700 ± 5 K	3%

The project team made a preliminary estimate of the expected results for each of the seven critical factors. It believed that its current technical approach would yield a box weighing 5.4 pounds, 10 percent better than the requirement. It had great confidence in the estimate (note that the team believed the current estimate would vary by no more than 0.2 pounds, and so it felt that a 10 percent design margin was ample). The preliminary estimates indicated the steady state power, spare memory, and the high temperature clock speed requirements would all be met and that there was plenty of margin to accommodate any surprises. However, the preliminary analysis indicated that the current design might or might not meet the requirement that the CPU clock operate at 2.0 mhz in a nominal temperature environment. The analysis suggested that the clock would operate somewhere between 1.7 mhz and 2.3 mhz, indicating that the analysis team could estimate the speed within no more than 15 percent. Such a wide range suggested there might be unknown or uncertain factors yet to be fully understood. The team needed to immediately begin an effort to resolve some of the uncertainties and to search for design changes that would give them some clock speed requirements margin. The preliminary analysis also indicated the current design approach would not meet the peak power requirement. The team immediately set out to explore design changes to reduce the peak power demand not just by one watt but by at least two watts in order to cope with the inevitable further surprises as the design matured.

The assembly was to be designed to cost less than $10,000 each to build, in quantities of 100 to 500 units. The cost estimate suggested the assembly would cost somewhere between $9200 and $10,200. That was not good enough. First, the analysis showed that the team might miss the $10,000 target, making some deem the project a failure. Second, driving the cost lower would create the opportunity for the firm to make greater than planned profits or to lower the price and increase sales. It decided to set an internal goal significantly below $10,000.

Within 60 days the project team was able to renegotiate the CPU nominal clock speed to be greater than or equal to 2.2 mhz rather than 2.5 mhz, instantly creating ample margin to be able to cope with any surprises as the design matures. They were also able to identify a way to reduce the peak power demand by two watts, thereby creating some requirements margin. Finally, they launched a design-to-target-cost team with the goal of reducing the unit cost by 20 percent. The organization funded the additional work because they became convinced the team had a good chance of achieving the goal and the recurring cost savings would repay the added project cost within the first 90 days of sales.

So, the team managed to identify the critical requirements parameters, understand the likelihood of achieving those targets, and modify its approach to give itself adequate margin to cope with the inevitable uncertainty and ignorance. Later, when the team learns that a particular power supply component is no longer available, it will have the flexibility to use a less efficient part and accept the slightly poorer power performance because it will have the adequate margin to do so. That will be a far less traumatic outcome than having no margin, discovering the component is no longer available, and then having to hurriedly redesign the power supply in a desperate attempt to meet the requirement. Adequate technical margin preserves the flexibility needed to deal with surprises.

Technical reserves must be monitored throughout the project life, not just at the beginning. Those inevitable surprises often lead to new understandings about the design and about the analyses used to establish the margins to begin with. Every month those requirements and margins are subject to change and to reinterpretation. Teams track the key requirements and their margin estimates continually, adjusting them as the team learns.

There are no planning tools or monitoring systems that address the notion of technical reserves. Systems engineering tools such as DOORS can be used to track requirements information, including margin. However, the project team must construct an ad hoc system that elevates those critical requirements out of the engineering tool set, making them readily visible to the project leadership team.

Resource (People, Skills, Facilities) Reserves

Money and time is of no benefit unless the team has resources to apply to the challenges that will inevitably arise. A project planned on the assumption of a 40-hour workweek and a 52-week year with no allowances for holidays, vacations, personal time, training, and so on, starts with a planned shortage of resources—that no one has yet admitted. After all, Christmas comes every year whether or not a project manager has learned to plan for it. A project planned assuming a 2000-hour work-year allows for those typical activities that temporarily redirect team members from the project work. A team that has planned for a staff of six mid-range software engineers and succeeds in securing two or three experienced, efficient senior engineers, along with three mid-range engineers, has created resource reserves more effectively than planned. Software project managers who get into trouble often complain they cannot use more software people because they do not have time to train them and integrate them into the team. The sin was committed when the project manager failed to understand that the software task was risky and that having additional resources was an appropriate, even necessary, precaution. A team that determines it can get by with only one set of hardware for both software development and hardware test and integration is building in a point of conflict and a work-activity chokepoint. If the hardware team or the software team runs into unexpected problems, its difficulties will necessarily have a negative impact on the other team. On the other hand, the prudent team builds enough additional equipment (the resource reserve) to minimize the likelihood of serious conflict.

Each project team should identify critical resource needs as a part of the project planning exercise. It should staff for those high-risk needs and develop contingency plans for acquiring additional resources depending on the perceived level of project risk as the project evolves. Resource reserves may include people, either at the general staffing levels or in special-skill positions that are critical to project success. They may include equipment such as test hardware and work stations. They may include facilities, such as laboratory workspace, access to test chambers, and office work areas.

There are no planning tools or monitoring systems that address the notion of resource reserves. Project teams must develop their own ad hoc approaches to identifying the needs, securing the resources, and using them effectively. One useful technique is for project teams to include in the initial project management plan review a summary of the critical resource needs, those single-point failures where the resources make or break project success. The team can communicate those critical needs to organizational leadership during the plan review. It can also highlight them during the periodic project reviews, thereby reminding leadership how important those resources are and that organizational commitments were made to the project team. Another useful technique is to highlight during the planning review where and when resource reserves will reduce risk, enhance opportunity, or potentially be needed to address changes. The team may be able to secure commitments to make those reserves available. Still another useful technique is for project teams to track the planned/promised staffing versus the actual staffing provided then articulate the direct impact on project performance if staffing is not made available as promised. The point of these techniques is to highlight the bad of resource shortages and the good consequences of adequate resources and resource reserves. Over time, the organizational culture will embrace the understanding that adequate resources enables project success.

ADJUSTING RESERVES

Recall the earlier comment that savvy teams track the key technical requirements and their margin estimates continually, adjusting them as the team learns new information. The same is true for financial, schedule, and resource reserves. Teams continually work to adjust them to fit their current understanding of the project outlook. For example, a project team had designed a set of electronic boxes for use on the International Space Station. It discovered that a supplier's component had not been built properly, which necessitated replacing the components in the boxes. Luckily, the team had been carrying a 60-day schedule reserve and the delay was only going to take 45 days. It was able to meet its commitments to NASA. But now the team had only two weeks of schedule reserve, and the project had another year of work ahead of it. The team immediately launched into a replan, attempting to create more schedule reserve. Its experience with the boxes had made it clear that adequate reserves are invaluable, and it was determined to create additional schedule reserves as quickly as possible. The team decided to use overtime to complete the component replacement and box retest as quickly as possible. Then they continued the overtime until they had rebuilt a 50-day schedule reserve. Successful teams create, monitor, use judiciously, and then rebuild adequate reserves throughout the life of the project.

HIDDEN RESERVES

Project plans sometimes include hidden or unacknowledged reserves that were created when the work was first proposed or planned. Some people are naturally conservative; others have learned through bitter experience that they will be punished for failure, and so they hide reserves hoping they will cover the unexpected as the work gets under way. Although this approach is better than having no reserves at all, it causes several problems. First, the project manager and the team as a whole has no idea how much reserve is present, nor do they know where it lies. As a result, politics rather than logic drives the senior leadership discussions about adequacy of project reserves. Second, the reserves are hoarded away, with each work activity leader trying to protect his or her piece of the work. As a result, reserves are not effectively used to address crosscutting risks or challenges. In effect, the team as a whole behaves as if it has no reserves, electing to not do smart work because it does not think it can afford to do so.

Although this situation is relatively common in project-management-based organizations, savvy managers can help the project find success by making better use of the reserves that exist. The project manager can review each work activity plan searching for potential conservatism in cost, schedule, technical margin, and resources. Then, instead of taking away that conservatism, the manager can negotiate a work activity "stretch plan" while also agreeing that the reserves will stay in place in case the more aggressive plan does not come to pass. The work activity leader retains control of the reserve agreeing to notify the project manager if it is used. The project manager must convince the work activity leader that he will not be criticized for using the now exposed reserves but he will be lauded for hitting the more aggressive plan.

Over time this approach can shift the project team culture to one of cross-collaboration that allows better overall use of available reserves.

ADAPTIVE (AGILE) PROJECT MANAGEMENT: ANOTHER APPROACH TO MANAGING PROJECT UNCERTAINTIES

In February 2001 a group of seventeen software development professionals gathered at the Snowbird ski resort in the Wasatch Mountains in Utah to socialize and to discuss their common challenges and frustrations in dealing with what they felt had become a cumbersome software development process. That interaction spawned the Agile Software Development Manifesto, a document that is credited with being the foundation for a new more streamlined approach to managing software development.[4] The frustration that gave rise to the Manifesto came out of a belief that the traditional development approach had become so encumbered by rigorous documentation and procedure that software development work was being hindered rather than facilitated. At about the same time, an article by Alan MacCormack outlined the history of IT development techniques, ending with what he called "evolutionary delivery."[5] He described the evolutionary development of IT development techniques as:

- Waterfall—follows a sequential flow while maintaining rigorous documentation as the development proceeds
- Rapid prototyping—rapid creation of a prototype that functions well enough for customers to be able to provide feedback about desired changes
- Spiral—iterative prototyping that incrementally moves closer to the customers final needs

- Staged delivery—development and delivery of functional blocks that are later integrated to form a system
- Evolutionary delivery—an iterative approach in which customers test working versions of the software after each iteration.

MacCormack recommended a set of evolutionary delivery operating practices that included early release of evolving design and code, daily build of code and fast turnaround on changes, and deeply skilled teams. The Agile Manifesto embraced MacCormack's approach and the document has since become the foundational document for a rapidly spreading movement to streamline project management. Of course, MacCormack was describing IT development techniques that are a subset of an IT project management schema. Nonetheless, the agile advocates embraced his recommendations.

Agile project management has caught on. It is still most often used in the software development world, especially for iterative development of operating systems, although it has begun to spread to other arenas including the development of some of the personal electronic devices that many of us use. GE Aviation has begun using agile project management in the development of some of their aircraft engines.

Agile project management emerged out of a frustration with overly burdensome rigor and documentation, but at its heart agile project management embraces and accommodates the uncertainty and ignorance inherent in many complex development projects (see Figure 6.4). Projects that begin with vague notions about the intended outcome, sketchy requirements, conflicting stakeholder agendas, and other environmental uncertainties find it difficult to accomplish their work using the predictive project management disciplines and techniques. It is,

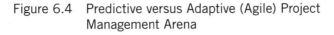

Figure 6.4   Predictive versus Adaptive (Agile) Project
Management Arena

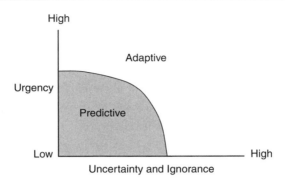

after all, difficult to develop an integrated project plan
to accomplish work for which the requirements are not
agreed or fully understood. Projects that launch with a
great deal of ignorance or many false assumptions about
the technologies they will use, the resources available to
them, or the capabilities of the staff may find that their
carefully crafted plans are soon irrelevant. Projects that
launch with a great sense of urgency find themselves delv-
ing immediately into the specifics of the tasks directly in
front of them, failing to develop the plans and monitoring
systems so necessary to the predictive project management
approach. Agile project management acknowledges uncertainty, ignorance, and urgency. The iterative nature of the
process accommodates the learning and maturation as the
project progresses. It can be a more effective approach to
dealing with inherently chaotic project environments.

Agile project management copes better with dynamic
environments because it embraces an iterative approach to
development. Teams begin working with an objective that
may be broadly defined. They also begin with an agreed
completion or product release date and an agreed budget
or staffing and resource plan. The team identifies those
pieces of the work that can be clearly defined and accomplished then proceeds as fast as possible to complete and

evaluate those pieces of work. Meanwhile, some members of the team tackle the definition of other pieces of work. The team knows its overall goal and resources but does not know what specific path it will take to accomplish the project. It tackles the work activities as they mature enough to be understood.

Agile project management is not a cure-all. It has its detractors who argue that it does not scale well. Large software projects are still being conducted with more traditional approaches. Agile techniques cannot make a fatally flawed project successful; an unachievable cost, schedule, and scope is still unachievable no matter what project management approach is used. Also, the Agile approach offers no advantage when requirements are relatively stable and unknowns arise infrequently. Additionally, some customers are unfamiliar with, or unwilling to consider, agile methods. The DOD project management bureaucracy is certainly not structured to embrace Agile techniques on anything but an experimental basis. Some customers and organizational leaders are intimidated by the loss of rigor and established control techniques they think Agile implies. Finally, Agile project management cannot be adopted instantly. Organizations need training, their cultures and bureaucracies need to adapt, and they need to develop expertise over time. Many environments are not ready for Agile project management whether or not it is appropriate.

ROLLING WAVE PLANNING

Project teams working in a predictive project management rather than an adaptive (Agile) project management environment must initially develop plans for the full project duration. There is no other way for them to determine the critical path schedule, to identify the key work activity inputs and outputs, to determine key work group interfaces, or to accomplish a host of other activities critical to predictive project management success. So, the project teams must initially develop a relatively detailed and full duration project plan if they hope to succeed.

However, teams should not assume that detailed plans remain valid for very long. Many subsequent military leaders have paraphrased Moltke's quotation that opened this chapter—the phrase "no plan survives first contact with the enemy" is often repeated in that community. Moltke's main thesis was that military strategy had to be understood as a system of options since only the beginning of a military operation was plannable. As a result, he thought military leaders should concentrate their efforts on understanding and preparing for an array of possible alternatives.

Project managers often adopt Moltke's observation as their own. Some of them recall that their project plans seem to develop cracks and flaws soon after work begins, or after first contact with the customer, or after being confronted with the reality of organizational resource constraints. These managers then leap to the assumption that planning is a waste of time. They believe their teams should instead dive immediately into the melee and hack their way forward. But this is wrongheaded. Dwight Eisenhower said, "Plans are nothing, planning is everything." Eisenhower recognized the great value of making plans, including contingency plans, of course. Integrated planning for the full project duration is essential. Once these plans have been established and all the learning and insights that derive from such planning have been gained, then a project team must deploy that plan in such a way that it accommodates the inevitable changes. Rolling wave is the technique for doing so.

Each project has a relatively clear planning horizon beyond which the path ahead becomes less and less certain. The planning horizon for a six-week project to upgrade the computer network within a building almost certainly extends through the end of the project. The planning horizon for the Apollo Program, a ten-year effort to land a man on the moon, had a clear vision and goals, but the path to achieving those goals was far from certain. The ten-year plan was filled with financial, technical, and political assumptions, many of which would be proven wrong. The team's clear planning horizon was initially only months, certainly no more than a year or two out. Beyond that point there were more questions than answers, and the plans were sure to change.

Project duration and complexity are not the only determinants of the distance of a clear planning horizon. A project with vague or conflicting visions has a very close-in planning horizon. A project with significant trade-offs or alternatives early in the project has a very close-in planning horizon. On the other hand, a three-year project to modify existing software and then test and deploy it may have a one-year, or even a two-year planning horizon because the task is clearly understood, the resources are available, and there are no significant alternatives to consider.

What happens when teams deploy plans too far out into the increasingly uncertain future? Nothing good and a lot of bad happens. Deploying detailed plans beyond the reasonable knowledge horizon leads to iterative change, or "iterative churn" (change activity without substantive benefit). A project team that begins work by developing jointly with the customer a set of specific requirements and specifications cannot know what work will be done to fulfill those not-yet-defined requirements. The detailed plans that follow the requirements definition period will very likely have to be redone once the requirements are established. The plans may have to be redone when the technical approaches are established. The plans may have to be redone again when the designs are simulated. So, detailed plans get made then tossed out and remade over and over again. The iterative changes waste project resources. The planning and re-planning adds non-value-added cost to the project. The effort also distracts the team from value-added work it could be doing that would advance the project toward its objectives. The iterative, but soon wasted, planning also impedes change control, a topic addressed in the next chapter, because teams tire of continually revising the plan. They eventually decide to make the changes hastily and sloppily, or they stop making them altogether. The result is a bad plan. As the plan becomes less and less relevant, team members find themselves doing work that is not in the plan. Thus, there is no way to monitor that off-the-plan work activity and its accomplishments. The team members are also not doing work that is in the plan. The project monitoring system is reporting on work that is not being done and is not reporting on work that is being done. Thus, people no longer trust or use the monitoring system. Both the plan and the monitoring system become a bureaucratic burden of little value to the team. All this leads the team to conclude that planning is not beneficial.

What happens when teams deploy detailed plans only as far into the future as they can reasonably predict? A lot of good and very little bad happens. The iterative re-planning is eliminated or minimized. Project resources focus on productive work. The plan stays relevant to the work. The monitoring system remains useful. The plans help the team make progress.

The following seven practices can help teams successfully use rolling wave planning:

1. Develop an integrated project plan (discussed in Chapter 4) with as much detail as necessary to establish the critical path, key work activity interfaces, cost estimates, and so on.
2. Preserve the integrated plan for future reference.

3. Determine the first detailed planning horizon. It may be a few months to a year or more
   beyond the project starting point.

4. Deploy that part of the integrated plan into
   the baseline project plan tools (e.g., Artemis,
   Microsoft Project) using as much detail as
   can be reasonably established. The rest of the
   plan should be aggregated into large planning
   packages, and then those packages should be
   inserted in the planning tool.

5. Document in the PMP its approach to iteratively rolling out increments of the plan. That
   approach should be reviewed and approved by
   senior management.

6. Begin planning for the next wave about 60
   days before the current wave ends. The team
   should revisit the upcoming aggregated planning packages, modify them to reflect current
   knowledge, disaggregate the ones in the next
   wave into the detailed planning level, and
   deploy that updated detailed version back into
   the plan tools.

7. Different parts of the project may operate on
   different waves. For example, the hardware
   design team may have full knowledge of what
   it needs to do and be able to deploy a one-year
   planning wave while the software team may still
   be debating a few critical requirements with
   the customer and so is only able to plan for a
   couple of months into the future.

Let's close with a few comments about how rolling-wave
deployments go astray. Certainly teams can go astray if
they fail to consider these seven recommendations, but
there are other perils as well. Some project managers, and
some organizations, use rolling wave as an excuse to reset

the project plan and wipe out otherwise bad performance, in effect giving the team a clean slate. They essentially replan the work frequently so the monitoring system will report good results. Project managers and organizational leaders need to guard against this kind of abuse because it gives a useful tool a bad name and only delays the inevitable bad news about the project. Rolling wave can also go awry if the organizational planning tools, techniques, and policies are overly bureaucratic. Effective rolling wave planning is a recurring activity that is efficiently done if the tools and bureaucracy are controlled but flexible and easy to work with.

SUMMARY

Uncertainty and ignorance are unavoidable attributes of the project management environment. Teams and their organizations must acknowledge, embrace, and deal with them. Failure to do so only creates additional unnecessary challenges. The following tools, techniques, and practices can help.

Teams must be willing to make assumptions, but they must also be *un*willing to make assumptions. Some assumptions are necessary while others are not. Some assumptions are critical while others are not. Teams must recognize what assumptions they have made and be prepared to deal with the consequences of being wrong. Sometimes a team will find that the consequences of being wrong will be fatal. That is when it must be unwilling to make the assumption instead taking the time to learn more and seek alternatives.

Teams must remember their assumptions and be willing to adjust them when new learning, new perspectives, or a changed environment warrants. It is futile and self-defeating to stick to an irrelevant or destructive assumption.

Teams must establish, maintain and adjust project reserves to the projects changing degree of uncertainty.

They must maintain appropriate levels of financial reserves, schedule reserves, resource reserves, and technical reserves in order to cope with their inevitable learning.

Teams should employ rolling wave planning. It accommodates new learning. It avoids wasted efforts. It maintains the integrity and value of the plans and the monitoring systems.

Teams should consider Agile project management if their culture and their project challenge are compatible with the approach.

This topic is an important underlying factor in subsequent chapters.

CHAPTER 7

HABIT # 6—EMBRACE BUT CONTROL CHANGE

"It is not the strongest of the species that survives, nor the most intelligent: It is the one that is most adaptable to change."

—Charles Darwin

The Central Artery Tunnel (CA/T) Project, otherwise known as the Big Dig, was a massive infrastructure improvement project in the heart of Boston, Massachusetts. The project included rerouting the city-center section of Interstate Highway 93 from above ground into a 3.5-mile tunnel, construction of the Ted Williams Tunnel under the Charles River to the Logan Airport, construction of a bridge over the Charles River, and development of the Rose Kennedy Greenway, a massive central-city park in the space vacated by moving I-93 underground. Initial plans called for constructing a rail connection between two major train stations but those plans were dropped as costs grew and schedules stretched, a significant reduction of the project scope. The project was conceived in the 1970s, but environmental impact studies did not get under way until 1983 and ground breaking occurred in 1991. Work was completed in 2006, many years late and many millions of dollars over budget.

The cost overrun was dramatic (see Table 7.1). In same-year dollars costs grew from a planned $2.8 billion to $14 billion. The final $22 billion tally (in 2006 dollars) included almost $7 billion in additional interest charges because the project took so much longer than planned to finish. The city will not pay off the total debt until 2038.

It is tough to quantify the extent of the schedule delays. Should one begin when the project was first conceived in the 1970s or with the onset of environmental impact studies, or with groundbreaking in 1981? Should the end of the project be deemed to have been in 2006, when the downtown tunnels were dedicated, or a couple of years later, when the litigation ended? Regardless, by all accounts, every phase of the project, from concept through final construction took far longer than originally planned.

There were quality problems as well. As early as 2001, the tunnel system was experiencing many thousands of small water leaks in the ceiling and in wall fissures that caused water damage to the structure and the installed systems. Criminal charges were filed against employees of the firm that supplied much of the concrete. In the summer 2006, a three-ton ceiling panel fell onto an automobile,

Table 7.1   Big Dig Cost Growth

	1982 ($billions)	2006 ($ Billions)
Original estimate	2.8	6.0
2006 estimate	8.1	14.6
2008 estimate	14.0	22.0

Source: Data taken from: No author given (2003). "Honeywell Wants More Money for Traffic-Monitoring System in Big Dig's I-93 Tunnel." Roads and Bridges e-news (source *Boston Globe* October 29, 2003) http://www.roadsbridges .com/Honeywell-wants-more-money-for-traffic-monitoring-system-in-Big-Dig -146-s-I-93-tunnel-NewsPiece5980

killing the passenger and injuring the driver. As recently as 2008, the *Boston Globe* reported that the tunnel system was still plagued with hundreds of leaks. State engineers believe it may take years to plug them all.

The prime contractor, Bechtel/Parsons Brinckerhoff, has repaid over $400 million to settle claims, and subcontractors have paid another $150 million or so. That is collectively less than 2.5% of the total project cost, but it no doubt represented a serious deterioration of profits, or in some cases additional losses, for the contractors.

Few would dare to assert the Big Dig was a successful project. It would be hard to find a happy member of the Big Dig stakeholder community. The project certainly failed to meet its triple constraint challenges of cost, schedule, and technical performance. Massachusetts taxpayers are no doubt unhappy about the cost growth and the continuing years of debt. Boston residents, as well as tourist and visitors during the 20 years it took to complete the project, were no doubt unhappy about the years of delays and the decades-long havoc the project wrought in downtown Boston. The prime contractors were certainly unhappy about the public conflict, the damage to their reputations, and the negotiated settlement of claims. Most of the subcontractors were also unhappy about the conflict, the damage to reputations, and the financial losses. There was little stakeholder satisfaction to be had on the Big Dig.

One subcontractor, Honeywell Technology Solutions Inc. (HTSI), a subsidiary of Honeywell International, had a $104 million contract to complete the integrated project control system (IPCS) providing roadway controls and fire and security systems for the project. The work involved installing 2.6-million feet of fiber-optic cable, 413 closed-circuit cameras, 135 electronic message signs, and devices to detect smoke in the tunnel. The IPCS work was done in two phases. The first phase was a $52-million contract to Transdyne, Inc., which developed the system software as part of the Ted Williams Tunnel work. HTSI outbid Transdyne for the second phase and won the contract for the rest of the Big Dig. Transdyne maintained that the software it developed was proprietary and refused to provide the source code to Honeywell for the second contract. The subsequent litigation between the state and Transdyne delayed the work for months. Additionally, the Honeywell and HTSI executives asserted that their project team often had to wait for other work to be completed; if the other work finished late, it had to accelerate its activity, at higher resulting cost, in order to meet the deadlines. They also asserted that the CA/T Project authorities changed the agreed work orders without compensating HTSI. The company claimed that the impacts caused a $130 million cost growth, raising the cost to more than double the original bid. The ensuing negotiations resulted in the contract being capped at $188 million, representing an over 80 percent cost growth.[1]

Even then HTSI was unhappy, believing it had lost a great deal of money by paying for work that should have been funded. During the roughly six years the company worked under the IPCS contract, it had three project managers. The third project manager made a serious attempt to clearly define and defend a baseline scope of work and insisted on change control. He also took on the task of trying to reconstruct the documents necessary to substantiate what subsequently became the HTSI claim of $130 million.

HTSI was not the only unhappy subcontractor, and the company's were not the only baseline and change control issues. For example, the 1997 version of the Bechtel design drawings, originally completed in 1994, failed to depict the 19,600-seat arena, instead showing an obstacle-free area for contractors to lay utility lines. That gaffe eventually required subcontractors to significantly alter their plans and complicated their work activity. This was only one of many design changes, albeit a very significant one, that was not captured, was miscommunicated, or was not negotiated in a timely fashion.

PROJECTS OFTEN STRUGGLE WITH CHANGE

The Big Dig illustrates the implications of challenging projects and the consequences of the incessant change they encounter, implications that are not uncommon across many types of projects and industries. Consider the project performance information in Table 7.2. The data shows that four of the five projects were completed later and at a higher cost than originally planned. The IT project was apparently completed within schedule and budget, but one does not know whether the project met all its original scope objectives. Perhaps it was "de-scoped" to keep it within budget. Perhaps some of the other projects had significant scope increases that caused the schedule to stretch and the costs to grow. Perhaps some of the projects incurred schedule and cost growth as a result of significant customer-directed change. Some of the projects may have encountered significant outside scope change but handled it well. One cannot know whether these projects were managed well or badly because one does not know whether the work scope grew, shrank, or stayed the same. The data in the table does strongly suggest that change, whether or not it is managed well, is

Table 7. 2   Were the Projects Managed Well?

Project	Time	Cost
Development of a new pharmaceutical drug	1.8X	1.0X
IT project to deploy an EVM system	1.0X	0.85X
DOD avionics development	1.1X	1.4X
Dam construction	1.6X	3.9X
Energy process plant	1.4X	2.8X

Source: Data taken from Rosenau, Milton D. Jr. and Githens, Gregory D. (2005). *Successful Project Management.* New York: John Wiley & Sons, Inc.

present in nearly every project, just as it was present in the Big Dig project.

Now take a look at the data in Table 7.3. It summarizes the performance of a group of projects in several different industries. This data indicates how much longer and how much more costly the sample of projects within an industry were, on average, than originally planned. The data, gathered from several independent studies illustrates that neither the Big Dig nor the commercial construction industry as whole has a corner on cost and schedule growth. Of course, the data provides little insight into whether the project's performances were a function of overly aggressive ambitions and optimistic planning, poor project performance, or highly dynamic and uncertain environments in which any predictions about future performance are risky.

Project change comes from every direction, and again, the Big Dig offers a good example. The planning, design, and construction phase stretched over more than twenty years, encompassing at least five major city- and state-election cycles. The political stakeholders changed several times. Prospective and current politicians made promises or revisited old decisions about the Big Dig, a dynamic that induced major changes in how the Big Dig vision, goals, and requirements were interpreted. The political dynamic also ensured that there could be no consensus, no matter

Table 7.3 Industry Project Performance Data

Project	Time	Cost
50 new products in drug firm	1.8X	1.6X
69 new products in drug lab	2.9X	2.1X
20 IT projects	2.1X	2.0X
34 DOD systems		
from "planning estimate"	—	2.1X
from "development estimate"	—	1.4X
10 major construction projects	—	3.9X
10 energy processing plants	—	2.5X

Souce: Data taken from Rosenau, Milton D. Jr. and Githens, Gregory D. (2005). *Successful Project Management.* New York: John Wiley & Sons, Inc.

how short-lived, about the project vision and requirements because politicians were eager to capitalize on even subtle differences that could win them votes. Prime and subcontractor leaders were coming and going, each with their own agendas and unique interpretations of what aspects of the project mattered. Each contractor leader advocated his or her interpretation of the Big Dig vision, goals, and requirements. Imagine the wave after wave of lobbying efforts as local real estate developers and property owners in and around the construction tried to gain or preserve advantage. Imagine the surprises once digging began: the unmarked or abandoned utility lines, the long-abandoned tunnels that had been forgotten, and the archeological finds of artifacts from the early history of the area. Imagine the complexities of temporarily routing and re-routing interstate and local traffic, thousands of cars per hour, as the construction progressed. Imagine the complex interaction between different contractors, and then imagine how those interactions were altered by every project change. Imagine how often the plans had errors, and got misinterpreted, and got interpreted differently. The Big Dig was awash in continual change.

The following paragraphs describe the various sources of change (see Table 7.4), and offer suggestions for dealing with them.

Table 7.4   Several Sources of Project Change

Vision changes
Requirements change
Technology performance
Supplier performance
Team performance
Funding levels
Market dynamics
Regulatory changes
Organizational strategic shifts
Perceptions
Politics

Project visions change. As discussed in Chapter 2, a project's vision may change and in turn, the project plan must be revised to reflect the new vision. Vision changes are far more frequent than stakeholders will ever admit. In fact, vision changes are often denied because stakeholders do not want to deal with the consequences. Visions also change subconsciously as people move in and out of the environment and as everyone responds to the challenges of trying to accomplish the original vision. So teams do not always have clear signals indicating change.

Chapter 2 offers guidance on establishing the vision baseline and detecting vision change. Here are a few additional tips. Some organizations ask project teams to schedule a project plan review after every major project milestone. Those reviews are a good opportunity to remind all stakeholders about the vision. Changes can be debated, negotiated, and agreed among the stakeholders. Project managers are the primary force in maintaining a shared vision. As such, they must also be responsible for detecting changes in the vision. Communicating and building consensus around a changed vision is just as challenging as is detecting that change. Project managers must foster adoption of the revised vision. They must also root out of people's subconscious any no longer appropriate dimensions or implications of the prior vision. Finally, they must lead a review of all past project work product and current work activity to determine what must be redone or revised to align with the changed vision.

Project requirements change. Another frequent and important source of change involves project requirements (see Figure 7.1). Certainly, changes in the project vision may alter the project requirements, but many other factors may also cause requirements to change. Some requirements get deleted. For example, the need driving a particular requirement may go away, or the project team and customer may agree that a particular requirement is unnecessary or too

Figure 7.1   Requirements Change

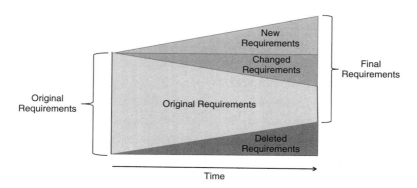

expensive. Some requirements change. The customer may learn something that leads to a reinterpretation of what is required or the project team and customer may renegotiate what is to be accomplished. New requirements arise. The users may identify a new requirement that had not been previously documented or the competition or market needs may shift mandating a revision to the product requirements.

Project teams must establish the requirements baseline as the standard against which to recognize needed changes. They must use the tools and techniques described in Chapter 3 to manage the way those requirements are deployed and how they are verified. Project managers must foster a culture of commitment to maintaining the currency and integrity of the requirements baseline, to identifying potential changes, and to adapting the baseline as appropriate.

Technology drives change. A project team working on the next generation e-reader, for example, may plan to use a display screen that has shown great promise, one that costs more than the screen already being used but that will be more readable in bright light. After getting under way, the team learns that the new screen is experiencing some premature failures, causing them to decide to stay with the proven screen. Additionally, the team may now discover that it can use existing display interfaces rather than design new ones. The lower-cost existing displays and the use of existing interfaces frees up money to enable the development of other features previously deemed unaffordable. Thus, the changes in technology influence several aspects of the project.

Supplier performance drives change. Certainly, a supplier's technical performance can lead to change. For example, the supplier providing the display described above may deliver late or early, deliver good or bad product, meet or miss specifications, interpret requirements differently than expected, or offer changes that solve interface problems. Any of these changes may impact the overall project.

Team performance drives change. Project teams seldom initially include all the individuals or expertise originally envisioned. Sometimes people are not available. Some people are not as experienced as they were thought to be. Teams are not always fully staffed on time. Teams may be raided to support higher priority challenges on other projects. The project challenges may turn out to be different from the ones anticipated, and the original team may be less qualified to handle the new set of challenges. The team may work more or less efficiently than anticipated.

Funding drives change. Other projects may run into trouble that requires leadership to divert funding from one project to another. The industry or the business unit may face a down cycle in sales and growth, forcing a decision to stretch out project funding. A project may become the beneficiary of available funds coming in from a troubled project that was shut down. Any changes in funding, up or down, can result in changes to many dimensions of the project baseline plan.

Market dynamics drive change. Competitors may unexpectedly introduce new products or features, forcing a revision to the project requirements or timelines. Apple's introduction of the iPhone, for example, certainly influenced its competitors' cell-phone development projects. Competitive pressures may lead to an overall drop in prices, forcing the project team to embrace a new, dramatically lower recurring price target for the product currently being developed.

Regulations drive change. Changes in safety requirements may force changes in project requirements. Changes in liability regulations may force requirements changes. Changes in work rules, company policies, or test requirements may also force the project to revise its plans.

Organizational strategic shift drives change. A project may be aligned with a corporation's strategy to develop a businesswide IT network; yet, soon after the project is under way the company may be acquired by a larger organization that already has an integrated IT network, one that will be expanded across your business unit, thus reshaping the technical approach and timeline for the project.

Perceptions change. Some stakeholders may have shifting views about the project and the importance of its mission. Their changes in perception may erode support for the project, forcing it to either demonstrate quick successes or suffer funding cuts.

Politics change. An executive champion for the project may be reassigned or retire or be fired, only to be replaced by someone else. His replacement may have had a different vision for the project but remained silent. Now the newly empowered executive decides to redirect the project toward his personal preference.

Change can occur from within the team as well as from without. Many of the change sources described above are factors outside the project team and force themselves on the team and its project plan, but another frequent and insidious source of change is *internal scope creep*. A project team may work hard to establish an integrated baseline plan and then tear that plan apart because of its lack of internal discipline. For example, a team established a technical baseline approach for the design of a gear train to be used in a sophisticated antenna positioning system. The technical requirements were challenging and the approach the team had selected was complex but achievable using specially treated metals, lubricants, and assembly methods. As the work got under way, a couple of team members decided they had found a better approach to machining a particular part, an approach which would make the part more durable. They instructed the machine shop to make the changes, the part was made, and the first gear train was assembled for testing. It turned out that their more durable part did not interact as it should have with the lubricant; the gear train overheated and failed the test. The ensuing investigation cost over $250,000 and it was nearly two months before the investigation team learned what had gone wrong and how it happened. Engineers have a tendency to want to change things because they know they can make them better or because they have been asked to make another change in the same area of the design, and the additional adjustment will be easy to slip in. Every member of the project team must understand that any change may have repercussions that are not obvious and can devastate the project. They must all embrace the notion of disciplined change control.

Project change continually comes from any of the directions described above and more. Teams that deny change or fail to recognize and control it pay a steep price because lack of change control leads to mass confusion, which in turn leads to serious mistakes that often cause projects to fail.

DISCIPLINED CHANGE CONTROL ENHANCES THE GOOD AND INHIBITS THE BAD

Project teams may exhibit any of three approaches to change control, only one of which offers sustainable success. Project managers can determine which approach is used through the attitude they display about change and through the rigor they demand.

The ostrich approach is common. The proverbial ostrich sticks his head in the sand hoping that what he cannot see will do him no harm. The ostrich-like project manager, and by extension the project team, pretends that change is not occurring. For example, a project team working to deploy an EVMS at several sites discovered that one of the sites lacks the capacity to collect cost account or work package level cost data, rendering the EVMS to be useless at that site. The team should have revised its deployment plans to accommodate the new insight, but the project manager and her supervisor knew there was significant executive pressure to have the system fully deployed across all the sites by year-end. They elected to press on with the original plan rather than face another confrontation with senior management. Of course, ignoring change does not make it disappear. Instead, it lies neglected until the impact of the change is even larger and more difficult to cope with. Toward the end of the project it became evident that the EVMS could not be supported at not only that one but several sites. The project was deemed a failure; it had cost nearly a million dollars and consumed important resources, but provided no benefit to the sites. The project vision was to establish an EVMS that would enable the aggregation of project performance data for all projects, with work spread across all sites. That vision could not be achieved. The team had stuck its head in the sand, ignoring the problem until it was too late to recover.

Sometimes an ostrich-like project manager who is unable to ignore a change may rationalize that it is actually within the project scope, telling his team it had misinterpreted the original requirement or plan. An example described earlier, one in which a project team was developing a fuel-control system for a new airplane, helps to illustrate this point. The customer had been vague about where the electronics box would be located on the aircraft, in the cockpit electronics bay where temperature and pressure variations were relatively mild or in an aft electronics bay were temperature and pressure variations were more extreme. The project team had made clear that its project baseline assumed the equipment would go in the cockpit electronics bay. In fact, the customer had approved a couple of design reports that documented that specific assumption. Several months into the project, however, the customer's technical leader denied that agreement existed and insisted that the fuel controller electronics had to go into the aft electronics bay. This change would force the project to spend about $250,000 on revising the previous work and doing the new work and would cause a five-month schedule slip. The project manager also knew that his organization had just submitted a bid to this customer for another major project. He did not want to be responsible for irritating the customer at such a critical time. So, he turned to his work activity leaders asking them to accept the change without adjusing their work activity agreements. This sort of denial leads to conflict and distrust between project managers and the work activity leaders. It also leads to dissolution of the integrated baseline plan. This form of the ostrich approach worsens the impact of changes and creates additional problems for the team. It does not work.

The "Dirty Harry" Callahan (Clint Eastwood) approach—"Go ahead, make my day"—is the second most common. Project managers who have suffered in the past from the consequences of uncontrolled change but have still not figured out how to deal with change constructively typically employ the Harry Callahan approach. These managers project the notion that they can "will" an end to changes. They make pronouncements like Harry's hoping to discourage change. For example, a project manager leading an effort to develop software for a complex data handling system was frustrated that the software test team kept finding new problems. In fact, the rate of new problems was increasing rather than decreasing, even though the scheduled delivery date was only a couple of months away. Acting out of frustration, the project manager made it very clear to the team that the number of new problems must taper off immediately. Of course, his mandate had no impact on the actual number of problems remaining in the software. What did happen was that the test team began ignoring intermittent problems and stopped looking so closely at test results. The number of reported new problems did decline. The team shipped the software on time. Of course, within a few weeks the customer had serious problems when it tried to integrate that software into its system, problems that should have been detected and fixed before the software was shipped. This caused a major crisis for the team when it had to find and resolve all those problems after delivery to the customer and ran up the project cost. What happens when project managers use the Harry Callahan approach to change management is that change continues to occur but is kept hidden or is ignored until, like in the ostrich approach, it festers and becomes too painful to ignore.

There is a better approach to change management, one that acknowledges the inevitability of change and constructively deals with it. (See Figure 7.2). This five-step approach seeks out potential change, analyzes its impact, negotiates its consequences with the originator, incorporates it into the baseline plan, and communicates its impacts to all stakeholders, inside and outside the team.

Figure 7.2   A Better Approach to Change Control

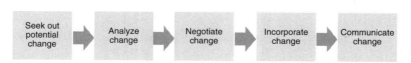

Project teams must seek out potential change. To do so they must have an established and well-understood project baseline, without which the need for baseline project changes can be argued subjectively, and the person best positioned politically often prevails. Team members follow suit when project managers and organizational leaders treat change as an inherent part of project life. They also learn to bury or mask change when their leaders reject it or handle it badly. Project managers must model the desired behavior and reward it when it occurs in others.

Customers must also become conditioned to recognize and acknowledge change. Some customer communities are more than eager to have a project team absorb changes so that the team rather than the customer can be held accountable for the consequences (overruns, delays, rework) of the changes. Project team discipline can condition customers to behave more fairly.

Some project managers insist on an open discussion of customer directed changes but then fail to do so with their internal project work activities. For example, a customer has decided that a software change should be tested more carefully before it is shipped from the supplier. The supplier project manager appropriately insists that the customer must acknowledge whether or not the work is outside the agreed scope and whether some consideration is appropriate. However, just two weeks earlier the supplier project manager had decided that one of the project work teams should do some additional analysis to verify an equipment calibration procedure. The project manager ignored the work team leader's request that the additional work be evaluated as potentially outside the agreed baseline for the work activity. Such behavior creates at least two problems. First, it conditions the team to believe that some people can disregard the project baselines, and so the baseline becomes a political device. Second, it conditions the team to pay less attention to managing those baselines and to seeking out potential changes. Project managers must be respectful of internal work activity baselines if they hope to condition their teams to defend external project baselines.

All project stakeholders, including the team members, must talk openly about changes, dealing with them as an unavoidable and important aspect of project life. Here ritual and procedure can be useful. For example, best practice project managers establish change identification and control procedures for the project. They insist that everyone understand the baseline. They maintain an on-going dialogue about with their team and the customer about potential change and the impact of change.

Project teams must analyze changes. Again, the changes can only be analyzed against an established and understood baseline plan. The team must have a disciplined process for conducting the analysis. It should be clearly understood how potential changes are submitted for consideration, how the analysis is accomplished, and how the change decision is determined. The process must engage the appropriate parties to evaluate potential changes. Appropriate parties should include those potentially directly affected by the change as well as experienced professionals who may be able to recognize change and consequences that the team members may not recognize. Not all change is bad. The process should investigate both the cost and the benefits of potential change, identifying all the consequences of implementing the change. Finally, the process should revisit the project risks and opportunities to assess whether the potential change impacts the probability or impact of any of those potential future events.

Teams often fail to acknowledge all the consequences of a potential change. Some consequences are obvious, for example, added work scope, additional material or equipment, and schedule impacts. Other consequences are less obvious but no less important, for example, completed work that may have to be redone, documents that may have to be revised, decisions that may have to be reevaluated, communications that may have to be withdrawn or revised, previously unneeded skills that must now be acquired. Still others may be contentious, such as when the mere act of evaluating a change requires the use of project staff on work that was not planned. That staff should be working on planned activity instead. So, teams should understand the cost of evaluating potential changes and consider how those costs will be covered. Best practice project managers establish a funded work activity within the project baseline, a work activity to be used for evaluating potential changes. They then negotiate with the customer whether work will be covered as a contract cost.

Project teams must always negotiate the consequences of changes. Let me repeat, project teams must *always* negotiate the consequences of changes. It is vital that customers and outside stakeholders appreciate all of the consequences of making changes. Failure to establish and maintain that appreciation can be devastating for the project. It is also vital that team members appreciate the consequences of their internal changes. Finally, it is vital that they believe their leadership will defend the project baseline against unofficial and unauthorized changes. Failure in any of these dimensions can doom a project to failure.

Negotiations need not always result in a financial consideration. In fact, non-financial considerations can be far more valuable than money. Sometimes specification relief, or schedule relief, or in-kind technical assistance, or some other consideration can be of tremendous value in eliminating a high probability risk or enabling a valuable opportunity. Sometimes negotiations may result in a promissory note, an "I owe you one," that can be redeemed later when the need is more critical. Occasionally, the project manager may elect to give the customer or other stakeholder a free change because doing so will build a stronger partnership with the customer or stakeholder. But, even when getting a "freebie" the customer or stakeholder must be made to understand the project consequences of their change so that each future change is understood to be a matter for negotiation. Project teams that fail to negotiate the consequences of change abdicate the authority to control change in the future. Change is pervasive and insidious. It will quickly overwhelm the undisciplined team.

Project teams must incorporate change into the baseline. Teams must work to the project baseline. A change is not a change until it has been incorporated into the baseline plan where it can be under the watchful eye of the project monitoring system. Exceptions should be rare and tightly controlled. Even the so-called "freebie" and "I owe you one" must be funded from project management reserve because the work activity leaders should always believe they have a mutually agreed commitment to accomplish a given scope of work for an appropriate amount of money and within an appropriate time frame. Inflicting work activity change without consideration is a sure way to disconnect work activity leaders from their commitment to accomplishing that work activity as agreed. So, the project team must have a rigorous process for implementing change into the project baseline that includes cost, schedule, and scope adjustments so as to maintain an integrated baseline project plan.

The consequences of doing work that is outside the baseline plan are dire. First, the mere act of permitting such work allows the team and the stakeholders to begin questioning what is or is not within the project scope. This results in differing versions of the baseline and, eventually, leads to no baseline at all. Second, the work being done outside the plan is likely being done by people who are not doing the work within the plan that they should be doing. Resource planning quickly goes awry. Third, the monitoring system ends up tracking the lack of progress of work that is not being done while also not tracking the progress of work that is being done. That makes the monitoring system subject to suspicion and allows people the justification for not being held accountable for their commitments.

Project teams must communicate change. The discipline of change management is itself the foundation of good communication about change. Good communication naturally occurs when the change-control process engages all the affected parties. The act of updating the baseline plan further communicates the occurrence of change. Best practice project teams adopt a formal approach to officially communicating change. They use the minutes of a formal change control board committee meeting, a change approval document signed by the project manager, or some other vehicle to make clear when a change has been accepted and is now part of the revised baseline plan. Finally, best practice project managers use change events as an opportunity to communicate to the team members the good and bad effects of significant changes. Doing so helps foster an environment in which every team member is alert for potential change and so is a guardian of the project baseline.

Occasionally, a change is so critical that work must be started before negotiations can take place. NASA asked a project team developing electronic boxes for the International Space Station to quickly modify, test, and deliver several additional boxes to its Russian International Space Station partners. The project manager asked for a formal request letter to ensure that the change request was appropriately documented. He then used project management reserve funds and some available schedule slack to integrate the additional work into the project baseline. The work activity managers each negotiated a revised baseline plan thereby keeping the internal baseline intact. The equipment was delivered on time. The NASA customers were delighted. A few weeks later the change was negotiated on the basis of the actual cost of doing the additional work. The additional funding was deposited in the project management reserve pool to replace the funding withdrawn earlier. The negotiations included a new agreement for key project milestones thus allowing the project to retrieve not only its financial reserves but also its schedule reserves. The work was done quickly but the baseline remained under control.

Stakeholders sometimes resist disciplined change management. Customers, whether internal or external to the organization, may resist it because they prefer to make changes without acknowledging the consequences. Organizational leaders may resist because they fear it will make customers unhappy, which may affect future business opportunities. Project managers may resist it because it puts them in the position of the "disciplinarian." Project team members may resist it because they would rather do work than track and negotiate changes. There is no shortage of opposition to disciplined change management.

Such resistance often arises because people confuse customer satisfaction with customer appeasement. Customers and other stakeholders have short-term needs and expectations and will naturally express their disappointment when those expectations are opposed. Project managers must remember that sometimes it is necessary to confront or disappoint the customer or stakeholder in the near term in order to be able to satisfy them in the long term. A customer may want to reinterpret a requirement or impose some additional work scope without having it be considered a formal change subject to negotiation. The project manager, feeling the pressure to keep the customer happy, may elect to accept the change even though it will cause problems. Later, when those difficulties are manifested in schedule delays or cost growth or compromised technical performance, the customer will almost certainly be very dissatisfied. Customers would much rather be disappointed in the short term than completely dissatisfied in the long term. Project managers must appreciate the difference between customer appeasement and customer satisfaction and behave accordingly, especially with respect to change management.

As we have seen, not every project starts with a solid baseline, fair-minded stakeholders, and a willingness to deal fairly with change. Sometimes a project manager has to gain control after the project has gotten started, after bad habits and inappropriate expectations have been established. Several years ago a veteran project manager took over a troubled project working to develop equipment for a government satellite. The project had experienced significant cost growth and schedule delays. The customer had become a bit of a bully and was imposing changes with impunity. The new project manager had been tasked to get the customer and the project back under control, and he immediately set about doing just that.

This project manager, let's call him Randy, began working on the project only a few weeks before a scheduled major design review. He had met a few of the customer leaders but was still a stranger to most of the customer's team and to some of his own team. On the day of the review Randy elected to sit in the back of the conference room just observing the proceedings and telling anyone who asked that he was there primarily to learn. The hours passed and Randy said very little.

After lunch a conversation began about a particular work activity and associated requirements. A customer technical leader asserted that the work should be done in a particular way and began to explain his interpretation of the requirements accordingly. Randy, our new and relatively unknown project manager, stood up at the rear of the room. He raised his hand politely and said something to the effect of, "Excuse me. I am Randy, the new project manager. Please forgive my ignorance but that comment seems to me to be a directed change of our previously agreed work scope. Perhaps I am wrong. On the table at the side of the room you will find some new forms that we will be using to collect and evaluate potential changes. We will be delighted to evaluate this potential change if someone will fill out the form and leave it with us. In the meantime, I realize that the discussions should proceed, so I suggest, just for the sake of today's discussions, that we agree the potential change is indeed a real change, that it will add six months to the project schedule, and that it will cost an additional one million dollars. Certainly, the change may turn out to have a different impact but for now let's just assume this is a one-million-dollar and six-month change. Thank you." Randy sat down.

There was complete silence in the room for nearly a minute. Finally, an awkward conversation resumed on a different topic and gradually the group moved on, essentially not responding to Randy's comment because they were so stunned by it. A couple of hours later another comment was made that prompted Randy to rise and repeat, almost verbatim, his previous statement. He asserted that this new conversation seemed to be addressing another potential change. He again suggested that everyone deal with the topic as if it were a change with a one-million-dollar and six-month impact to the project baseline. Again the audience was stunned, but no one replied directly to Randy's comments. Randy gave this guidance a few more times before the end of the review two days later.

After the review had ended, the customer's executives went to Randy's supervisor to complain about his behavior. The supervisor was of course prepared for the meeting because he and Randy had anticipated that the customer would complain if Randy tried to restore discipline. After listening patiently to the customers, the supervisor asked if they had filled out the change-evaluation forms as Randy asked. They said, "Of course not." The supervisor slyly said that it seemed unfair to fire the new project manager simply because he asked that potential changes be evaluated. The supervisor said that, perhaps, if the customer submitted the change for evaluation it would turn out that Randy was wrong and the customer was right about the work activity and the requirement. Wouldn't it be better to discuss the matter then? The executives left frustrated.

Over the next few weeks the customer did formally submit two change-evaluation forms, electing to not submit the other potential changes discussed during the review. Randy's team evaluated the two potential changes. They concluded that one was a minor change that would have minimal impact because that specific work had not yet begun and the plan could be easily modified. They concluded that the second change would have a $50,000 and four-week impact on the baseline. They informed the customer about both potential changes and offered a timeline for negotiating the one change. It was negotiated and the work was incorporated into the baseline.

Several months later, during another review with the customer, a customer comment prompted Randy to rise and begin his speech. A customer executive interrupted Randy, saying, "Yeah, we know Randy—one million dollars and six months. We'll fill out the forms later."

The point of this story is that projects can be brought under control, even if they have started badly. Randy was able to quickly establish and enforce a necessary discipline. Certainly the customer was unhappy that it could no longer introduce change with impunity but it also sheepishly agreed that the chances of overall project success improved when such discipline was imposed. The project subsequently received two consecutive supplier-of-the-year awards for meeting all cost, schedule, and technical objectives. Focusing on satisfaction instead of appeasement can be rewarding.

SUMMARY

There are relatively few change management tools outside the engineering discipline to assist project teams. The engineering requirements development tools and document/drawing configuration control tools are helpful. The disciplines and techniques surrounding them can be adapted for broader project change control. The EVM disciplines and tools can also be helpful when used correctly. The team must supplement these tools with their own set of ad hoc tools, techniques, and disciplines to construct a total project change control system.

The most powerful of these is commitment and discipline. Team members must be aware of the perils of unmanaged change and remain alert for it. Discipline and commitment can be developed through training, through project manager focus and role modeling, and through a rigorous identification, review, approval, incorporation, and communication process. Project teams find themselves taking on ever more challenging and fast-moving projects in increasingly dynamic environments that demand even greater commitment and discipline.

CHAPTER 8

HABIT # 7— CONTINUALLY ACT TO INFLUENCE THE FUTURE

"I was thinking of my patients, and how the worst moment for them was when they discovered they were masters of their own fate. It was not a matter of bad or good luck. When they could no longer blame fate, they were in despair."

—Anais Nin

"So, after all, we are but puppets, creatures of our fate, not commanding it but being molded by it."

—Eleanor Roosevelt

Eleanor Roosevelt and Anais Nin were opposites in many ways, certainly in their worldviews: in one we shape our future; and in the other our environment shapes our future and us. Geneticists and neurobiologists ask to what extent many of our individual preferences and emotions are genetic predispositions. So far the answers are elusive, but it may just be that we each have a genetic "set point," a preferential spot on the emotional stability spectrum, the happiness and contentment spectrum, and even the fatalism spectrum, where we prefer to dwell. Events may knock us off that preferred set point from time to time, but we seem to quickly find our way back to where we are predisposed to be. Whether it is influenced by genetics or experiences or both, our predisposition has little to do with whether our actions can in fact influence the future, but it does influence how we choose to respond to challenges, whether we decide to take action or instead ride along with the winds of fate.

Project managers, like anyone else, have a variety of pre-dispositions. Some behave as if their success or failure is determined by the luck of the draw; those fortunate enough to be assigned to easy projects or who have lucky breaks succeed. Others are certain they can influence the project stakeholder community, the execution challenges, and the team itself to thereby influence the project outcome. A veteran executive at an organization that had successfully dealt with many very challenging projects once observed, "There are two kinds of project managers; reporters and influencers. [...] I already get the newspaper. I don't need another reporter." He sought out, promoted, and supported people who viewed the world as malleable to their actions.

Organizations also tend to have a worldview about projects. Recurring traumatic project experiences can make it very easy for organizational leaders, project managers, and project teams to develop a fatalistic worldview about project success and failure. Some see projects as a terrible ordeal they only hope to survive while others see projects as an activity within their control, or at least within their influence. Indeed some projects start out fatally flawed or soon become so. Certainly, the Big Dig (see Chapter 7) was fraught with peril from the beginning. A significantly flawed vision can doom a project. A disconnected or overly aggressive plan can doom a project. Chronic under-staffing or a lack of critical expertise can doom a project.

Some organizations have a recurring history of nightmarish projects that take far too long, cost far too much, and ruin careers. The people in those organizations often develop a fatalistic attitude, ascribing their failure to the gods rather than to their own actions. On the other hand, organizations that experience project success tend to believe their actions contributed to that success. Their leaders invest in building a culture, processes, disciplines, and skills that positively influence project performance. That investment and the ensuing project successes foster a virtuous reinforcing cycle of taking action, seeing positive consequences, additional investment in competence building, more powerful action taking, and so on. The result is an organization and employees who believe they can influence their environment, who actually do influence their environment because they believe they can do so.

Project managers who demonstrate a positive worldview more often find success. If nothing else, the preceding chapters have made the point that the project environment is challenging; the project vision, goals, and requirements may be unclear or conflicting; the project plan may be disconnected or impossibly aggressive; there may be a shortage of funding and resources, critical assumptions may turn out to be invalid, and teams drown in wave after wave of change. Projects are by their very nature a demonstration of intent to coerce the environment into compliance toward a specific vision and goals. The complex and fragile project environment naturally deteriorates toward chaos. A proactive and influencing worldview is the force that counterbalances the environment's decline.

So, how does one encourage, develop, and expand a proactive worldview in a project manager and within the team? In this chapter we look at how R/O management disciplines and techniques can facilitate this worldview. We also look at how the appropriate use of project reserves operates as an enabler and facilitator, and how leaders can shape the organizational and project cultures. We close with a brief description of the project manager's personal responsibility for fostering this action-taking worldview within the project team.

RISK AND OPPORTUNITY MANAGEMENT IS A CORE ACTION-TAKING DISCIPLINE

The Project Management Institute identifies *project risk management* as one of its nine essential project management knowledge areas.[1] Risk management is perhaps only second to EVMS as an acknowledged project management discipline. However, as we have seen, EVMS only succeeds when the underlying fundamental concepts are in place. The same is true of risk management. It is a discipline that can be, and quite often is, deployed without an understanding of the underlying principles. Risk management only has value if the project has an integrated baseline plan against which to assess risks and opportunities. Risk management can be used to report on what the team perceives as the likely project cost, schedule, and scope outcome, but it can also help influence that outcome if the team has discretionary resource reserves with which to take action.

Proactive risk management serves to keep the team aware of the road ahead, not just the pavement beneath its wheels. Teams that systematically address the uncertain future can then try to influence that future; teams that focus only on today's task quickly feel victimized by their ever-changing environments. Thus, risk management can facilitate an action-taking team perspective.

Many risk management deployments focus exclusively on the risk dimension, as if there is no possibility that any future state could possibly be better than the one represented by the current plan—only bad things will happen, not good things. This adjustment in focus, to include a discussion of the potential good as well as the potential bad, can be the single most powerful agent for moving a project team closer to an action-taking perspective. The more balanced perspective pushes back the depression.

Organizations and project teams benefit in yet another way from embracing opportunity as well as risk management. As teams and their organizations come to realize in hard factual terms that they persistently create project plans that are so aggressive they have virtually no potential to succeed and every potential to fail, they begin to accept the need to develop more realistic and achievable project plans. They move away from the notion of continually striving to do the impossible and toward the notion of balanced projects with viable opportunities for success.

Project R/O management is an ongoing endeavor. Many teams address project risks at the proposal or start-up phase, and then their attention fades as the challenges of each day overwhelm them. Fewer teams, the consistently more successful ones, make it a practice to persistently assess R/Os as the project evolves.

But merely acknowledging and reporting potential R/Os is not enough—the organization needs influencers, not just reporters. The project must embrace an R/O management posture rather than a reporting posture, identifying potential threats and opportunities then acting to influence their outcomes.

Successful R/O management is made up of four distinct activities. First, the *identification activity* involves the recognition of future conditions, events, or results that, if they occur, will have a significant impact on the overall project outcome. As we saw in Chapter 6, every project faces many R/Os. Project teams set the stage for action taking when they identify their specific challenges and opportunities. Second, the *assessment activity* involves quantifying the likelihood and impact of each identified project R/O, given the current baseline project plan and its assumptions. Together, identification and assessment yield a description of what the team believes could happen and the consequences, thereby accomplishing the reporting function. The third, *action-taking activity* identifies alternative actions that can be taken to lessen the likelihood or impact of the risks and to increase the likelihood or impact of the opportunities, and then selects the most cost-effective actions and incorporates them into the project plan. The result is a revised plan that is more likely to succeed. The team took actions that should improve its chances of project success. Finally, the ongoing *management activity* involves the iterative adjustment of R/Os and the consequential adjustment of actions as the project evolves. It also includes an accounting and reporting function, associated with the ever-changing R/Os and response actions.

For example, a project team has been tasked to modify an existing software program that is used to operate and monitor a chemical manufacturing process, making several changes and adding new functionality. The project also includes testing and installing the modified software. The customer has directed the project team to hire an independent verification and validation (IV&V) subcontractor to assess the new software. Such IV&V activity is usually required when the customer feels it must have a fully functional software system with no hidden flaws or performance problems and is willing to pay an independent contractor to verify the performance of the software. The idea behind the IV&V is that third-party testing is more likely to uncover problems than testing done by those who designed and developed the software, who are so familiar with it that they may overlook problems they inadvertently created. The initial plan for this project included the IV&V activity, and no significant risks or opportunities had been identified. However, several months into the project the team has learned that the IV&V subcontractor recently laid off several engineers, raising a new concern about the activity. The project team has identified this concern as a new risk—that the subcontractor's IV&V work would be accomplished late or would be unsatisfactory to the end customer (see Table 8.1).

The team estimates that such a problem would force a two-month delay in the project critical path schedule and cause the team to miss the scheduled delivery of the final software, forfeiting a $200,000 on-time delivery incentive. It would also incur additional labor costs and have to accomplish work-around activities that would all together cost them about $800,000 more than planned. The team believes, based on its current understanding of this risk, that there is a 40 percent chance the risk event will occur. Thus the net risk, that is, the full impact of the risk event if it occurs, times the likelihood of it occurring, is $400,000. There is a 40 percent chance the team will incur a two-month schedule delay and a $1 million cost growth.

At this point, the team has identified and assessed a new project risk that emerged after the project was under way. Now it moves to the action-taking stage, to determine

Table 8.1   Risk Example

Software Independent Verification and Validation (IV&V) vendor capability. The current vendor has recently lost several experienced engineers to layoff. There is a concern that the IV&V subcontractor activity may take longer than planned or that the result may become suspect after completion.

Gross impact	Probability	Impact

Two months schedule critical path delay
    Loss of $200,000 completion payment
Two added months of staff at $150,000/
    month = $300,000
Panic review and rework of IV&V = $500,000
$1,000,000 total ($200,000 loss of profit plus
    $800,000 cost growth)
	40%	$400,000

what it can do to mimimize the likelihood or impact of this newly identified risk. Table 8.2 describes four potential response actions the team thinks are worth considering. This team has demonstrated good practice in that it has identified several viable actions rather than just coming up with a single action then implementing it.

The four alternate responses shown in Table 8.2 each has its own strengths and weaknesses. Some may be more advantageous than others. The team may find it can implement more than one of the alternatives or that some of them are mutually exclusive.

The first response, replacing the subcontractor with another one, is a typical "brute-force" approach. The project team may be able to identify a different, more stable, subcontractor to do the work, but it would also have to terminate the contract with the current subcontractor, which can be an expensive and messy task. They would also have to deal with the cost and delay of finding, and

Table 8.2   Response Alternatives

Alternative responses	Advantages	Disadvantages
1. Replace IV&V subcontractor	More reliable subcontractor	Termination costs, re-compete costs
2. Investigate subcontractor capability	Inexpensive Substantial risk clarification (reduction or increase)	Subcontractor may resist. Tough to verify capability.
3. Supplement subcontractor staff	Substantial risk reduction	Experienced internal staff unavailable Subcontractor may insist on compensation. IV&V liability shifts to project team.
4. Incentivize subcontractor	Some risk reduction Pay for performance only	Subcontractor may be incapable of earning incentive.

then placing under contract the new subcontractor, who would need additional time to learn about the software to be tested. Finally, there is the risk that the new subcontractor will have its own shortcomings that will only become evident much later. This first alternative may be the most obvious but it may not be the best choice.

The second possibility is to investigate and monitor the current IV&V subcontractor's capability. After all, the project team has concerns about the current subcontractor's ability to perform but little actual knowledge about the truth of the layoff rumors or the impact of those layoffs on the subcontractor's ability to do the job. Perhaps a bit of investigation will disclose that the risk is much smaller than supposed. This approach offers the advantage of being relatively inexpensive. It also replaces rumor, inference, and assumption with facts that may allow the team to dismiss the risk as insignificant or minor. It may also disclose that the risk is real and immediate; in this case it is better that the team learns the facts of the situation as early as possible. But this alternative has disadvantages as well. Subcontractors do not always welcome customers that have probing questions about their internal operations. They may be reluctant to divulge their true capabilities for fear of losing the contract. They may be overly optimistic about their capabilities and so mislead the investigators. Although an investigation of the subcontractor's true capabilities may be a quick and inexpensive response, it is a fact-finding initiative rather than a future-influencing initiative.

The third alternative is to supplement the subcontractor's staff with additional temporary engineers. The project team would be able to learn firsthand about the subcontractor's capability and to monitor ongoing performance much more intimately. The additional staffing would certainly reduce the risk probability and impact. On the other hand, it is not always easy to get such engineering talent pulled off existing projects and relocated to work with sub-contractors. Such talent may be in great demand inside the organization and the team may be unable to get them reassigned to work with the subcontractor. Additionally, the subcontractor may view the visiting engineers as an unnecessary burden and insist on compensation for training them and integrating them into its team. Finally, and most importantly, relocating engineers from the software-development project organization risks invalidating the IV&V activity. The customer may feel that the presence and involvement of these engineers annuls the independence of the IV&V activity. Therefore, this response could significantly reduce the risk but it could also suddenly turn it from a probability into a certainty, hardly the desired result.

The team identified a fourth alternative, incentivizing the subcontractor. The notion is that perhaps the subcontractor would be motivated to assign its best talent and management priority to this particular activity in return for the potential to earn a large bonus for on-time delivery of an accepted IV&V certification. The benefits of this alternative are that it appears to offer risk reduction and that the bonus is only paid out if the subcontractor succeeds. On the other hand, the subcontractor may be simply unable to accomplish the work and offering a bonus would have no real effect on the risk likelihood or impact. Instead, it would merely allow the project team to feel as if it had done something, when in fact it had not.

This team elected to more rigorously evaluate the potential costs, benefits, and risks of all four alternatives, choosing not to dismiss any of them right away (see Table 8.3). They determined that the first alternative, engaging a different IV&V subcontractor would be expensive, costing about $350,000 in termination and re-competition costs. They also concluded that although hiring a new subcontractor might be less risky, it didn't completely eliminate

Table 8.3   Response Alternative Analysis

Risk	Alternative actions	Cost	Key milestones	Net benefit
Software IV&V (3-month delay, net)	1. New subcontractor	$350,000	• Cancel current contract 4/4/11 • Issue new request for bids 4/24/11 • New subcontractor award 6/1/11	$50,000
$400,000	2. Investigate capability	$30,000	• Dispatch team 3/3/11 • Verdict 3/10/11	$120,000
	3. Supplement subcontractor staff	$85,000	• Subcontractor informed 3/3/11 • Staff relocated 6/10/11	$215,000
	4. Incentivize subcontractor	$150,000	• Subcontractor informed 3/10/11	$100,000

Note: The project team selected option number three as the most effective.

risk because the new subcontractor may have its own undisclosed problems. Additionally, the transition from one subcontractor to another would inject new schedule and technical transition risks. The team estimated that risk would decline from $1 million at 40 percent probability to $1 million at 10 percent probability. Thus the project risk profile would improve by $300,000 but at a cost of $350,000. The term determined that this most obvious response alternative would actually increase rather than decrease the project cost. The team would be better off taking its chances that the risk would not materialize after all. This is an example of the most obvious response sometimes being both crude and costly. It reminds us that teams should explore several alternate responses for each R/O before settling on a specific approach to shaping their project future.

The project team evaluated the other three candidate actions in a similar fashion. It determined the cost of implementing the action. It discussed the time required to implement the action and the key milestones that would have to be accomplished. It also estimated the net benefit to this particular R/O item assessment and then to the overall project estimate-at-completion. They concluded that alternatives two, three, and four each offered some benefit.

The team elected to immediately implement alternative two, investigate the subcontractor's capability, seeking to replace rumor and inference with facts and data. Perhaps what it learned would allow it eliminate or significantly reduce the risk. The team felt it was important to learn the facts of the situation as early as possible, the definition of project efficiency.

The team also elected to go forward with alternative number three, supplementing the subcontractor's staff, if the subcontractor investigation confirmed the risk was real. It reasoned that this was the most effective way to actually improve the subcontractor's, and thus its own, odds of succeeding. However, it immediately discussed the planned action with the customer, explaining the risk, the alternatives, and the merits of the approach. The customer concurred with the rationale and formally agreed that the activity would not jeopardize the independence of the IV&V activity if specific review points were added to the effort. They were thus able to mitigate the weaknesses of this alternative, making it the most attractive alternative.

What makes for a good choice? How does a team decide whether an alternative is worth pursuing? The short answer is that teams should make decisions using relevant experience and a determination of facts rather than anxieties and hopes, subject however, to a few general guidelines. It is clear by now that R/O management involves a great deal of educated guessing about the future, about what could go wrong or right, about probabilities, about the extent of consequences, and about the cost and benefit of alternative actions. These guesses may be crude because there may be little real and valid data available. So, teams should look for actions where modest costs will yield large benefits. An action costing $0.2 million that reduces a $1 million risk by 10 percent is not worth doing. Who wants to spend $200,000 now in the hope of gaining only a $100,000 improvement in what is only a probable, not a certain, future event? Statistically, one is far better off accepting the risk. A different candidate action may cost only $20,000 to implement and yield an estimated 50 percent improvement in the $1 million risk, moving it from a 70 percent probability to a 20 percent probability. That is a $0.5 million improvement in the net R/O, and thus in the project EAC for only a cost of $20,000. The team does not need to know whether the risk is actually $1 million or only $0.8 million. It does not matter if the probability is actually 85 percent instead of 70 percent, or if the cost of the action is really $30,000 instead of $20,000. This is clearly a smart alternative. It should be done. Teams should seek out relatively low cost actions that provide real and substantial leverage. They should reject expensive actions unless the R/O are massive. They should only fuss about the math when the benefits of the actions are modest compared to the costs of implementing those actions.

This software project team identified a new risk, investigated and selected appropriate alternatives to reduce that risk, then implemented the appropriate alternatives thus taking actions that influenced the likelihood of project success. The team was not a victim of its environment. Instead, it was a shaper of its environment.

Funded R/O actions such as this yield lower project cost and thus generate more profit or additional project financial reserves. Assume the software project described above was originally bid at a contract target price of $10 million including $1 million of fee and $9 million of project cost, often called the contract budget baseline because it is the baseline against which project cost performance is measured (see Table 8.4). The initial project plan shown in the middle column included an assumed project management financial reserve of $0.5 million, leaving a budget at completion of $8.5 million. The initial plan also included an R/O analysis that estimated the sum of the net risks and net opportunities to be $0.8 million. Thus, the most probable estimate at completion for this project was $9.3 million indicating the team anticipated spending the entire budget plus incurring the net R/O offset by the management reserve.

Several weeks after the project got under way the team identified and implemented an action plan for the IV&V risk as well as a couple of other risks and one of the identified opportunities. Their total actions resulted in the status described by the right column in Table 8.4. The contract target price remained the same; the customer was not asked to spend more money. The fee/profit remained the same; the project team organization was not asked to spend more money. The contract budget baseline remained the same; the overall project yardstick was unchanged. The actions the team elected to employ did cost $0.1 million, an amount taken from the project management reserve. However, those funded actions resulted in an overall improvement of the R/O probabilities and impacts, reducing the net risk from $0.8 million to $0.2 million. So, an expenditure of $0.1 million

Table 8.4   Funded Actions Equal More Dollars

	Before action	After action
Contract target price	$10.0M	$10.0M
Fee/profit	$1.0M	$1.0M
Contract budget baseline	$9.0M	$9.0M
Management reserve	$0.5M	$0.4M
Budget at completion	$8.5M	$8.6M
Net risk/opportunity	$0.8M	$0.2M
Estimate at completion	$9.3M	$8.8M

created an estimated overall project improvement of $0.5 million.

This approach to funding R/O influencing actions works whether or not the project has an initial management reserve. It can even be used to create reserves. Every project should have a baseline plan and an assessment of the uncertainty surrounding that plan. Perhaps the project described above was bid at $9 million plus $ 1 million of fee. Perhaps the project team believed the actual cost, considering known R/Os, would be $ 9.5 million, or a $ 0.5 million overrun. Every action the team takes to improve the likelihood or impact of a R/O improves the project EAC, which is offset by the cost of the actions taken. Smart actions should reduce the project R/O, and thus the project EAC, significantly more than the cost of the actions. If not, the actions would be imprudent. Thus, teams that continually monitor and attack R/Os improve their projects odds of success, generate lower EACs, and free up dollars that can be used to take additional prudent risk reduction and opportunity enhancement actions. It is a virtuous cycle of improvement in the likelihood of project success.

RESERVES EMPOWER ACTION TAKING

Project reserves empower teams while also making them more accountable for project success. As discussed in Chapter 6, reserves allow project teams to cope with the inevitable uncertainty and ignorance that is so pervasive in their environment. Reserves, be they financial, schedule, resource, or technical, also encourage and enable teams to take risk-mitigating and opportunity-enhancing actions.

A team working to design and install a new system for tracking assets as they move through a distribution center has a tight budget and an aggressive schedule. The team members are enthusiastic about the project. They have a partially integrated plan for accomplishing the identified work scope, a plan with no reserves to deal with any surprises. They have identified several project risks and one or two opportunities that combine to yield a probable overrun of about 20 percent, but the project is just getting started and the team is optimistic that they will be able to overcome any challenges that come their way.

One project risk involves a concern that the interfaces between the various subsystems may not work as described in the documentation. Some of the interfaces have been modified in the past and the documentation has not always been updated carefully. A few interfaces have never been adequately documented, so the team has relied on engineers and operators to describe how those interfaces operate. The team members know this risk is present and they have described the potential impact in their risk assessment, suggesting the cost could be as high as $200,000 and the schedule delay as long as six months, depending on when the potential problems become real.

The team has begun discussing what it might do to mitigate this risk, but it has not yet decided on a viable plan. Someone learns that a senior engineer not presently assigned to the project has a great deal of experience working on the various interfaces, and she is currently idle while waiting for another project to get under way. The team thinks it would be a good idea to bring her on board for a few weeks to review the interface documentation, test the interfaces it is most worried about, and propose design solutions. She could quickly turn uncertainties into facts, whether good or bad. This would be the most efficient way to find the problems and to design workarounds. But bringing the engineer into the project will cost money the team does not have and will cause a two-week critical path schedule delay while the analysis is conducted.

The project manager decides that the team cannot afford the cost or schedule impact. The project started with a very aggressive budget and schedule. There is no project financial management reserve and no schedule reserve. In fact, the team is already behind schedule and leadership has been complaining about the 20 percent cost risk estimate that was not covered in the budget. The project manager decides to hope that the interface problems will not be so difficult to overcome because dealing with the problem now will create additional conflict with management and make the project be further overrun and behind schedule. When comparing the immediate and real consequences of dealing with the risk versus the uncertain and future consequences of not dealing with it, the project manager chose defer his pain. Notice also that he chose to defer project learning, a project sin that often has catastrophic consequences.

The lack of project reserves has discouraged the project manager from taking action to reduce the likelihood and impact of a known risk. The project manager has embraced the fatalistic view that the fates may be kind or unkind to his project rather than embracing the view that his team can and should take prudent actions to influence their future. He has embraced this fatalistic view because he does not think he has the resources to do otherwise.

When organizations insist that teams establish and maintain appropriate project reserves, they enable those teams to take action because the resources are available. They also foster team creativity and innovation because teams believe they have the flexibility to act on what they come up with. They reinforce team empowerment and thereby reinforce team accountability for project success. Teams that have no discretionary resources often do not feel accountable for project success or failure but teams with such resources and the authority to use them typically embrace that accountability for project success, seeing it as an opportunity to demonstrate their competence.

CULTURE ENABLES TEAM ACTION TAKING

The discussion has so far focused on R/O management and project reserves, two specific disciplines or techniques that enable teams to take action to influence project outcomes. Tools, techniques, and disciplines are more useful when they exist within a culture that appreciates and supports their effective use. As described in Chapter 1, project work activity is different in several important ways than process or task work activity, and those differences suggest the need for particular cultural attributes including a much stronger than typical emphasis on empowering project teams to act independently, a focus on problem solving and shared learning, supportive systems, and timely resource decision making.

The very nature of the project team structure points toward an organizational focus on empowerment. Teams are created to bring together expertise from various functional line and staff groups to focus on a unique work activity that crosses many organizational boundaries. The project manager must be empowered to work across those boundaries in order to accomplish the project vision and goals. Empowerment implies several things. First, it implies that project managers are accountable for project success. They bear the burden of leading the team through many foreseeable and unforeseeable challenges. Second, empowerment implies trust. Project managers must be trusted to determine what must be done, to set priorities, to build consensus, to lead their team, and to make the tough decisions that enable project success. Third, empowerment also implies tolerance for mistakes. Project management is risky business. Success is far from assured. Critical decisions must often be made with scant information. Project managers must know that they will not be sacrificed at the first sign of a bad outcome.

The organization must foster a project team culture that values problem solving and shared learning rather than self-protection and blaming. First, it must reward sharing and knowledge-transfer efforts, not just results. Significant results may not occur for a while. It is important to reward efforts and to celebrate even the small gains. Learning and knowledge-sharing efforts can be rewarded in several ways. Improvement in team and individual behavior can be publically recognized. Teams can meet frequently with senior leadership, giving them opportunities to interact. Leaders can describe the projects as learning and exploration experiences, reminding people that the failed projects may be more valuable learning experiences than a successful project. Second, the organization can celebrate signs of improvement by hosting luncheons for individuals and teams that demonstrate the appropriate behaviors. Such recognitions communicate to others what behaviors will be rewarded, what the organization values. They also serve as a way to spread knowledge to other groups where it might prove useful or insightful.

The organization must implement, maintain, and improve support systems and infrastructure. An organization that elects to deploy an EVMS capability must appreciate the underlying needs that will determine whether the system will be effective or will merely be another hurdle that project teams must find a way to scramble over while trying to find project success. The organization must implement the people, process, and tools changes as a whole rather than just install a tool hoping it will somehow magically change behaviors and existing process demands. Organizations must also acknowledge the importance of flexible systems and processes that can be adapted to accommodate the unique demands of each project. Organizations that are proficient at quickly finding and implementing the right balance of process or system discipline and rigor versus process or system tailoring for each project are much more likely to find project success than those who are not as proficient.

Project-based organizations must be timely and effective decision makers. The project environment is awash in change and learning. Nearly every day every project team makes discoveries and finds itself coping with change that demands a reevaluation of resource allocation and priority decisions within the projects and between projects that are trying to use shared resources. Organizations that are quick to acknowledge, process, and share their learning can make faster and better decisions. Organizations that allow information to flow as needed rather than be constrained by functional boundaries or hierarchy can make faster and better decisions. Organizations that understand the condition of their resources, anticipate future resource conflicts, then work diligently to have the appropriate resources available have less difficult decisions to resolve and thereby less often cause otherwise avoidable project trauma.

So far the focus has been on organizational culture influence on the action-taking habit rather than project team culture. The project manager sets the tone for the team's action-taking perspective. The project manager must role model an action-taking attitude and disciplined behavior, the habits described here being good examples of such behavior. The team behaves in a fatalistic way when the project manager does so and it behaves in a proactive influencing way when the project manager does so. Certainly, the project manager's challenge is lessened when the organizational culture is reinforcing, but project managers must hold themselves and their teams accountable for an action-taking bias whether or not the broader organization enables them.

Large, complex projects can develop their own unique culture, sometimes purposely behaving in a manner that contradicts the broader organizational culture. The difference can become a point of pride for the team. The project managers on these large projects must pay even more attention to the project culture fostering an environment wherein key leaders and decision-makers feel empowered and accountable for success. Doing so can be less challenging when the broader organizational culture is appropriate but successful project managers find a way to foster such a culture even when the broader organizations is not supportive.

SUMMARY

Teams that have an action-taking bias tend to succeed more often than teams that feel they are victims of their environment. A robust R/O management discipline helps teams become more aware of the alternative futures before them and helps them uncover the information and perspectives that enable them to influence which of those alternative futures will come to pass. That awareness and insight facilitates an action-taking orientation. Adequate project reserves also encourage an action-taking bias because they make action taking a viable alternative within the team's control. They no longer have an alibi for inaction. When project teams operate in an environment with a supportive culture where these disciplines are practiced effectively, they tend to find success because the take action to shape their future.

CHAPTER 9

HABIT # 8— CONTINUALLY COMMUNICATE

"The single biggest problem in communication is the illusion that it has taken place."

—George Bernard Shaw

Effective communication either enables or debilitates all the other habits. One must be able to communicate effectively if he or she hopes to have project success.

At the risk of belaboring the point, I'll repeat that project teams are learning entities. The primary standard of project efficiency is how fast it learns what it does not know and then adapts to that new learning. Teams that learn early have a much better chance of success than do teams that learn late. Learning is accomplished through communication. It occurs quicker and is applied faster when communications paths are open, wide, and free flowing.

This chapter looks at three broad topics. First, it summarizes challenges of effective human communication, reminding us that effective communication demands discipline and attention. Second, it sets the stage for a discussion about the unique challenges of communicating in the project management arena, addressing the tools and techniques that can make that communication more effective. Third, it focuses on the communications challenges that arise with geographically dispersed project teams, a rapidly growing trend.

COMMUNICATION IS CHALLENGING

Communication is more than just an exchange of facts, data, and information. We also communicate in order to relate events, letting others know what transpired so they can apply that learning or help us interpret the meaning of the events. We also communicate in order to clarify meaning, helping others understand what message is being delivered. We share our experiences and our perspectives, hoping to be better understood and to better understand others. We share our emotions and our aspirations, hoping to gain sympathy and support.

The process of communication is often described as a bidirectional effort in which the sender and receiver interact to assure full comprehension of the message. However, in practice some of these activities are largely unidirectional. Project teams communicate unidirectionally all the time. The test team may transmit its test results to the customer via a formal report or a casual e-mail. The project manager may receive a proposed budget from a work activity leader. In both instances information is transmitted (communicated), but there is not always a reciprocal communication back to the source. Project teams also communicate bidirectionally, or interactively. The test team that has reported its test results to the customer may then participate in a conference (bidirectional communication) with the customer to discuss those results. The project manager may receive a proposed budget from a work activity leader, and then meet

with the leader to talk about the key assumptions and conditions surrounding the proposed budget. Both instances
involve an the communication of information and ideas in
an effort to arrive at shared interpretation. Interactive or
bilateral communication is more challenging and complex
but much more potent and thus more important.

The communication process includes several inter-
locking components (see Figure 9.1). The process is successful when it accurately and completely communicates a
message from the mind of the sender to the mind of the
receiver, avoiding distortion that may arise from any component or interface. Notice that the communication process as depicted does not concern itself with the form or
content of the message, assuming that the message is clear
and has been accurately and fully captured and placed in
the relevant context.

Also notice that the process is inherently "noisy," and
noise can distort a message as it moves through the various components. The message itself may be noisy. That is,
it may be vague, out of context, or contradictory making
it difficult for either the sender or the receiver to understand. The sender may garble a message, even one that
is clear and in its relevant context, just as a receiver may
garble a message that has been accurately received.

Figure 9. 1   The Communications Process

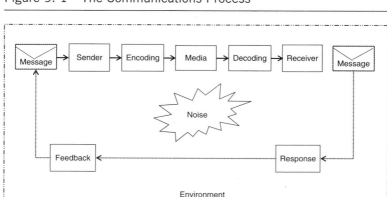

For example, we humans often interpret differently what are called "words of estimative probability," a phrase coined by Sherman Kent, an early contributor to the formal discipline of intelligence analysis. Analysts often find themselves dealing with people whom Kent described as "poets" or "mathematicians"; that is, with people who naturally gravitate to word and phrase probability statements like "almost certain" or "probably not" (poets) and those who prefer numerical probability statements like "30 percent give or take about 5 percent" (mathematicians). Kent developed a table of the relationship between the two perspectives to help analysts effectively communicate the same message to both constituencies (see Table 9.1).[1] Kent's approach was not adopted, but it continues to be used to illustrate the dilemma. Physicians face a similar challenge when explaining medical risks to patients before asking them to sign informed consent forms. Some patients are more comfortable with "poetic" terms while others prefer concrete "mathematical" terms, and doctors need to be able to communicate the same level of risk to both kinds of patients. Guidelines often provide quantifying associations, for example considering that the statement "frequent occurrence for patients" is equivalent to "will occur in 10 percent to 50 percent of patients" or that the statement "rarely occurs" is equivalent to "will occur in less than 1 percent of cases."

Table 9.1   Kent's Words of Estimative Probability

Word/Phrase	Probability	Range of probability
Certain	100%	± 0%
Almost certain	93%	± 6%
Probable	75%	± 12%
Chances about even	50%	± 10%
Probably not	30%	± 10%
Almost certainly not	7%	± 5%
Impossible	0	± 0%

Source: Central Intelligence Agency (2002). Kent and the Profession of Intelligence Analysis, Center for the Study of Intelligence. November, 2002.

These attempts at equivalency address a real concern, but they often fail to solve the problem. Numerous studies have shown that individual human interpretations of word/phrase statements of probability differ widely; similarly, some people have a poor understanding of the correct meaning of mathematical statements of probability (see Table 9.2). One of two engineers or managers who have worked together for months may quantify the phrase "we doubt" as being equivalent to a 10 percent likelihood; whereas the other may interpret it as being equivalent to 60 percent. No wonder miscommunication is so rampant. Individuals may have a conversation, nod in agreement, then go their separate ways, each having an entirely different idea about what was agreed or understood during the conversation. Successful communication is difficult.

Table 9.2   What Does That Mean?

Statement	10%	20%	30%	40%	50%	60%	70%	80%	90%	100%
Almost certainly										
Highly likely										
Very good chance										
Likely										
Probable										
We believe										
Better than even										
We doubt										
Improbable										
Unlikely										
Probably not										
Little chance										
Almost chance										
Highly unlikely										
Chances are slight										

Finally, note that the communications process always operates within a particular environment that influences whether the process is appreciated, how effectively it can operate, for whom it operates effectively, and inevitably generates additional noise that can skew the message. Certainly, the project management environment exerts its influence on the communication process, as does the organizational and industry environment in which the project operates.

Communication is more than what we say. It is not what we say but the way we "speak" with our voice, eyes, face, and body that counts (see Figure 9.2). Our body language transmits more than half of what the other party "hears" when we interact face-to-face. Professional poker players often say that they do not play the cards as much as they "play" their opponent, interpreting the opponent's body language for indications that he has a powerful hand or is bluffing. In conversational settings, a person who has been listening intently but then begins playing with his ear lobe or scratching his chin has likely stopped believing what is being said and is distracted. Each of us knows there are times when it is wise to avoid our significant other even though not a word has been spoken. Our facial expressions are very telling. Some of us are stoic and expressionless while others have dynamic facial expressions, communicating a great deal about how we feel about a topic, our sincerity, our enthusiasm, or our sympathy. Some of us should never play poker. In some cultures direct eye contact is a sign of truthfulness

Figure 9.2   How We Communicate

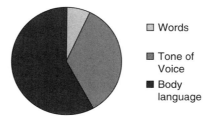

- Words
- Tone of Voice
- Body language

or interest in what is being said. Tone of voice is also a powerful means of communication. We all know how difficult it is to stay attentive to someone who is speaking in a monotone, or whose voice has an exceptionally high pitch, or who seems to lack enthusiasm for the subject. We also appreciate how someone's positive or appealing tone of voice can draw us in, making everything that person says seem credible. Only about 7 percent of what we communicate is passed along through the words we choose.

Broadcasting is not communicating. Yet, we continually constrain our communication bandwidth when we choose to deliver a message. In our rush to transmit a message we often substitute broadcasting for communicating; that is, we send an e-mail message assuming the intended receivers will take the time to read it and will understand it. Or, we distribute a training package instead of conducting a live training event because it is cheaper, quicker, and less difficult. We tell ourselves that people will be able to learn what we want them to learn by reviewing the material on their own, even though we know better. Successful organizations and leaders understand that when we eliminate over 90 percent of the communication process bandwidth—body language and tone of voice—we also severely compromise our ability to convey the message correctly.

We often send conflicting messages. Our communications are influenced by what we say or write; by how clearly we deliver our message. They are also influenced by what we do. Our actions communicate whether our stated message is credible. For example, a project manager may clearly communicate a desire for open and frank discussion without retribution, but one instance of shutting down such discussion will belie that message. Project managers must remember that they are communicating through not only what they say but what they do, what they pay attention to or neglect, and what they reward or punish.

PROJECT COMMUNICATION IS UNIQUELY CHALLENGING

Time and time again in post-project assessments, project teams list communication as one of the areas most in need of improvement. On troubled projects, project team members often feel that if the communication had been better, the project would have run smoother. Communication is often more difficult because of the challenges unique to project management.

Project teams are ad hoc formations, assembled from individuals working in various disciplines and perhaps working on multiple teams, meaning that communications systems need to be established from scratch. Projects often include cross-functional or interorganizational teams. Project teams may not reside in the same geographic location. They are embedded in existing communications networks established by their functional groups. Managers must establish new networks and adapt existing networks to coordinate their project's activity. Each communication system must be unique because its aggregation of people is unique, as are all project visions, requirements, plans, and environments.

Another challenge is that the stakeholder community of customers, subcontractors, functional departments, and so on, forms uniquely around each project. As we saw in Chapter 2, some projects have internal-to-the-organization customers, and others have external customers. Some require heavy involvement from the engineering department; and others, less. On some projects it is necessary to interface with a wide array of potential product end users, who may all consider themselves legitimate stakeholders; others may have only one potential user/stakeholder. The project manager must determine the makeup and the unique communications needs of the stakeholder community.

Some projects are composed of a small, intimate team that has worked together on other projects, making the challenge of assembling a tailored project communication system relatively straightforward. On the other hand, some complex projects bring together large numbers of people working with each other for the first time, creating an entirely different set of demands for the communications system.

Additionally, projects are increasingly international, "Virtual" teams are being assembled with members located at sites around the world, using different systems and tools, operating in different organizational cultures, and coming from different social cultures. This ever more important topic is further addressed later.

Finally, the fact that project team efficiency is all about flexibility and rapid learning creates a unique demand on the communications system because teams do not know ahead of time what information and messages are apt to be important and which are trivial. The project communication system must facilitate the free flow of a great deal of information to many constituents in order to increase the likelihood that sudden insights or revelations will occur, sparking new learning and rapid adaptation of that learning across the project. The result is a lot of information flow, most of which each individual cares little about. What one person deems important may to be buried in a sea of the seemingly unimportant, which in fact is very important to team members. Thus, the project communication system must both facilitate the flow of a large amount of traffic and at the same time facilitate the highlighting of specific parts of the traffic.

Project teams typically communicate with four groups of stakeholders, each of which may be a quite complex subgroup, consisting of multiple constituents with their own agendas, cultures, and demands. Teams must communicate with their own organizational leadership who has expectations of the team, who wants to be kept informed about progress, and who controls resources the team needs to succeed. Teams must also communicate with the functional groups within the organization, groups whom they rely on to provide staff and facilities, to buy materials, or to provide technical processes and tools. Teams may also need to communicate with external suppliers whom they rely on to provide critical subsystems, components, or technical expertise. Finally, teams may have an external customer who has expectations of the team and who wants to be kept informed about progress.

Teams must also establish and nurture a healthy internal communication system that enables them to share plans, performance progress, new learning, changes, and so on, quickly and accurately. Project managers must select and deploy the appropriate information and communication technologies, but they must also work equally hard to establish and nurture the appropriate learning and collaborative culture that will value and use the technology.

Figure 9.3   Project Communications Paths

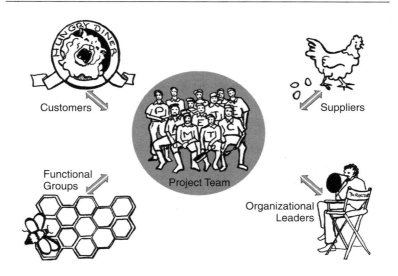

Project managers must keep in mind that their communications systems, whether internal or external, must flow in two directions because it is just as important to receive important information and messages as it is to send them. For example, the project team must send customers information about project status and outlook, risks and opportunities, potential and real scope changes, needs and expectations, and a host of other topics. The team must also be able to learn about potential changes coming from the customer community, about risks and opportunities that may impact the project, about how much progress the customer has made toward its commitments to the project team, about the customer's satisfaction with and confidence in the project team, and a host of other topics (see Figure 9.4).

The project communications system is both formal and informal. The formal components include plans, monitoring and controls, reports, design documents, status reviews, tollgate reviews, surveys, and a host of other mechanisms. The informal components include personal relationships, making oneself available for ad hoc discussions, sensing sessions, liasons, and so on. Even the rumor

Figure 9.4   Customer Communications

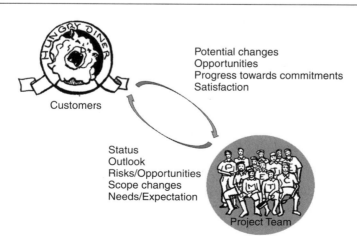

Potential changes
Opportunities
Progress towards commitments
Satisfaction

Customers

Status
Outlook
Risks/Opportunities
Scope changes
Needs/Expectation

Project Team

mill has a distinct informational value. Certainly, rumors may be true or false but those that thrive and spread rapidly and widely often accurately reflect what people either fear or wish for; otherwise, they would not bother to repeat them so actively. Rumors tell leaders what their teams care about, and that insight can be invaluable.

VIRTUAL TEAMS ADD ADDITIONAL CHALLENGES

A virtual project team consists of independent individuals or groups of people working toward a common goal while separated by geographic distance and time zones. The members of the team rely heavily on information and communication technologies to compensate for the separation. The benefits are significant. Organizations can bring together specialists, experience, and capabilities from around the world to attack complex challenges.

Virtual teams may be large and extremely complex. The International Space Station (ISS) project involved team members from five different space agencies including the National Aeronautics and Space Administration, the European Space Agency, the Russian Federal Space Agency, the Japan Aerospace Exploration Agency, and the Canadian Space Agency. The $150 billion-plus project involved hundreds of organizations and firms as well as tens of thousands of individuals located around the globe, and above it, for that matter.

Virtual teams are often small with a relatively straightforward purpose, yet still present real communications challenges. Trane established a virtual team to design a next-generation commercial air-handling system with about 30 participants located in Kentucky, Wisconsin, and the Czech Republic.

The ISS project team faces many far greater challenges than does the Trane project team. Yet, the two virtual project teams share some very similar challenges in principle.

All virtual teams, no matter their size or scope, share similar challenges. They must overcome geographic dispersion, time zones, organizational and national cultures, work practices, and technology differences to name only a few. Field engineers often talk about the "geographic transformer." They comment that the mere separation from the home office causes a level of anxiety, distrust, and misunderstanding that garbles communication, distorting even simple and innocuous messages. Time zones differences mean that individuals have to disrupt their daily schedules to communicate with far-flung team members whom they do not know. Conversations may take place before or after the work day, during when family members are present and directly express their unhappiness with the arrangement. Cultural differences, whether organizational or national, cause confusion and misunderstanding. In the U.S. "yes" typically means "I agree" while in Japan "yes" means "I understand." It does not indicate agreement. This one difference continually confuses communications between members of virtual project teams. Organizational work practices may differ widely within the same firm. A business site that does a lot of development work may have a robust system for collecting and reporting work activity costs; another site that is primarily a manufacturing operation may have no such systems. Project team members at the first site may be unable to understand why their counterparts at the other site are unable or unwilling to provide requested information. That lack of appreciation for inherently different operational practices breeds misunderstanding, distrust, and poor communications within the team.

Line Duby and Daniel Robey,[2] who teach at HEC-Montreal, one of Canada's leading business schools, describe five paradoxes faced by virtual teams that complicate how they communicate internally and with the external stakeholder community, and offer strategies for coping with those paradoxes.

Paradox # 1—Virtual teams, although geographically dispersed, require the physical presence of other members. Time and again team members indicate that topics that should in theory have been adequately addressed over the phone or via videoconference became confused and led to conflicts, but were typically resolved once people were able to meet face-to-face. The nonverbal cues may tell us whether someone understands us or is confused, whether they agree with our position or have merely stopped trying to dissuade us, and whether they know more than they are sharing. Additionally, physical presence allows team members to develop a personal social bond, leading to a level of trust that fosters more open communication.

Virtual teams are established to connect disparate resources and capabilities around a specific project, but they are also often promoted as a way to avoid travel and relocation costs. Thus the paradox: teams need face time in order to develop the trust and understanding that opens up and strengthens the communications channels that make it possible for them to function when they are not together.

The manager of a virtual project team must constantly balance the amount of face-to-face time necessary to address problems efficiently and to keep communications healthy. More face-to-face time is needed early when teams are forming and developing relationships. Later, those trusting relationships and successful problem-solving experiences may enable the teams to rely more on indirect communication techniques. For example, people may initially come to expect a quarterly face-to-face meeting and so manage how they bring up and address issues accordingly. Problem solving may be disrupted and anxieties may be raised if the quarterly meeting is cancelled. Later, when trust has been established this anxiety may lesson and indirect communications may be sufficient.

Paradox # 2—Structure enables flexibility. Virtual teams often add and drop staff as needed to address new challenges or to adapt to changes but that flexibility can quickly deteriorate into chaos. The various organizations and their shifting agendas can also cause confusion and disruption. Hence the paradox: structured communications systems and channels can bring a level of stability that helps the team remain flexible rather than chaotic.

As described in earlier chapters, project managers need to continually monitor the processes within and without the project to assure they remain in control yet flexible enough to accommodate real project needs. Thus clear and detailed plans that can be readily adapted to new requirements keep the project team stable and foster healthy communications.

Paradox # 3—Interdependent work is accomplished by independent actions. Virtual teams often strive to break work activity into independent pieces in an effort to reduce task interdependencies, in part because they fear or distrust the complex communications challenges that arise when the work is tightly interdependent across locations. Hence the paradox: teams established to foster interconnectivity and interdependence strive to avoid it.

Project managers must design their project work activity boundaries with this paradox in mind. The manager must ensure that the necessary and strategically valuable interdependencies remain in tact, taking special care that the communications paths are supportive: more face-to-face meetings, more collaborative work sessions, more temporary transfers of key talent back and forth among the distant work teams, and so on. On the other hand, project managers should identify work activities that can be conducted relatively independently of other remote groups and allow that, avoiding the burden of unnecessary communications challenges. Above all, project managers must else establish a collaborative culture through their selection of staff, the behaviors they reinforce, the priorities they set, and a determined effort to encourage inputs from the disparate parties.

Paradox # 4—Virtual work activity is accomplished through social interaction. Virtual teams strive to compartmentalize their work activities to minimize the difficulties and complications of long-distance collaboration. Yet, it is the very interaction they seek to avoid that can make project success possible; hence the paradox that virtual work relies so heavily on social interaction. Project managers must make it clear that work activity leaders are responsible for developing and maintaining healthy social connections.

Paradox # 5—Trust is built by overcoming distrust. The members of virtual teams may begin with a great distrust of one another, especially if they have not worked together successfully in the recent past. Trustworthiness is judged by performance. Those who perform well early in the project earn the trust of others while those who do not perform well or cause hardship confirm the initial distrust. Thus the paradox that trust is built on a foundation of mistrust.

Project managers must recognize and accept this typical phenomenon of virtual teams. Managers must create early opportunities for work groups to demonstrate to one another their competence, that they can be depended upon to perform, and that they are willing to collaborate. They must also monitor these early activities very closely to assure success because failures, even failures caused by forces beyond the work group's control, will reinforce the initial distrust and thereby handicap the project for the foreseeable future.

PROJECT COMMUNICATION PLAN

PMPs, described in Chapter 4, should include a communication-plan section describing the project's communications strategy, policy, and systems. A strong plan describes how the project will establish effective and efficient communications with project stakeholders, explaining what communications channels will be used and how they will be controlled to ensure they remain effective. A good communication plan generally includes four elements: communication objectives, target audiences, key content for the communications, and communication method and frequency.

The project manager and the project leadership team are responsible for developing a tailored communications strategy and plan. Just as no two projects are identical, no two communications plans are identical. Project managers can use the following topics to develop a plan most appropriate for their objectives, their stakeholders, and their environment.

What are the communications objectives?—The team should review the project vision and goals as a reminder of what it is trying to accomplish and why it is important. That review sets the stage for a discussion about what it hopes to achieve with the communication activity.

Who is the target audience and who are the target sources?—With whom does the team want to communicate? Remember that the communication should address not only to whom it wants to send messages, but also from whom it wants to receive messages. Consider internal and external stakeholders.

What is to be communicated?—Determine what messages the team wants to deliver to each stakeholder. The team may want to influence stakeholders by giving them information that will shift their position on some topics. Determine what they may want to know. Stakeholders may have information curiosity or needs that do not seem especially relevant to the project team, but satisfying the customer's itch may be worthwhile. Determine what you want to learn from them. Remember that communication involves receiving of information as much as it does the transmission of information.

What are the key messages?—Determine the key themes. For example, one key theme of every project is the continual communication of the project vision to all stakeholders and the continual testing of stakeholder buy-in to that vision. Another key theme may be to openly share the team's progress in dealing with a specific major project risk or opportunity that could dramatically change the project outlook.

How frequently will communication occur?—Determine how often the communication should happen based on the need for current information and the cost or complexity of accomplishing the communication.

What communication channels are available or must be developed?—Consider whether to rely on only one communication path or to use multiple paths in order to triangulate critical communications. Consider how the stakeholder prefers to receive information.

Who is responsible for the communication?—Who will be responsible for making sure that the communication occurs, for validating the communication, and for adapting the communication approach as the project evolves?

How will the communications effort be monitored and adapted?—What metrics or figures of merit will be used to ensure that communications are effective? How often will the communications plan be evaluated?

SUMMARY

It is not possible to overstate the importance of open, robust, and honest communication within a project team and between the team and its external stakeholders. Team members assert time and again that their difficulties involve either the lack of communication or miscommunication. Yet, no one ever suggests that failure or even difficulty was caused by too much communication. Teams should strive to overcommunicate because the risk of failure in that direction is nil while the risk in the other direction is pervasive and serious. Today's project teams are more and more frequently virtual teams spread across geography, time, and cultures. Hence, communication takes on an even more important role while at the same time it is dramatically more difficult to accomplish.

Project managers should spend time during the initial planning stages to develop a communications system tailored for their unique project and its environment. They should use the Communications Plan as a tool for capturing that plan and for communicating it to the appropriate parties. They should include in the project monitoring system a means to test the effectiveness of the communication plan. They should frequently review and adapt the plan as the project evolves and its communications needs change. The should keep in mind that in the heat of battle there is always a great temptation to broadcast rather than communicate because it is quicker and easier—it is rarely effective however.

Effective communication is a difficult and challenging endeavor in any arena. It is both more important and more difficult in the project management arena. Managers who take the challenge lightly do so at their own peril.

EPILOGUE

Being a project manager is much like being a bronco rider at the rodeo. Some days you draw the wrong horse, one that has decided he will not be ridden, and on that day you will eat dirt. Other days you draw a horse that does not feel particularly spirited, one that just wants to get the ride over with and return to the stable. On that day you will score poorly because you are denied an opportunity to demonstrate your skill. Some days you draw a spirited and feisty horse that challenges your skills, but your skills prevail. On those days you look great up there. On those days you score well because you are able to demonstrate your full range of skill and expertise. Projects are like those rodeo horses, some more challenging than others. Project managers are like broncobusters, some more skilled than others. The trick is for the project manager to be paired with a horse that challenges but does not overwhelm his or her skill level. Even so, on some days some horses just won't be ridden by anyone.

Organizations must foster a culture that understands the challenges of projects. They must become skilled at recognizing horses that will not be ridden and acknowledging that fact. They must develop organizational skills, processes, and disciplines that enable rather than inhibit project success, and then establish a culture that appreciates the learning nature of project work and uses the organizational resources appropriately. Organizations must also develop individual project managers' skills and practices that enable them to ride progressively more ornery horses. They must shape their environment making project success more likely rather than becoming a victim of recurring poor project performance.

Project managers must develop their own skills to manage progressively more challenging projects and to survive, perhaps even thrive, when the organizational and stakeholder environments are less supportive than they might be. They must also recognize and embrace their responsibility for influencing the project environment as well as leading the project team, a daunting responsibility, but theirs nonetheless. Managers who continually develop their competence practicing the eight habits will more often find project success.

THINGS TO DO NOW!

Project managers can take actions now to help their project succeed. The following paragraphs offer one significant step that a project manager can take now to start down that road.

Habit # 1—Foster and nurture a shared project vision

Articulate a project vision and share it widely. A stakeholder community that has already embraced a vision will benefit from the reminder and from the reassurance that the project manager and team have embraced that vision. A stakeholder community that has no consensus vision will perhaps be able to come together around the project manager's vision thus making project success more likely. Finally, the project team members will benefit from the clarity of a single vision to guide their internal efforts even if the stakeholder community remains divided.

Habit # 2—Translate the project vision into coherent requirements

Review project requirements and specifications to find and close TBDs. Closing open requirements and specifications as soon as possible reduces project risk and improves project productivity. Teams should develop a plan for driving to closure any that cannot immediately be resolved. Delay is a nasty enemy of project success. The review will also cause the team to revisit many of the requirements, and in the process it may uncover lingering confusion or misunderstanding that can be cleared up, thereby avoiding future problems.

Habit # 3—Build an integrated plan for accomplishing the vision

Expose the disconnects in your current plans. Most project plans were never integrated, meaning the budget, schedule, and work scope were defined independently of one another. The plans that were initially integrated often come apart as the project unfolds. Teams often know these disconnects are present but have been conditioned to keep quiet about them. The project manager can bring these disconnects into the light so that the project team can begin to address how to move toward reintegration. Hopefully, the organizational leadership and stakeholders will embrace a frank discussion of the disconnects and how to resolve them. If not, at least the team can adjusts its actions to move closer to an integrated plan.

Habit # 4—Continually monitor performance against the plan

Identify the ten most important project activities and validate they are being monitored appropriately. Project metrics are often the result of a collision between organizational convention and external stakeholder demand. The result may not address some of the areas most important to achieving project success. Building a comprehensive project monitoring system takes time. But, project managers can begin now by taking action to assure the team is tracking the most important activities. That work will lay a foundation for further improvement later.

Habit # 5—Acknowledge and accommodate both uncertainty and ignorance

Foster dialogue about accuracy and underlying assumptions rather than precision and method. People get wrapped up in the mechanics of how information is generated, massaged, and formatted. They become slaves to the process, forgetting what they are trying to learn and how confident they should be about the information. Project managers can begin today by asking questions about critical assumptions and confidence factors, by acknowledging openly the range of uncertainty and ignorance.

Habit # 6—Embrace but control change

Insist that the project team work to the baseline plan. Change tends to be identified and discussed when team members are forced to do only work that is within the approved baseline plan and thus being tracked by the monitoring system. It is much easier to track and control change once it is brought into the open. The change control system may initially be too slow and bureaucratic to accommodate all the change activity but the project manager can begin the second step of streamlining the change control process. The first step is to force change into the open, and insisting that people work only on what is in the plan is a quick and clear way to do so.

Habit # 7—Continually act to influence the future

Take action on identified risks and opportunities. Teams become much more proactive when they see the project manager is willing to allocate resources to influence the future rather than just to cope with what arises. It sends a signal that discussion about uncertainty and ignorance is okay, even welcomed. Being willing to act on opportunities as well as risks sends a signal that the project prospects are not all bad and that the team can have an impact on the outcome. Project managers need not initially have reserves in order to take action. A few dollars spent to reduce a significant risk or enhance a significant opportunity will improve the project EAC, no matter what the accounting system may indicate. Eventually those smart actions will pay off and will be recognized.

Habit # 8—Continually communicate

Talk less, listen more. The project manager job attracts and encourages type A personalities, people who want to provide direction and leadership. Projects need that. But, project managers also need to understand their external stakeholders and their team members who often possess a massive amount of knowledge that can influence project success, but who can also have attitudes and biases that enable or constrain project success. A project manager who listens more will learn more. A project manager who listens more will seek to strengthen and widen the incoming communication paths. People will feel they are being heard. In return they will be more open to listening to the messages from the project manager.

Project management is challenging work, very challenging. These eight habits are neither simple nor easy to practice, but they have time and again helped managers find success in the face of daunting project challenges. May you find them useful.

SAMPLE PROJECT VISION STATEMENTS

The GVSC Project will demonstrate to the satellite prime contractor community a fully functional computer chip set one year before the competitor does. We believe this will enable us to win the first two new satellite computer opportunities and secure for us a leadership position in the marketplace.

The ABD project will replace all currently identified obsolete parts through replacement parts selection and minimal redesign, all within the $5 million budget and within 18 months. Any newly identified obsolete parts replacements will be outside the scope of this project.

The LDB project will install and test a new fiber-optic local area network within the facility. Our first priority is to cause minimal interruption to users. Our second priority is to complete the work within six weeks and for a cost of less than $50,000.

The GX project intends to build a custom rotary mechanism that will operate on an earth-orbit satellite for ten years, allowing the National Oceanic and Atmospheric Administration to gather data for use in global weather prediction. This one-of-a-kind mechanism will be fully tested and delivered not later than 15 December 2013, for a target cost of $13 million.

The JFX project will redesign the current flight data recorder to reduce the weight by five pounds and lower the unit production cost by 20%. We will successfully complete testing on the redesigned box within 18 months and at a total cost of less than $3 million.

SAMPLE PROJECT REVIEW FORMAT

PROJECT REVIEW GUIDELINES

These project review guidelines are purposely written as guidelines rather than as a policy or procedure because it is recognized that every project is a unique activity with its own set of important topics, monitoring needs, and communications needs. The project manager is responsible for reviewing these guidelines then recommending to senior leadership a project review format most suitable for their particular project. The project manager is also responsible for recommending modifications as the project progress dictates.

Every project must present a monthly project review to (insert key organizational leader titles). The reviews will have a common, with mutually agreed flexibility, set of templates. Leaders can decide how best to spend their review time and on which projects or project elements to focus their discussion. However, a current complete monthly review "package" is required for each project.

The following elements must be addressed in every review package unless explicitly agreed by senior leadership (exceptions will be rare):

1. Project overview—a brief description of the project vision/goals, customer, contract structure, etc.
2. Highlights/Lowlights since last review—a brief summary of key events, learning, etc. since the last review.
3. Top Level schedule and status—a summary schedule identifying current status and critical path.
4. Key Customer Issues—a brief summary of the current customer/external stakeholder concerns or issues.
5. Identification of significant scope changes and their implication—a summary of any identified or pending scope changes and the estimated impact of those changes to the overall project outcome.
6. Schedule and cost performance—a summary of the inception-to-date performance, current month performance, estimate at project completion performance, and explanation for variances to plan (typically EVMS data (CPI/SPI, CV/SV, EAC, etc.).
7. Key metrics—a review of the key project metrics as agreed in the approved project management plan.
8. Financial - varies for type of program; elements to be considered include "burn rate," estimate-to-completion, impact to financial plan (revenue, margin), and status of financial reserves.
9. Technical requirements—a summary of key technical requirements status/margin versus goal and any key technical issues.

10. Staffing status, plan and issues—a summary of current staffing versus agreed plan and highlight upcoming needs.
11. Risk and opportunity—a review of the current project risk/opportunity outlook.
12. Project review action log—a review of the log of open actions (organization, leadership, or project).

Additional elements may also be addressed as agreed by leadership and the project manager. Examples include but are not limited to:

1. Project background and/or platform background—a brief summary of the project history, how it fits in a larger project or mission scheme.
2. Key schedule topics—a summary of contract delivery schedules and status, critical supplier schedule, etc.
3. EVMS data—a summary of EVMS data when such data is required by customer or leadership (trend charts, monthly performance data, etc.).
4. Detailed staffing projections—a summary of staffing needs broken out by discipline, to report on significant up/down staff change progress, etc.
5. Product design requirements—a more extensive summary of requirements status, outlook, and margin. Typically required for technically challenging and complex projects.
6. Design-to-Production transition—a summary of status versus plans and current actions/issues.

7. Design-to-Target-Cost—a summary of status versus plans and current actions/issues.

8. Recovery initiatives—a summary of any special initiatives aimed at recovering project performance deterioration. Required as agreed by leadership and the project manager.

9. Other—other items appropriate to address program peculiarities.

The attached templates may be adapted or supplemented as appropriate to enhance the project review.

NOTES

PREFACE

1. Rosenau, Milton Jr. (2005). *Successful Project Management.* New York: John Wiley & Sons, Inc.
2. Cleland, David (1990). *Project Management: Strategic Design and Implementation.* New York: McGraw-Hill, Inc.
3. Mintzberg, H. (1979). *The Structuring of Organizations.* Englewood Cliffs, NJ: Prentice-Hall.

1 PROJECT MANAGEMENT

1. Economist Intelligence Unit (September 2009). "Closing the gap: The link between project management excellence and long-term success." PM Network, March 2010, Newton Square, PA.
2. The Standish Group, 1995. The Standish Group Report—Chaos. http://www.projectsmart.co.uk/docs/chaos-report .pdf, assessed 12/31/2010.
3. United States Department of Defense, 2011. Fiscal Year 2011 BudgetRequest,2011.http://comptroller.defense.gov/budget .html, assessed 12/20/2010.
4. Breakbulk Online http://www.breakbulk.com/breakbulk /construction-spending-estimates-revised-down-2010, assessed 12/20/2010.
5. McManus, John, and Wood-Harper, Trevor, 2008. "A study in project failure," The British Computer Society http:// www.bcs.org/server.php?show=ConWebDoc.19584, assessed 12/31/2010.
6. The Standish Group, 1995. The Standish Group Report: Chaos. http://www.projectsmart.co.uk/docs/chaos-report. pdf, assessed 12/31/2010

7. Eng, George J.P. (2007). A presentation titled cost/ schedule overrun in mega construction projects. www .docstoc.com/docs/4274029/CostSchedule-Overrun-in -Mega-Construction-Projects 12/27/2010

8. MercoPress, South Atlantic News Agency, "Global construction to outpace GDP growth in next 20 years with China and India leading". March 5, 2011.

9. Miller, Roger and Lessard, Donald R. (2000). *The Strategic Management of Large Engineering Projects.* Boston, MA: The MIT Press.

10. Rosenau, Milton D. Jr., and Githens, Gregory D. (2005). *Successful Project Management: A Step-by-Step Approach.* New York: John Wiley & Sons, Inc.

11. Mayne, Eric, 2009. "Ontario tops in production; Toyota's Georgetown plant most prolific in N.A.," , WardsAuto.com, assessed Dec. 23, 2009.

12. Gaddis, Paul. O., 1959. "The project manager," Harvard Business Review, May-June 1959

13. Stretton, Alan, 2007. "A short history of modern project management," second edition. PMI World Today, October 2007 (vol. IX, Issue X) http://www.pmforum.org/library /second-edition/2007/PDFs/Stretton-10-07.pdf, assessed 12/28/2010.

14. Morris, Peter W.G., 1994. *The Management of Projects.* London: Thomas Telford Services Ltd.

15. Drucker, P. (1985). *Innovation and Entrepreneurship.* New York: Harper & Row.

16. *A Guide to the Project Management Body of Knowledge: (PMBOK Guide),* fourth edition, 2008. Project Management Institute, Newton Square, PA.

17. *A Guide to the Project Management Body of Knowledge: (PMBOK Guide),* fourth edition, 2008. Project Management Institute, Newton Square, PA.

18. *A Guide to the Project Management Body of Knowledge: (PMBOK Guide),* fourth edition, 2008. Project Management Institute, Newton Square, PA.

19. Augustine, Norman R. (1997). *Augustine's Laws,* sixth edition. American Institute of Aeronautics and Astronautics, Inc.

20. *A Guide to the Project Management Body of Knowledge: (PMBOK Guide),* fourth edition, 2008. Project Management Institute, Newton Square, PA.

21. Drucker, Peter F. (1973). *Management: Tasks, Responsibilities, and Practices*. New York: Harper & Row.
22. Rosenau, Milton D. Jr., and Githens, Gregory D. (2005). *Successful Project Management: A Step-by-Step Approach*. New York: John Wiley & Sons, Inc.
23. *A Guide to the Project Management Body of Knowledge: (PMBOK Guide)*, fourth edition, 2008. Project Management Institute, Newton Square, PA.

2 HABIT # 1—FOSTER AND NURTURE A SHARED PROJECT VISION

1. Christenson, D & Walker, D. (2010) http://www.zulanas.lt /images/adm_source/docs/2_Christenson_paperENG.pdf
2. Senge, Peter M., (1990). *The Fifth Discipline: The Art and Practice of The Learning Organization*, New York: Doubleday.
3. Weick, K.E. (2001). *Making Sense of the Organization*, Oxford, England: Blackwell Publishers.
4. Miller, R. and D. R. Lessard (2000). *The Strategic Management of Large Engineering Projects*. Cambridge, MA: The MIT Press.
5. A gate is an electronic switch that allows or prevents the flow of current in a circuit. As a matter of perspective one might think of the design challenge as follows. Draw a vertical line from top to bottom on a blank 8 1/2" by 11" sheet of paper. Now try to draw 1,000 lines on the paper without any of the lines touching. Quite a challenge! Now draw those 1,000 lines in intertwined loops and turns, but still without touching one another. Nearly impossible! Now attempt to draw those 1,000 lines on the edge of the paper! That's more or less the challenge faced by the design teams in the 1980s. The challenge has grown more than a 100-fold since then.
6. Senge, Peter M., (1990). *The Fifth Discipline: The Art and Practice of The Learning Organization*, New York, Doubleday
7. Christenson, D. and Walker, D. (2004). Understanding the role of "vision" in project success, *Project Management Journal*, Vol. 35, No. 3, September, 2004, pp. 39–52.
8. Christenson, D & Walker, D. (2010) http://www.zulanas.lt /images/adm_source/docs/2_Christenson_paperENG.pdf
9. Briner, W., Hastings, C., and Geddes, M. (1996) *Project Leadership*, 2nd edition. Farnham, United Kingdom: Gower

3   HABIT # 2—TRANSLATE THE PROJECT VISION INTO COHERENT REQUIREMENTS

1. "History of Helicopters." Infoseek. Internet. 25 Dec. 1997. http://www.helis.com, assessed Jan. 12, 2011.
2. Edwards, Vernon (2002). "The True Story of the Wright Brothers'Contract(It'sNotWhatYouThink.)"WIFCON.COM http://www.wifcon.com/anal/analwright.htm, accessed Jan .5, 2011.
3. Edwards, Vernon (2002). "The True Story of the Wright Brothers'Contract(It'sNotWhatYouThink.)"WIFCON.COM http://www.wifcon.com/anal/analwright.htm.accesssed Jan. 5, 2011.
4. Forsberg, K., Mooz, H., Cotterman, H. (2005). *Visualizing Project Management*. Hoboken, NJ: John Wiley & Sons, Inc.
5. 3Back (2010). blog.3back.com, assessed June 9, 2010.
6. 3Back (2010). blog.3back.com, assessed June 9, 2010.

4   HABIT # 3—BUILD AN INTEGRATED PLAN FOR ACCOMPLISHING THE VISION

1. Rinkworks (2011). "Things People Said: Bad Predictions" http://www.rinkworks.com/said/predictions.shtml, assessed Jan. 14, 2011.
2. Schrage, Michael (1999). Speech about software acquisition and program management given at Computerworld, Feb. 8, 1999.

5   HABIT # 4—CONTINUALLY MONITOR PERFORMANCE AGAINST THE PLAN

1. Augustine, Norman R., (1997). Augustine's Laws. Reston, VA, American Institute of Aeronautics and Astronautics, Inc.
2. Drucker, Peter (1973). *Management: Tasks, Responsibilities, Practices.* New York: Harper & Row, Publishers.
3. Robbins, Stephen P. and Coulter, Mary (2009). *Management*, 10th edition. London: Pearson Prentice Hall.
4. Goleman, Daniel (1995). *Emotional Intelligence.* New York: Bantam Books.
5. Project Auditors LLC (2011). http://www.projectaudi-tors.com/Company/Project_Management_Quotes.html, assessed Jan. 18, 2011.

6. Drucker, Peter (1973). *Management: Tasks, Responsibilities, Practices.* New York: Harper & Row, Publishers.
7. Drucker, Peter (1973). *Management: Tasks, Responsibilities, Practices.* New York: Harper & Row, Publishers.
8. Drucker, Peter (1973). *Management: Tasks, Responsibilities, Practices.* New York: Harper & Row, Publishers.
9. Kerr, S. (1975). "On the Folly of Rewarding A, While Hoping for B." *Academy of Management Journal* 18(4): 769–783.
10. Augustine, Norman R. (1997). *Augustine's Laws.* 6th edition. Reston, VA: American Institute of Aeronautics and Astronautics, Inc.
11. Project Auditors LLC (2011). http://www.projectauditors.com/Company/Project_Management_Quotes.html, assessed Jan. 18, 2011

6 HABIT # 5—ACKNOWLEDGE AND ACCOMMODATE BOTH UNCERTAINTY AND IGNORANCE

1. Lehrer, Jonah (2009). *How We Decide.* Boston: Houghton Mifflin Harcourt.
2. McGowan, Kathleen (2009). "How Much of Your Memory Is True?" *Discover Magazine* (special online issue) August 3, 2009. (citing Karim Nader)
3. Augustine, Norman (1997). *Augustine's Laws.* 6th edition. Reston, VA. American Institute of Aeronautics and Astronautics, Inc.
4. Highsmith, Jim (2001). History: The Agile Manifesto. http://agilemanifesto.org/history.html (Feb. 12, 2011).
5. MacCormack, Alan (2001). "Why Evolutionary Software Development Works." *Harvard Business Review.* April 30, 2001.

7 HABIT # 6—EMBRACE BUT CONTROL CHANGE

1. No author given (2003). Honeywell wants more money for traffic-monitoring system in Big Dig's I-93 tunnel. Roads and Bridges e-news (*Boston Globe,* Oct. 29, 2003) http://www.roadsbridges.com/Honeywell-wants-more-money-for

-traffic-monitoring-system-in-Big-Dig-146-s-I-93-tunnel
-NewsPiece5980

News Release, Joe DeNucci, Office of the State
Auditor. (2005) State House Boston, Mass. Feb. 17,
2005   http://www.mass.gov/sao/Press%20Releases/2005
/bigdigipcscontractpr.pdf

8 HABIT # 7—CONTINUALLY ACT
TO INFLUENCE THE FUTURE

1. *A Guide to the Project Management Body of Knowledge: PMBOK
Guide*, fourth edition (2008) Project Management Institute,
Newton Square, PA.

9 HABIT # 8—CONTINUALLY COMMUNICATE

1. Central Intelligence Agency (2002). Kent and the Profession
of Intelligence Analysis, Center for the Study of Intelligence.
November, 2002
2. Dube, Line and Robey, Daniel (2008). "Surviving the
Paradoxes of Virtual Teamwork". *Information Systems Journal*
No. 19: 3–30.

INDEX